BURIED BENEATH THE CITY

BURIED
BENEATH
THE CITY

AN ARCHAEOLOGICAL HISTORY
OF NEW YORK

NAN A. ROTHSCHILD, AMANDA SUTPHIN,
H. ARTHUR BANKOFF, AND JESSICA STRIEBEL MACLEAN

COLUMBIA UNIVERSITY PRESS
NEW YORK

Furthermore:
a program of the J. M. Kaplan Fund

Columbia University Press wishes to express its appreciation for assistance given by
Furthermore: a program of the J. M. Kaplan Fund in the publication of this book.

Columbia University Press
Publishers Since 1893
New York Chichester, West Sussex
cup.columbia.edu

Library of Congress Cataloging-in-Publication Data
Names: Rothschild, Nan A., 1937– author. | Sutphin, Amanda, author. |
Bankoff, H. Arthur, author. | MacLean, Jessica Striebel, author. |
New York (N.Y.). Landmarks Preservation Commission.
Title: Buried beneath the city : an archaeological history of New York / Nan A. Rothschild,
Amanda Sutphin, H. Arthur Bankoff, and Jessica Striebel MacLean.
Other titles: Archaeological history of New York
Description: New York : Columbia University Press, [2022] | Includes bibliographical
references and index.
Identifiers: LCCN 2021036732 (print) | LCCN 2021036733 (ebook) | ISBN 9780231194945
(hardback) | ISBN 9780231194952 (trade paperback) | ISBN 9780231551090 (ebook)
Subjects: LCSH: New York (N.Y.)—Antiquities. | Excavations (Archaeology)—New York
(State)—New York. | New York (N.Y.)—History.
Classification: LCC F128.39 .R68 2022 (print) | LCC F128.39 (ebook) | DDC 974.7/1—dc23
LC record available at https://lccn.loc.gov/2021036732
LC ebook record available at https://lccn.loc.gov/2021036733

Book design: Chang Jae Lee
Cover illustration: James Gulliver Hancock
Cover artifacts from left to right:
1) Black Lead-Glazed Teapot, Stadt Huys Project, Qi#203971:
https://archaeology.cityofnewyork.us/linker/collection/7/203971
2) Smoking Pipe, South Ferry Project, Qi#115653:
https://archaeology.cityofnewyork.us/linker/collection/7/115653
3) Dipped Pearlware Pitcher, Van Cortlandt Project, Qi#199563:
https://archaeology.cityofnewyork.us/linker/collection/7/199563
4) Commemorative Medal from the 1758 Battle of Louisbourg, South Ferry Project,
Qi#104227: https://archaeology.cityofnewyork.us/linker/collection/7/104227
5) Gutta-Percha Comb, Seneca Village, Qi#210746:
https://archaeology.cityofnewyork.us/linker/collection/7/210746
6) Glass Bottle, Van Cortlandt Project, Qi#:199715:
https://archaeology.cityofnewyork.us/linker/collection/7/199715
7) Brass Barrel Tap Key, 7 Hanover Square, Qi#208291:
https://archaeology.cityofnewyork.us/linker/collection/7/208291
8) Printed Whiteware Teacup, Stadt Huys Project, Qi#201505:
https://archaeology.cityofnewyork.us/linker/collection/7/201505

CONTENTS

Preface   ix

Introduction   1

1. Indigenous Peoples Before the City   17

2. Dutch Beginnings, 1624–1664   51

3. The British Colonial City and the Nascent Republic, 1664–1800   87

4. Growing Pains, 1800–1840   139

5. Development of the Modern City, 1840–1898   167

Conclusion   213

Appendix A: The New York City Landmarks and Historic Districts
Discussed in the Book   221

Appendix B: Archaeological Sites Within New York City Discussed in the Book   231

Acknowledgments   245

Notes   249

Works Cited   265

Index   285

Regional map of New York City

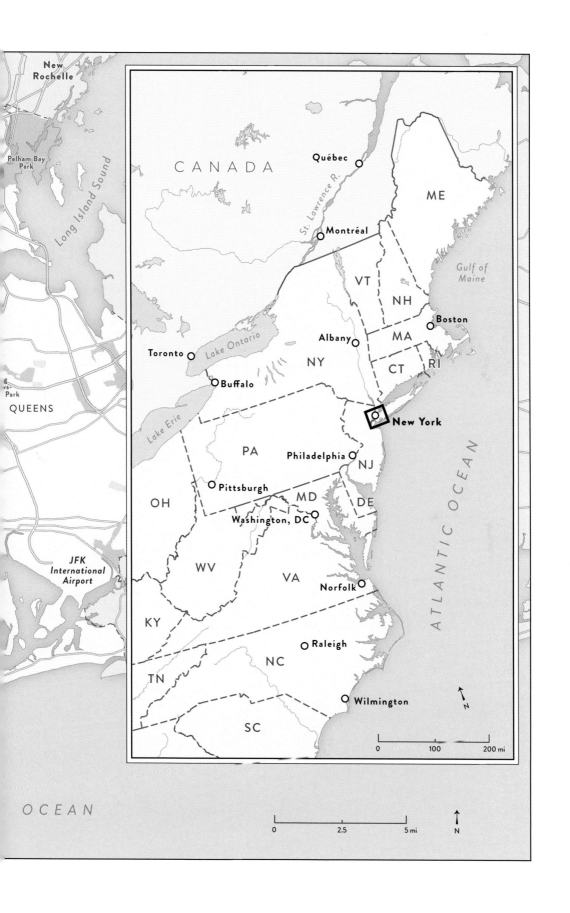

PREFACE

Buried Beneath the City emerged through a collaboration between the New York City Landmarks Preservation Commission's Archaeology Department, represented by Amanda Sutphin, director of the department, Dr. H. Arthur Bankoff, special advisor to the chair, Dr. Jessica Striebel MacLean, urban archaeologist, and Dr. Nan Rothschild, research professor at Barnard College and professor emerita at Columbia University. The book uses artifacts and information uncovered in archaeological investigations in the five boroughs of New York City to help understand and illuminate the history of the city and its people.

The Landmarks Preservation Commission (LPC) is the largest municipal preservation agency in the nation. It is responsible for protecting New York City's architecturally, historically, and culturally significant buildings and sites by granting them status as landmarks or historic districts and regulating them after designation. The agency is comprised of a commission of eleven commissioners, ten volunteers and a paid chair, all of whom are appointed by the mayor with the advice and consent of the city council, and supported by a staff of approximately eighty preservationists, researchers, architects, historians, attorneys, archaeologists, and administrative employees.

The commission was established in 1965 through groundbreaking legislation signed by the late Mayor Robert F. Wagner, in response to the losses of historically significant buildings. Most notable among these was the old Pennsylvania Station, which was demolished in 1963. There are now more than 37,500 designated buildings and sites in New York City across all five boroughs; most of them are located in over 150 historic districts.

LPC prioritizes designations that tell the stories of all New Yorkers and that reflect the city's history and communities. Archaeology can help reveal what the lives of everyday people of the past were like, as will be demonstrated throughout this book. The work of the Archaeology Department will be discussed in chapter 1. The Landmarks Preservation Commission is one of the few city agencies in the United States to have an Archaeology Department. After many years of effort to consolidate the city's archaeological collections in one central location, in 2014 the department established the NYC Archaeological Repository: The Nan A. Rothschild Research Center ("Repository") to curate the city's archaeological collections and to make them accessible to archaeologists, researchers, teachers, students, and the public. It is still an important part of the department's work. Located in Midtown Manhattan, in space donated by The Durst Organization, the Repository houses hundreds of thousands of artifacts from sites throughout the city and is open by appointment to researchers and scholars. As part of this project, the LPC worked with the Museum of the City of New York from 2013 to 2016 to create a comprehensive database of these collections, so they are available digitally to everyone. The Repository also launched a public website in 2016. Besides catalog information about the artifacts, the website has online exhibits, quizzes, and other features; it also accepts queries from the public. The collections in the Repository reveal the results of excavations and site assessments over the past forty years. The archaeological reports can be found online at the Landmark Preservation Commission's website. Almost all of the artifacts discussed in the book are curated in the Repository.

Archaeologists often seem to write only for other archaeologists. This book, on the other hand, is for anyone interested in New York City and its past. While containing technical material, it never forgets that history, especially as revealed through archaeological excavation, has a lure of its own. People are connected to their place, their city, their neighborhood, and they want to connect even to those who lived there before them. It is intriguing to know that mundane objects that were new in the past can still tell us something about their former users or owners, no matter that they are now battered and broken fragments.

BURIED BENEATH THE CITY

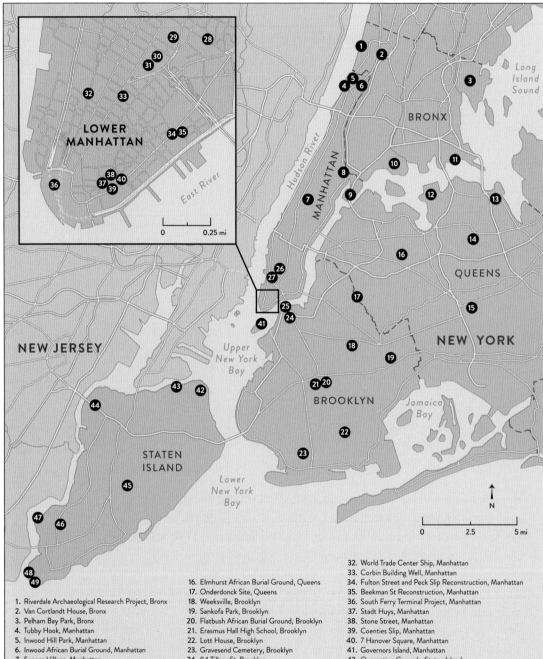

LOWER MANHATTAN

Hudson River

East River

0   0.25 mi

29   28
30
31
32   33
34   35
38   40
37   39
36

BRONX

Long Island Sound

1
2
5
4   6

MANHATTAN

10
8
7   9
11
12
13
14
16

QUEENS

26
27
25
24
41

NEW JERSEY

Upper New York Bay

17
15

NEW YORK

18
19
21   20

BROOKLYN

Jamaica Bay

22
23

STATEN ISLAND

Lower New York Bay

45

43
42
44

47
46

48
49

N

0   2.5   5 mi

1. Riverdale Archaeological Research Project, Bronx
2. Van Cortlandt House, Bronx
3. Pelham Bay Park, Bronx
4. Tubby Hook, Manhattan
5. Inwood Hill Park, Manhattan
6. Inwood African Burial Ground, Manhattan
7. Seneca Village, Manhattan
8. Harlem African Burial Ground, Manhattan
9. Ward's Island, Emigrant Refuge, Manhattan
10. Hunts Point Burial Ground, Bronx
11. Throgs Neck, Bronx
12. College Point, Queens
13. Bay Terrace, Queens
14. Old Towne Flushing Burial Ground, Queens
15. King Manor, Queens

16. Elmhurst African Burial Ground, Queens
17. Onderdonck Site, Queens
18. Weeksville, Brooklyn
19. Sankofa Park, Brooklyn
20. Flatbush African Burial Ground, Brooklyn
21. Erasmus Hall High School, Brooklyn
22. Lott House, Brooklyn
23. Gravesend Cemetery, Brooklyn
24. 84 Tillary St, Brooklyn
25. Empire Stores, Brooklyn
26. Washington Square Park, Manhattan
27. Spring Street Presbyterian Church
    Burial Ground, Manhattan
28. Five Points, Manhattan
29. African Burial Ground, Manhattan
30. Tweed Courthouse, Manhattan
31. City Hall Park, Manhattan

32. World Trade Center Ship, Manhattan
33. Corbin Building Well, Manhattan
34. Fulton Street and Peck Slip Reconstruction, Manhattan
35. Beekman St Reconstruction, Manhattan
36. South Ferry Terminal Project, Manhattan
37. Stadt Huys, Manhattan
38. Stone Street, Manhattan
39. Coenties Slip, Manhattan
40. 7 Hanover Square, Manhattan
41. Governors Island, Manhattan
42. Quarantine Grounds, Staten Island
43. Sailor's Snug Harbor, Staten Island
44. Old Place Neck, Staten Island
45. Richmond Hill, Staten Island
46. Sandy Ground, Staten Island
47. Port Mobil, Staten Island
48. Aakawaxung Munahanung (Island Protected from the Wind)
    Archaeological Site, Staten Island
49. H.F. Hollowell Site, Staten Island

INTRODUCTION

*B*uried Beneath the City is a special kind of book. It is a hybrid: an archaeology book about history and a history book about archaeology. It is a book about the place we call New York City, in all its diversity but also in its continuity over the past fourteen millennia. This history is seen through artifacts, the bits and pieces found in backyards, construction sites, street beds, and parks. It is a book meant to expand one's understanding of the concepts and uses of archaeology, to increase one's appreciation of the myriad ways of city life, past and present, to marvel that so much of the city's material past has been saved, and to reflect on how much has been lost.

Archaeology is the study of material objects (artifacts) and their relationships to each other and to nonmaterial parts of culture. "Culture" in this sense is best thought of as information about the world and how to live in it. Artifacts are objects made, used, or modified by humans, whether in the past or present. They are the embodied material evidence of this cultural information; they indicate what their makers and users thought was important or proper or useful for life in the world as they saw it. Archaeologists also study features, which are large structures that cannot be moved, such as wells, house foundations, and even the heavily modified landscape of the city itself, since cities and their modified landscapes are artifacts of human creation as well.

Understanding the past, whether approached through archaeology or history, relies on our empathy and our imagination. Except for the limited span of our own lives, we were not witness to the events that eventually shaped our present. Our understanding of the past is filtered through someone else's descriptions. This is not the same as being there or seeing it. Just as written records form the basic data of the historical record, artifacts and sites form the basic data of the archaeological record. *Buried Beneath the City* is about all of this.

The book is arranged chronologically. The chapters cover the period when Indigenous Peoples occupied the land by themselves, followed by European contact, then, in turn, the Dutch city, the English city, the period following the Revolutionary War, and the later nineteenth century. It uses the collections of the New York City Archaeological Repository: The Nan A. Rothschild Research Center. Today New York City includes five boroughs: Manhattan, Brooklyn, Queens, Staten Island, and the Bronx. But before the incorporation of all the boroughs in 1898, New York City primarily meant Manhattan. Because many of the sites excavated in Manhattan yielded very large collections, most of the artifacts in the Repository come from Manhattan, and in some ways the Repository's collections unintentionally emphasize that borough's role in the city's development (figure 0.1).

This island between the Hudson and East Rivers has seen geological and topographic changes over the past ten thousand years, as well as huge changes in the patterns of life and culture, including material culture, of its inhabitants. The shoreline has changed drastically, partly from natural causes like the rising sea levels from melting glaciers, and partly from human activity, like the landfilling that broadened the width of the island (figure 0.2). Hills were lowered, valleys filled, streams diverted, lakes and swamps drained. These changes can be traced both archaeologically and historically.[1] While the history of the past four hundred years is richly documented, the archaeology of the ever-changing city and its peoples is less so. Even New Yorkers are often surprised that there is archaeology to be done in the city. Many assume either that there are no archaeological remains left in New York or that archaeology is concerned only with the period before Europeans came to this land.

The archaeological record complements the written history, which we call the documentary record. New York is rich in documentary sources: European colonial court and land records, diaries, travelogues, maps, paintings, and more. This gives us a precise view of how the tapestry of commerce, society, and politics developed, with all the threads of social, economic, and ethnic diversity that characterize it.[2] New York City also has a wealth of landmarks that are designated for preservation by the New York City Landmarks Preservation Commission. They all provide information about the past—the Empire State Building in Midtown Manhattan, for instance, or the Fort Greene Historic District in Brooklyn. Designation recognizes the site's importance, preserves it for later generations, and allows us to experience spaces that embody the past. Most of the city's designated buildings and sites date from the nineteenth and twentieth centuries. But New York City's archaeological resources help tell the stories that predate many of the city's buildings. All of the New York City designated landmarks mentioned in this book are listed in appendix A.

There exists no documentary record before European contact. This is where archaeology comes in, as it can reveal the undocumented millennia when Indigenous Peoples inhabited this region. These traces and oral traditions are our only links to the most distant past, when there were no written records and no enduring standing structures.

FIGURE O.1

The website of the NYC Archaeological Repository: The Nan A. Rothschild Research Center provides public access to the archaeological collections owned by the City of New York and excavated in the city's five boroughs.

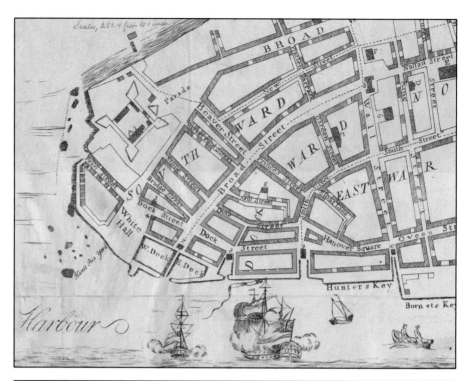

FIGURE 0.2

The Stadt Huys and 7 Hanover Square block highlighted on the James Lyne or Bradford Plan (*top*) and the Francis Maerschalck Plan (*bottom*) in 1728 and 1755. The distance of the 7 Hanover Square block from the waterfront illustrates the process of making land along the waterfront. Today, 7 Hanover Square is two full blocks from New York Harbor as opposed to what is shown on these eighteenth-century maps.

Maps courtesy of Norman B. Leventhal Map & Education Center of the Boston Public Library and the Library of Congress Map Division.

Artifacts and Documents

Artifacts have a life of their own. They are made, used, discarded, lost or buried, found or excavated, and sometimes curated. Each of these stages in the life of the artifact can tell us something about its past and its relation to people. There are artifacts illustrating religion (St. Catherine Labouré medal, figure 0.3), economics (merchant token, figure 0.4), social status (porcelain, figure 0.5), and recreation (bone die, figure 0.6); there are also features like the Battery, an eighteenth-century defensive fortification at the southern tip of Manhattan. While at times it may be difficult to draw out the information, it is there. And with it, we can reveal history and test the existing record.

What more can be learned about the past through archaeology? Is not the history of New York completely documented in the written records? Why do urban archaeology at all? Archaeologists often use documents to frame questions that can only be answered by excavation and artifacts. While invaluable to history, documents such as historical maps, tax records, diaries, wills, and newspapers may include mistakes and biases. Remember, Columbus thought he had discovered India. Or documents may contain little or nothing on whole parts of the population, such as women, enslaved people, the sick, or the poor. Archaeologists realize that documents and maps have their own biases and must be read with a critical eye. Indeed, some maps and documents, in both the past and the present, have specifically and purposefully omitted documentation of such minorities as a means of majority control. Thus, without the artifacts, those people are denied their history. For example, excavation of enslaved people's cabins at Thomas Jefferson's home at Monticello in Virginia has helped to tell a fuller story of the lives of the enslaved people who lived there.[3] Many times, documents simply omit the mundane aspects of day-to-day life, such as what people ate and when. Sometimes artifacts can correct misapprehensions. Beer bottles in a minister's garbage may contradict our belief that he was a teetotaler. Although using historical documents is a necessary part of the research strategy of historical archaeology, it leaves gaps—especially gaps in the facts of everyday life—that can only be filled by artifacts and sites that take us much closer to historical reality. This is as true in cities as in caves, as true today as it was thousands of years ago, and as true in New York as it is in Cairo. Archaeologists dig in New York to retrieve these lost bits of information.

Since an artifact is the result of the rules generated by cultural information, the more we know about the context of the artifact, the more information we can infer from it. Single artifacts from unknown or undocumented locations are naturally less valuable to us than artifacts from well-documented excavations. An artifact found "in context" tells us exactly where it was found, what type of soil it was deposited within (figure 0.7), and what other artifacts or objects it was found alongside. In turn, comparing it to other artifacts from similar contexts lets the archaeologist determine its age or use or its relationships to historical people and events. But when an artifact's context is unknown, meaning it has been taken from its original location without any information about where or how it was found, there is much less we can learn.

FIGURE O.3

Nineteenth-century Saint Catherine Labouré Miraculous Medal excavated from near Tweed Courthouse (a New York City landmark). The Catholic medal commemorates the appearance of the Virgin Mary to Catherine Labouré on November 27, 1830. The front (*left*), depicts the Virgin framed by the words "Ô Marie, conçue sans péché, priez pour nous qui avons recours à vous," or "*O Mary, conceived without sin, pray for us who have recourse to thee.*" The reverse (*right*), has a circle of twelve stars, a letter M surmounted by a cross, the Sacred Heart of Jesus crowned with thorns, and Immaculate Heart of Mary pierced with a sword. Found during the Tweed Courthouse excavations.

Qi#3754 CHP (Qi# is the NYC Archaeological Repository catalog number.)

FIGURE O.4

American one cent merchant token commissioned in 1794 by William Talbot, William Allum, and James Lee, partners in an East India trading company located at 241 Water Street in New York City. The token was redeemable for 1 cent worth of goods or tender "Payable at the Store of Talbot, Allum, & Lee," as is stamped on one face of the token. The tokens served as a substitute for legal tender or currency, which was difficult to obtain in the new nation and fluctuated in value. This side depicts the standing image of liberty and reads "LIBERTY & COMMERCE."

Qi#2386 CHP

FIGURE 0.5

Chinese export porcelain serving platter manufactured in China sometime between 1785 and 1853, found during excavations at Van Cortlandt House in the Bronx (a New York City landmark). The existence of costly Chinese porcelain, such as this piece known as Canton porcelain, tells us not only something about the economic status of the owner but also that the United States, as a newly formed country, had independently entered the global marketplace.

Qi#199138 VCP

FIGURE 0.6

Bone die excavated from Tweed Courthouse. The six-sided die is numbered 1 to 5 and one face, illustrated here, is curiously drilled with thirteen holes. A friendly game or high-stakes gambling, the die suggests many possibilities for eighteenth-century gaming.

Qi# 3901 CHP

Many of the artifacts illustrated in *Buried Beneath the City* are from well-excavated contexts, sites like Seneca Village or the 7 Hanover Square Block (figures 0.7 and 0.8), where they have helped date and illuminate the activities of the inhabitants who lived centuries before us. Material recovered through archaeology can also tell us about the changing environment. For example, the shrinking size of oyster shells found in New York sites indicates progressive overharvesting as oysters were collected before they reached maturity. This practice correlates with the deterioration of the riverine and coastal environment because of sedimentation and pollution. All archaeological sites covered in this book are described in appendix B.

A Brief History of Archaeology in New York

Archaeologists have been digging in New York for more than a hundred years. Many of the early archaeological pioneers were avocational archaeologists rather than professionals. Archaeology as a profession did not emerge until the late nineteenth century. The collections of the Museum of the American Indian–Heye Foundation—now housed near the Battery in the former U.S. Customs House that became the National Museum of the American Indian—have their origin in these early excavations. The same is true for many of the collections curated by the American Museum of Natural History and the New-York Historical Society. These early excavation projects were almost always focused on Indigenous Peoples' sites or sites associated with the American Revolutionary War. We discuss this early work in chapter 1, but it is worth noting that, although many of the practitioners were excellent fieldworkers, the ethical and culturally sensitive standards of today were not always evident in their excavations. Some of them used methodologies that would be considered inappropriate today, and some used methods that would have been considered inappropriate even at the time. Professional standards and practices, as well as the possibility of field training and advanced degrees, developed during the twentieth century.

By the 1970s, archaeology's predominant practitioners were either university archaeologists or independent archaeological contractors working in response to the changing regulations governing construction firms or developers; this latter group were often called contract archaeologists. As the number of archaeologists working in the city grew, they gradually adopted the idea, first offered by NYU archaeologist Bert Salwen, that archaeologists should do "archaeology *of* the city, not only archaeology *in* the city."[4] In other words, the city became the object of study, not just the place where the archaeologist dug. Soon, the periods of interest expanded from the area's earliest habitation all the way to the nineteenth century. The city itself was the site, and its archaeological record an inseparable part of the study of its development (figure 0.8).

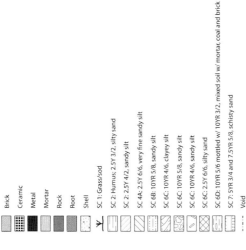

All Angels'
Profile 2.4a
West Wall of Test Cut M and
Test Cut M North Extension

Key

Brick
Ceramic
Metal
Mortar
Rock
Root
Shell

SC 1: Grass/sod
SC 2: Humus; 2.5Y 3/2, silty sand
SC 2: 2.5Y 4/2, sandy silt
SC 4A: 2.5Y 6/6, very fine sandy silt
SC 6B: 10YR 5/8, sandy silt
SC 6C: 10YR 4/6, clayey silt
SC 6C: 10YR 5/8, sandy silt
SC 6C: 10YR 4/6, sandy silt
SC 6C: 2.5Y 6/6, silty sand
SC 6D: 10YR 5/6 mottled w/ 10YR 3/2, mixed soil w/ mortar, coal and brick
SC 7: 5YR 3/4 and 7.5YR 5/8, schisty sand
Void

Note:
Ground surface of the northwest corner is 1.351 m above site datum.

0   20
Centimeters

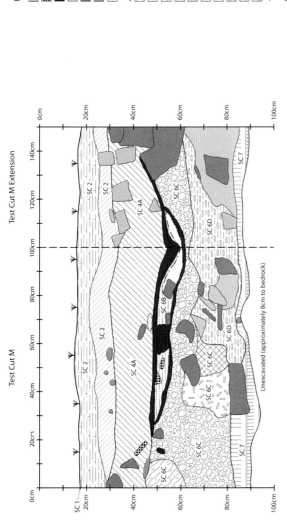

FIGURE O.7

Wall profile from 2011 Seneca Village excavation. Profiles are graphic representations of the vertical face of an excavation unit that show the stratigraphy and any features that have been uncovered. This profile illustrates the stratigraphic layers related to the creation of Central Park (layers SC 2 and SC 4A), covering the foundations of the Charlotte and William Godfrey Wilson house (SC 6B and SC 6C). The artifacts found in the stratigraphic level SC 6B represent the artifacts the Wilson family left behind when relocating their home after being displaced through eminent domain for the construction of Central Park (a New York City landmark).

Profile rendering by Hun·er Research, Inc.

FIGURE 0.8

The 7 Hanover Block (*foreground*) and the Stadt Huys block (*top right*) excavations, conducted between 1979 and 1981, were among the city's first comprehensive large-scale excavations and provided access to three hundred years of city history. With Water Street to the left and Pearl Street to the right, the foundations of the eighteenth and nineteenth buildings that once fronted Pearl Street can be seen emerging from the ground. 7 Hanover Block Project, NYC Archaeological Repository.

REGULATIONS AND ARCHAEOLOGICAL REVIEW

New York City has always experienced periods of intense development when the city seems to change overnight. One of these periods was in the mid-twentieth century when even Pennsylvania Station, a colossal train station modeled after the public buildings of Ancient Rome, was torn down after barely fifty years of service. In partial reaction to this destruction, Landmarks Law, Title 25, Chapter 3 of the New York City Administrative Code was enacted, establishing the New York City Landmarks Preservation Commission (see preface) charged with the designation and protection of the city's historic sites. Other protections followed: federal (National Historic Preservation Act 1966, National Environmental Policy Act 1970), state (State of New York Environmental Quality Review Act 1975), and city (New York City Environmental Review Act 1977), all of which required that public projects and applications requiring discretionary government approval consider the impacts of their proposals on a range of resources, including "archaeological". These acts, in effect, created the field of urban archaeology and the necessity of contract archaeology. The Landmarks Preservation Commission's first archaeologist was hired in 1980, and its Archaeology Department was created in 2002. It remains one of the few such departments in the United States.[5]

The department reviews proposals submitted by other government agencies or developers subject to the regulations noted above. If it is deemed that the proposed construction may impact archaeological resources, the department then oversees the ensuing archaeology but does not undertake the work itself. LPC archaeologists regulate and set the guidelines and standards for archaeological work conducted in the city.[6] One initial and notable result of this process was the excavation of the Lovelace Tavern (figure 0.9), on the Stadt Huys Block on Broad Street, one of the earliest taverns in New York. It was even used temporarily as City Hall, and its excavation illuminated a poorly documented slice of life of the seventeenth-century Dutch and English city.

Archaeological Process in New York City Under Landmarks Preservation Commission Oversight

1. **Archaeological Documentary Study:** Once a potential site is identified by LPC, a study is completed by a consulting archaeologist of all relevant historical documents, including previous archaeological reports, tax documents, wills and property records, and maps. A study such as this determines whether significant archaeological resources may exist at the site. The information produced is collected in a report that describes the analysis and its findings. Significant resources are those that can reveal new information about the past.

2. **Archaeological Testing:** If the previous step indicated that the site may have significant archaeological resources, the next step is to sample the site. This may mean borings, hand-excavated trenches, mechanical excavation, deep testing, or

FIGURE 0.9
Overview of northeast corner of the Lovelace Tavern foundation, which lies under a wall from a nineteenth-century building. Found during the Stadt Huys Excavations conducted from 1979 to 1980.
The Stadt Huys Block Project, NYC Archaeological Repository.

whatever appropriate technique can determine the presence and integrity of archaeological resources at a site. This multistep process includes a scope of work, the field testing itself, an analysis of what was found, and preparation of a final report by a consulting archaeologist or cultural resource management firm.

3. **Archaeological Excavation:** If the testing has determined that a site has potentially significant resources, often the project is redesigned to preserve the archaeological resources in place. If that is not possible, then it is essential that the site's archaeological information be preserved, which is best achieved by an archaeological excavation involving the scientific removal of earth in archaeologically sensitive areas by an archaeological team. This multistep process includes a scope of work, the excavation work, the analysis of what was found, and the creation of a final report and curation plan.

4. **Curation Plan:** If significant archaeological artifacts are recovered, they must be appropriately curated in archaeological repositories so that they are available for further study and exhibition. It is also important that project records be appropriately archived as they are essential when examining or reexamining archaeological material from a site.

ARCHAEOLOGICAL TECHNOLOGY

What are the tools of the modern urban archaeologist? Simply looking at the archive of New York City's archaeological reports shows how archaeological methodology in the city has developed over the past four decades. Computers, and especially laptops, have transformed documentation and recording. New standard forms have arisen for artifacts, contexts, and excavation units, which ensure that proper uniform measurements and other data are taken in the field and allows us to compare data sets among different excavations. A few online national archaeological databases have been created for archaeologists to share and record their findings. We have new technologies such as ground-penetrating radar (GPR), which can investigate objects and structures beneath the ground without ever breaking the surface, like an X-ray for the earth (figure 0.10). We now use dendrochronology (tree-ring dating) on the principle that matching the pattern of thick and thin rings within a tree (which correlates to the rainfall in a given year) to those of other trees of known age will allow us to determine construction dates of Colonial structures and landfill, such as those found in Battery Park. Total station electronic (laser) theodolites automate surveying and map making. Geographic information system (GIS) programs, using precise information from satellites, give the archaeologist precision in identifying locations and has simplified the process of drawing overlay maps to show changes in the use of a site or

FIGURE 0.10

A ground-penetrating radar (GPR) survey being conducted at Drake Park in Hunts Point in the Bronx to identify and delineate burials located underground without excavation. Each orange flag marks a transect, or slice, that was recorded using radar pulses and combined to create a complete map of the subsurface. Historical records indicate that this site contained an enslaved African burial ground adjacent to the one pictured here for enslaver families, which was verified using GPR technology.
Photograph by Jessica S. MacLean, 2016.

a part of the city through time. Historic maps online can be georeferenced to show the landfilling that created new land for wharfs and structures in the early nineteenth century, which have been excavated in Lower Manhattan (Battery Park). We will see this array of archaeological technology throughout the book.

The analysis of artifacts once they have been excavated has also changed dramatically. More collections and museums are digitizing their repositories with online photos and illustrations, and this has encouraged faster and more precise identification of artifacts. This can help establish dates, origins, and often producers of artifacts such as pottery and clay pipes. Archaeologists can also better trace the paths and growth of New York commerce through mass-produced items such as sugar molds and oyster jars. Preferences in types of cookware can indicate possible ethnic differences even within the same block or tenement. Identification of artifacts through association with other known artifacts elsewhere can lead to the attribution of this context to a specific profession, such as doctor or artist. Artifactual data can correct impressions erroneously found in texts, as in the newspaper accounts that claimed Seneca Village was a deeply impoverished community.

New techniques of analysis are also providing significant information. Portable and readily available X-ray fluorescent (XRF) spectrometers allow archaeologists to compare the elemental composition of similar or identical artifacts in the field and in the lab, thus giving another glimpse into their origin and trade patterns. This technique shoots a beam of charged particles into a sample—a pottery piece, for example—and produces a readout of the elements it contains and their percentages, which can be extremely helpful when it is difficult to tell whether, for example, a piece of stoneware pottery was imported from Germany or locally made.

All of these developments have made archaeology more useful in documenting New York's past. But even earlier projects with simpler technologies have added to the rich archaeological picture of this city.

OVERVIEW, *BURIED BENEATH THE CITY*

Over the past hundred years, archaeologists have unearthed all sorts of sites in New York City, from places that were used for thousands of years before the city emerged to residential and commercial sites of the past few centuries. They have unearthed Colonial fortifications, buried ships, and burial grounds. Some archaeological projects were granted a single opportunity, over a given amount of time, to excavate before the site was developed, potentially sealing the ground below it forever. And some areas, such as City Hall Park, have been excavated several times—each excavation turning up new artifacts and new information about the lives of the past.

The artifacts in this book tell the stories of life in New York in different times. They help us understand the lives of ancient paleolithic hunters and Woodland-era Indigenous Peoples who fished, gathered shellfish, and farmed. Through artifacts and archaeology, we can see their environment and how they used the land and its natural resources before the city emerged. Archaeology also shows us Dutch life during the settlement of New Amsterdam and English life when it became New York for the first time. We can see the growing diversity of the city in the artifacts, which themselves also illustrate the meaning and utility of the concept of ethnicity. Some colonists saw themselves as English, some as Dutch, and some as something different. Enslaved people, coming from different regions in Africa and forced into differing cultures in the New World, were as diverse as the colonists. Even the post-Revolutionary period brought an influx of immigrants from within and outside the country, and new canals tied the rapidly growing city more firmly to the economic and social lives of the American heartland. Population density and diversity increased alongside each other. New York never had a homogeneous population. Rich and poor, merchants and laborers, Dutch, English, Indigenous Peoples, enslaved and free Africans, people of ethnic groups from around the world had to, live, die, work, and play together in New York, whether they liked it or not.

The lives of the people who lived in New York are written into these artifacts and, along with them, the particularly urban problems of disease, clean water, keeping law and order among an ever increasing and diverse population, disastrous fires, and the raising and educating of children. All of these can be found in the stories told by the artifacts from every period of New York's history. We hope this book helps you hear them.

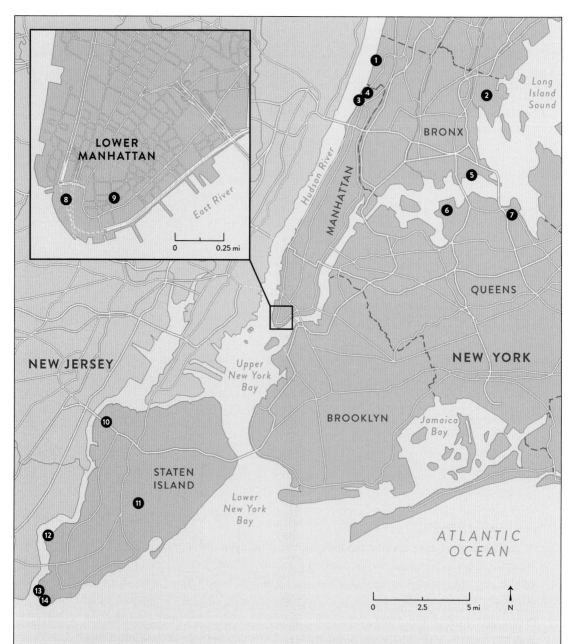

LOWER
MANHATTAN

East River

0   0.25 mi

Hudson River

MANHATTAN

BRONX

Long
Island
Sound

QUEENS

NEW YORK

NEW JERSEY

Upper
New York
Bay

BROOKLYN

Jamaica
Bay

STATEN
ISLAND

Lower
New York
Bay

ATLANTIC
OCEAN

0   2.5   5 mi   N

1. Riverdale Archaeological Research Project, Bronx
2. Pelham Bay Park, Bronx
3. Tubby Hook, Manhattan
4. Inwood Hill Park, Manhattan
5. Throgs Neck, Bronx
6. College Point, Queens
7. Bay Terrace, Queens
8. South Ferry Terminal Project, Manhattan

9. Stadt Huys, Manhattan
10. Old Place Neck, Staten Island
11. Richmond Hill, Staten Island
12. Port Mobil, Staten Island
13. Aakawaxung Munahanung (Island Protected from the Wind)
    Archaeological Site, Staten Island
14. H.F. Hollowell Site, Staten Island

1

INDIGENOUS PEOPLES
BEFORE THE CITY

Indigenous Peoples and communities populated the New York City region for at least fourteen thousand years before European colonists arrived in the sixteenth century. They used the land in very different ways than present-day New Yorkers do, and their cultural understandings differed from European attitudes toward all manner of things, including property ownership. Their lifeways were not singular nor static, but rather constantly adjusting in response to a changing environment, technologies, and interactions with new people and objects. There are no Indigenous documents from these times through which we might understand the thoughts and intentions of these people. Indigenous Peoples' oral traditions and ethnohistorical accounts gleaned from written histories from the time of European encounter provide perspectives on Indigenous history and cultural knowledge. Archaeology provides another perspective on the past, telling the material story of Indigenous lives through their material culture reflected in traces of homes and hearths, tools, and the fragmentary remains of foods.

Archaeologists have divided the long history of Indigenous Peoples in the region into chronological eras defined by cultural patterns, tool technology, and, to a lesser extent, climate change.[1] We do not know how those eras were defined by those living in them.[2] The commonly used archaeological eras are Paleo-Indian (12,000–9500 BP [years before present, defined as 1950]),[3] Archaic (9500–3000 BP), Woodland (3000–500 BP), and the Early Colonial period (500–250 BP), also called the Contact period, which covers the period in the seventeenth and eighteenth centuries when Indigenous Peoples in the region first began to encounter newly arrived Europeans and enslaved Africans (figure 1.1).[4] This chapter presents the current state of knowledge; but the story is incomplete, and new discoveries, new technologies, and new forms of analysis continue to expand what we know of the area's earliest occupants.

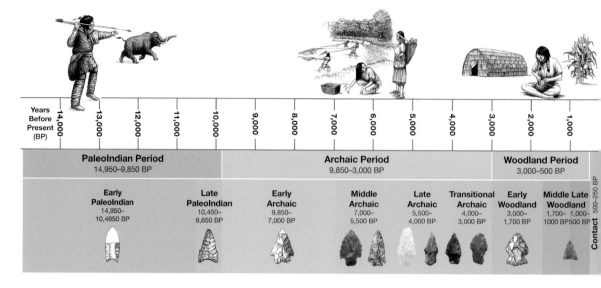

Years Before Present (BP)														

FIGURE 1.1

Timeline of Indigenous Peoples' periods in the area now known as New York City and the surrounding region, as defined by archaeologists.

Image by Sarah Moses, LPC.

THE IMPORTANCE OF THE CHANGING ENVIRONMENT

Our modern climate did not appear until about five and a half thousand years ago. Sixteen thousand years before that, "New Yorkers" would have had to walk a hundred miles from Manhattan to reach the shores of the Atlantic.[5] Twenty-one thousand years ago, Manhattan and its environs were covered by a glacier, the Laurentide Ice Sheet, two thousand feet high, much higher even than any skyscraper today. The glacier extended to what is now the southeastern shoreline of Staten Island, connecting the borough to Long Island and beyond to the lower arm of Cape Cod. Sea levels were one hundred meters (about 330 feet) lower than they are today. The Hudson River estuary, which begins in Troy, New York, where the fresh water of the river meets the saltwater of the Atlantic, and which made New York the most magnificent harbor of the Northeast, was carved out by glaciers at this time.[6]

As the climate warmed, the glacier receded northward, meltwaters flowed southward, and a familiar landscape gradually emerged. The open tundra–like vegetation and cold-loving trees like spruce, fir, birch, and alder gave way to pine and the deciduous forests of oak, hickory, and beech. Mammoth, mastodon, caribou, giant beaver, and sloth called the region home, then disappeared as a result of environmental change and animal and human predation.[7] Six thousand years ago, sea levels started to stabilize, and the coastline began to resemble that of today. By four thousand years ago, tidal salt marshes had developed along the shores of what would become the city's five boroughs. These marshes were home to a diverse and rich ecosystem of plants and animals.

This chronicle of environmental change is integral to the human story of New York City. The city is and was home to Indigenous Peoples who have lived in this region for at least fourteen thousand years. Over the millennia, humans have had an intimate relationship with the changing environment. Evidence of these ancient landscapes—environmental and human—survives beneath the city's streets and in the city's coastal waters.[8] As our ability to reconstruct environmental conditions has grown more precise, we have acquired a greater understanding of environmental conditions over various periods and their impact on culture. Humans have always had a dynamic relationship with the natural environment. The environment has influenced the choices people make about where and how to live; in turn, people have shaped environmental characteristics to support their way of life. As the historian William Cronon put it, "the environment may initially shape the range of choices available to a people at a given moment, but then culture reshapes environment in responding to those choices. The reshaped environment presents a new set of choices for cultural reproduction, thus setting up a new cycle of mutual determination."[9] It is this cycle of mutual determination that archaeologists work to understand.

THE ARCHAEOLOGICAL RECORD

New York City is part of an Indigenous cultural landscape that reflects a long, vibrant, and complex history. Only a few archaeological sites, however, inform our knowledge of the city's deepest past and oldest inhabitants. Most of the Indigenous Peoples sites that have been found in the city are located in areas of low population density today at the edges of the city—few have survived in historically intensely developed areas. There are several reasons for this. First, the earliest sites of Indigenous Peoples are small and primarily composed of perishable organic materials vulnerable to the acidic local soils. Second, the sites are difficult to locate because they were occupied by relatively few people, who left little trace of their presence, unlike the heavy material footprint of today's city. And third, because the habitation sites of Indigenous communities were situated in the same locations preferred by Europeans and later New Yorkers—at the intersection of rivers, along protected coastlines, on well-drained soils, or near freshwater sources—these sites were often destroyed in the early years of the city's modern history.[10]

EARLY EXCAVATIONS IN THE CITY

Excavations of Indigenous sites (which also included the disturbance and removal of burials and associated cultural objects) began in the late 1890s and early 1900s, when the neighborhoods outside of southern Manhattan were being developed. These neighborhoods included Inwood in Upper Manhattan, Pelham Bay in the Bronx, and College

Point in Queens. Most Indigenous Peoples' artifacts excavated during this period were collected through the efforts of so-called avocational archaeologists early in archaeology's professional development.

The term *avocational* is used to differentiate earlier archaeologists, who employed a variety of standards to govern their work, from today's professional archaeologists who work pursuant to generally recognized standards of conduct. In the late nineteenth and early twentieth centuries, the profession of archaeology was in its infancy, and most practitioners conducted fieldwork abroad even if they lived and worked in New York City. Many of these local pioneers were excellent recorders and diligently wrote down what archaeologists call the *provenience data*—the vertical and horizontal location of where artifacts were excavated. Avocational archaeologists have varied widely, from individuals who do high-quality work, keep careful records, and are committed to the conservation and preservation of sites to others who are only interested in finding valuable artifacts and keep no records. New York City is fortunate to have had several careful and responsible individuals who excavated a number of Indigenous Peoples sites when it became clear that the sites were endangered by development. William I. Calver and Reginald P. Bolton were among the first of these, working early in the twentieth century. They were followed by others like Arthur C. Parker, Julius Lopez, Edward Kaeser, and Stanley H. Wisniewski (figure 1.2), to name but a few. Some of these men

FIGURE 1.2
Avocational archaeologist Stanley H. Wisniewski excavating at the Graham Court Site in College Point, Queens, in 1934. Wisniewski and his childhood friend Ralph S. Solecki excavated various sites in the Bronx and Queens as teenagers, documenting and cataloging their finds as they worked. After World War II, Solecki went on to become a professional archaeologist specializing in the study of early humans and Neanderthals in the Middle East. Wisniewski became an engineering draftsman but continued his avocational research on the side. The NYC Archaeological Repository contains a collection of artifacts they discovered during the 1930s. Image courtesy of the Queens Borough Public Library, Archives (aql:4405). Ralph Solecki Photographs.

had regular day jobs but surveyed for sites on weekends, salvaging important information. These avocational practitioners were thoughtful and diligent excavators, but it is important to acknowledge that they were working prior to the advent of the ethical and professional standards in archaeology that guide current practice. It must also be noted that there were other excavators who carelessly disturbed many sites, including burial grounds. Today, it is preferred to leave the sites where Indigenous Peoples lived alone; in cases of unavoidable development impacts, then any work should include consultation with Tribal Nations to establish culturally sensitive excavation procedures.

At present, recent discoveries are concentrated in less developed areas of the city like Staten Island's Old Place Neck Site, but Indigenous sites would have been everywhere in today's five boroughs.[11]

Paleo-Indian (at Least 12,500–9500 BP)

The end of the Wisconsin glaciation marks the appearance of the first human inhabitants of the region, Paleo-Indians, who were hunter-gatherers living in small bands of fewer than fifty.[12] They were descendants of those who migrated into North America across the exposed land of the Bering Strait, along the Pacific Rim, and possibly by boat across the Pacific. They occupied temporary camps and workstations and frequently moved in pursuit of game animals and raw materials for food, shelter, and tools. Back then, all the land that now constitutes the city was full of plants and animals accustomed to the cold, dry climate. Paleo-Indians hunted big-game animals, many now extinct, including mammoth, mastodon, musk ox, caribou, elk, and moose, along with giant beaver and sloth, supplemented in the off-season with smaller game, fish, and wild plants.[13] In 1891, construction workers digging the Harlem Canal found a mastodon tusk, the first evidence that these animals had lived here. In 1925, workers in Inwood, a neighborhood near Manhattan's northern tip, recovered additional evidence of mastodons in the city, including teeth and bones.[14] Recent studies have also found mammoth and mastodon teeth south of the Hudson River channel and on the continental shelf east of the New Jersey shore and south of Staten Island, Brooklyn, and western Long Island. These finds further support the presence of these large mammals in the valley lowlands that have been drowned by the rising sea level.[15]

The archaeological record of Paleo-Indians is scant. Stone tools are mostly what has survived: fluted spear points, knives, scrapers, drills, and gravers—an engraving tool for bone. The distinctive fluted spear points of Paleo-Indians, known as Clovis points, typically range from three to five inches in length. They are usually made of chert, jasper, or argillite, all rocks that fracture in a predictable way when struck with another stone, producing a sharp edge. Paleo-Indians fashioned these lanceolate-shaped projectile points by removing flakes in one direction from the base toward the tip, leaving a long channel or "flute" on either side of the stone point midway up the body (figure 1.3, *left*).[16] The two-sided or bifacial fluting was where they tied the point to a wooden spear shaft.

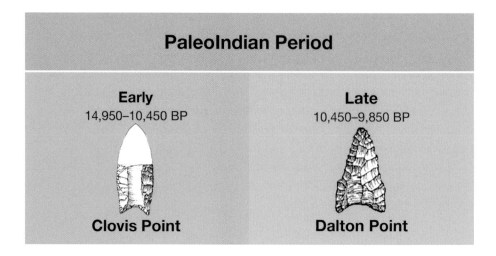

FIGURE 1.3

A fluted eastern Clovis projectile point (*left*) and a Dalton point (*right*). The channel, or "flute," on the Clovis point is a hallmark of early PaleoIndian projectiles, while the Dalton point marks the transition from the Paleolithic to the Early Archaic period in the New York City region. Projectile points like these were found at the Port Mobil and Old Place Neck archaeological sites in Staten Island, indicating that people occupied Staten Island, at least seasonally, a minimum of 12,500 years ago.

Image by Sarah Moses, LPC.

In New York City, only two archaeological sites have yielded Paleo-Indian artifacts: Port Mobil and the Old Place Neck site, both on Staten Island.[17] At Port Mobil, twenty-one Clovis points were found by avocational archaeologists.[18] The Old Place Neck site yielded a single Late Paleo-Indian Dalton-like projectile point made around ten thousand years ago (figure 1.3, *right*).[19]

Archaic Period (9500–3000 BP)

As the ice age ended, the climate in the New York City area warmed. Bridging nearly seven thousand years, the Archaic period marked a time of significant environmental change and cultural innovation. Deciduous hardwood forests of oak and maple gradually replaced pine and hemlock forests. The mammoth, mastodon, giant sloth, and beaver hunted by the Paleo-Indians became extinct. The elk, moose, and caribou left, migrating northward following the glaciers to cooler climes.[20] They were replaced by a wide variety of smaller animals, such as white-tailed deer, bear, beaver, rabbit, and turkey, as the ecology of the warming region diversified. Indigenous Peoples culture during the long Archaic period changed too. Populations increased, and Archaic peoples gradually became less mobile, migrating only seasonally and returning to the same settlements time and time again.[21]

Archaeologists subdivide the Archaic era into four periods based on these environmental and cultural changes: the Early, Middle, Late, and Transitional/Terminal Archaic periods. By the Middle Archaic period, humans had begun exploiting marine resources, especially shellfish. Stone tools emerged that served new functions, such as wood-working, and the presence of nonlocal lithic materials, or stone, provides evidence that trade networks had opened. The first stone bowls, a revolution in cooking technology, appeared at the end of the Archaic period in the Northeast.

EARLY ARCHAIC (9500–7000 BP)

The Early Archaic climate was warmer than that of the preceding Paleo-Indian period. Dense pine and oak forests stretched across most of the region, and glacial lakes trans-formed into marsh- and swampland.[22] These habitats attracted the smaller animals noted above. The habitats also hosted important plant resources, including sedges, reeds, bulbs, and seed-producing plants.

Archaeologists have identified a distinctive bifurcated-base stone projectile point style—a deep center notch in the base giving the appearance of rounded ears (figure 1.1, Early Archaic)—as characteristic of the Early Archaic. It was first manufactured by people in the southeastern United States about a thousand years before the technology migrated north, appearing in the Lower Hudson River Valley between nine and ten thousand years ago. This Early Archaic tool form was used for hunting local big game.[23] The tool kit of the Paleo-Indian, predominately used for hunting and skinning an array of animal species, was now supplemented by new types of tools indicating emergent activities such as woodworking, basket making, and hide rendering, among other innovative activities. Woodworking tool forms such as chipped stone axes and adzes (figure 1.4) appear in increasing numbers in the archaeological record beginning in the late Early Archaic and extending through the remaining Archaic phases.[24]

FIGURE 1.4
A trio of chipped stone axes, a tool form used for cutting and rendering wood that first appears in the Archaic period. The left axe was collected by Anthony Woodward in 1889 at 129th Street and Broadway in Manhattan. The right pair was collected by Reginald Pelham Bolton at the turn of the twentieth century from a site in Inwood, Manhattan.
The axes are in the collection of the National Museum of the American Indian, Smithsonian Institution (039239.000 and 121782.000). Photograph by NMAI Photo Services.

Almost all the evidence of Early Archaic occupations to date has been found in Staten Island. Mostly this is because this borough is the least developed, so there are more undisturbed sites for excavation. Evidence of Early Archaic occupations has been discovered at Ward's Point, Richmond Hill, the H. F. Hollowell site, and the Old Place Neck site.[25] These are significant because the spear points and bifurcated projectile points associated with Early Archaic peoples were found in deeply buried stratified deposits— what archaeologists call *in situ*—rather than on the ground, which are called *surface* finds. In situ finds tell archaeologists more about how the sites were formed, used, and abandoned. Charcoal found with in situ stone artifacts lets us carbon-date the artifacts, confirming the Early Archaic date assigned to these stone tools.

Radiocarbon Dating

Radiocarbon dating is a scientific method of determining the age of organic materials like animal bone, leather, and wood charcoal that originate from living things. It cannot be used to date inorganic material like stone or metal. Radiocarbon, or C-14, is a heavy form of carbon that is absorbed by living organisms. When the organisms die, they stop absorbing carbon. The nucleus of the unstable heavy carbon then decays, breaking down at a predictable rate that acts as a clock measuring how long it has been since that organism was living. Radiocarbon dating was invented in 1950 and revolutionized archaeologists' ability to date sites and artifacts. It is impractical for use on historic sites because there are other technologies better suited for dating more recent sites.

At Ward's Point, (today's Aakawaxung Munahanung [Island Protected from the Wind] Archaeological Site, a New York City landmark) at the southeastern tip of Staten Island in Conference House Park, for example, archaeologists dug up a series of hearths at the lowest level of the site—where the oldest artifacts were found—providing a rare glimpse into daily life eight thousand years ago. Near the hearths they also found evidence that they were the center of all sorts of domestic activities, including butchering and cooking food and making tools. Fire-reddened and cracked stones found in and around the hearths are evidence of cooking (figure 1.5)—more specifically, grilling and boiling. In one of the oldest cooking methods in the Americas, stones were heated in the hearth and then dropped into a skin or other container filled with water, boiling whatever was on the day's menu. Simmering and boiling was regulated with the addition of freshly heated stones.[26] Archaeologists also found chipped-stone knives and broken spear points for butchering, stone scrapers used to prepare animal hides for clothing, hammer stones and chert cores indicating tool manufacture, and four ground stone celts, stone axes that were used for woodworking.

A

B

FIGURE 1.5
Fire-cracked rock from the Riverdale Archaeological Project exhibiting the telltale fire-reddening (A) and hairline cracks (B) that indicate heating. Fire-cracked rocks can indicate the presence of a cooking hearth or rocks that were heated and used to cook food by boiling. This type of cooking practice would have been used at most Early to Middle Archaic sites like Ward's Point (Aakawaxung Munahanung [Island Protected from the Wind] Archaeological Site) in Staten Island.
Qi#211876 RPAP and Qi#211877 RPAP

MIDDLE ARCHAIC (7000–5500 BP)

In the Middle Archaic, although sea levels continued to rise, the shoreline was still somewhat distant. The woods were filling with deciduous oak, chestnut, and hemlock trees.[27] People began to stay in place longer, establishing larger seasonal base camps that were supplemented by foraging camps targeted to specific resources, such as coastal fishing and shellfish-gathering sites and inland quarries and hunting camps.[28] The period also marks a significant change in the lifeways of Archaic peoples: hunting and gathering expanded to include newly available marine resources, creating a diverse food base that archaeologists call a broad-spectrum diet. We can see this change in the evidence of shell middens—heaps of discarded fishhooks, bones, and shellfish such as oysters and clams along the New York coast and the tidal region of the Hudson River. Ground stone tool technology also began to appear in the Middle Archaic period.

At Dogan Point, about thirty miles north of the city on the Hudson River, archaeologists excavated a Middle Archaic shell midden they radiocarbon-dated to between 6900 and 4400 BP, establishing it as one of the earliest shell mounds ever found in the Northeast.[29] No shell middens of this antiquity have yet been found in New York City or the coastal sediments adjacent to the city. It is likely, however, that such sites are there, lying buried beneath New York City's natural accretion and modern landfill and development. Stone projectile points dating to the Middle Archaic have been found on Staten Island at Ward's Point (in Conference House Park) and two other nearby sites. A Stanly Stemmed point found in College Point, Queens (figure 1.6), is the oldest artifact in the

FIGURE 1.6
A Stanly Stemmed projectile point (front and back) from the Middle Archaic period, approximately 7,000 to 5,500 years old. This small spear point predates the use of the bow and arrow in the region by several thousand years. Originally it would have been hafted to a long wooden shaft. Its serrated edges and barbed ears were intended to be difficult for prey, whether game or fish, to dislodge. The point is made of yellow jasper, a raw material readily available to Native communities in New York City through trade from Delaware River region quarries or other quarry locations.
Qi#22 CPQ

NYC Archaeological Repository. These finds, however, were collected from the surface, not recovered from a stratified site, so we cannot precisely date their creation.

LATE ARCHAIC (5500–4000 BP)

While most artifacts for the Early and Middle Archaic peoples have been found in Staten Island, archaeologists have found stone tools from the Late Archaic period in Staten Island, Queens, the Bronx, and Manhattan. The population may have increased during this era, as rising sea levels stabilized and rich estuarine environments developed and expanded.[30] Newly established tidal marshes and flats provided a steady supply of food that included shellfish, fish, migratory birds, and plants, expanding the diet further.[31]

Following a settlement pattern established in the Middle Archaic, archaeologists believe that Late Archaic peoples lived in villages in river valleys, moving to coastal sites in the warm months and to interior hunting camps in winter. They stayed intermittently at fishing stations and other sites where specific food or material resources could be obtained in the warm months.[32] Pollen and other botanical evidence from soil cores indicate that forests in Manhattan had by then fully transformed into stands of oak and chestnut, which became habitat for deer, bear, raccoon, and turkey.[33] Referred to as mast forests, these trees produced acorns and chestnuts—called mast—which became an integral part of the Late Archaic diet along with shellfish.[34] Artifacts from Late Archaic sites in New York City reflect this changing diet, including mortars and pestles for grinding nut meats, steatite bowls for stews, and an array of spear and arrow points of varying sizes suggesting that specific tools were used to hunt specific animals.

At the beginning of the twentieth century, the archaeologists Alanson Skinner and Amos Oneroad excavated two sites in northern Manhattan—Tubby Hook in Washington Heights and Inwood Hill Park in Inwood. These sites, along with Ward's Point on Staten Island, provide evidence for repeated seasonal occupation by Indigenous Peoples who returned to these locations intermittently over thousands of years.[35] Late

Archaic shell middens (dumps) found at both sites and a rock shelter at the Inwood site indicate that they served as seasonal camps. Artifacts found at Inwood include Late Archaic chipped stone spear points and knives and ground stone tools that were used for woodworking. The archaeologists found stone axes (figure 1.4)—also indicative of woodworking—at both Washington Heights and Inwood and elsewhere in the city. These tools would have been used to make dugout canoes, paddles, dwellings, fish weirs, and other wooden objects.[36]

In 1989, archaeologists working in Riverdale Park in the Bronx unearthed an Indigenous Peoples' site that included evidence of Late Archaic and Early Woodland occupations. Among their finds was a distinctive Late Archaic Vosburg-type projectile point dating from between three and five thousand years ago (figure 1.7). The gray chert spear point was likely used for hunting large game such as deer and bear; it would have been hafted to a wooden spear shaft and thrown by hand or with the aid of an atlatl, or spear-thrower, pictured in the upraised arm of the man aiming at a mammoth in figure 1.1. Each projectile point tells the narrative of its manufacture from a rough stone core to a bifacially (two-sided) flaked-stone point. A photograph may not capture the flake scars, so a line-and-stipple drawing as in figure 1.7 is still the best way to record chipped-stone artifacts. The Riverdale Archaeological Collection spent years in temporary storage. Part of the impetus for the creation of the NYC Archaeological Repository was to bring collections like the Riverdale project, excavated on land owned by the Parks Department, into a centralized climate-controlled storage location where they could be protected, inventoried, and made accessible to researchers and the public.

Archaeologists interpret the differences in artifact styles and types from the Late Archaic as evidence of the development of group territories that maintained distinct

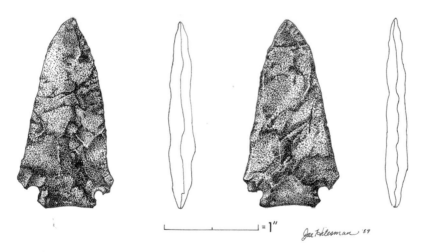

FIGURE 1.7
Late Archaic Vosburg corner-notched spear point excavated from Riverdale Park in the Bronx in 1989. The point would have been used to hunt deer and bear. Its sharp basal ears and downward projecting shoulder barbs make it difficult for prey to dislodge it (Justice 1987, 115).
Illustration by Jae Hilesman, 1989. Qi#211894 RPAP

FIGURE 1.8
From left to right: Three side-notched Lamoka projectile points made of quartz and gray chert and a closely related Wading River–type point, also known as a stemmed Lamoka, characterized by its long-stemmed base, at the far right. These points were excavated from Riverdale Park in the Bronx and College Point in Queens (second from left).
Qi#211891 RPAP, Qi#23 CPQ, Qi#211892 RPAP, Qi#211893 RPAP

traditions.[37] Many archaeologists believe that projectile point style is a signature of group identity, although there are also functional determinants of different point styles—certain points are better for hunting certain prey.[38] Late Archaic sites, for example, are mainly associated with Narrow Stemmed Tradition projectile points.[39] These are best illustrated in the example of the Lamoka points from the Riverdale Park Archaeological Project and from College Point in Queens that date from the Late Archaic into the Transitional Archaic period (figure 1.8). These small points would likely have been hafted or bound to arrow shafts for use with a bow, a technology that first appeared in the Transitional Archaic, to hunt small game like rabbit or turkey, and were in use for nearly three thousand years from the Transitional Archaic until the Late Woodland period (4000–500 BP).

THE TRANSITIONAL ARCHAIC (4000–3000 BP)

The Transitional, or Terminal Archaic period, overlaps with the Late Archaic and the beginning of the Early Woodland period. In the latter period, horticulture was introduced into the region from what is now the southeastern United States. In the Transitional period, the estuarine and forest habitats stabilized, and sea levels had risen to be only about fifteen feet lower than they are today.[40] Archaeological evidence of the Terminal Archaic is found more often than information from earlier periods. This increased database allows us a more nuanced peek into the lives of the Transitional Archaic Indigenous Peoples beyond simply their diet, technology, and the changes in their landscape.[41] The Transitional Archaic is the first period for which we have evidence of burial traditions, and through these we can begin to understand the complex social and ritual life of Indigenous communities in the region.

New artifacts introduced in the period indicate that it was a time of technological and cultural innovation. We can see three new cultural traditions arising among Indigenous Peoples living in the region based on distinct types of projectile points. The Laurentian Tradition, characterized by the Vosburg type (figure 1.7), appeared first during the Late Archaic. So too did the Small Stemmed Tradition, as seen in the Lamoka type (figure 1.8), used to hunt small game like rabbits and turkey, and the Susquehanna Tradition characterized by Orient points, long fishtail-like projectile points that have been found in four of the five boroughs.[42]

The cultural implications of the new projectile point types that emerged in the Transitional Archaic period are puzzling. The appearance of new technological developments always raises questions for archaeologists. Do these three types reflect the migration of new peoples into the region? Or are they the result of expanded trade networks introducing new materials, or new tool technologies, or new beliefs to groups in the Northeast? Or some combination of these?[43] Consensus holds that the emergence of these projectile types illustrates the expansion of, and participation in, trade networks over great distances, as an expansion of trade is seen elsewhere across North America during this period.

Handheld ground stone tools (versus hafted ground stone tools, which were used for different purposes) continued to develop in the Late to Transitional Archaic period, as in the example of a ground stone pestle, hammerstone, and mano from Bay Terrace, Queens (figure 1.9). The wear, or use pattern, on the stone indicates that it was a multifunction tool used in at least three different ways. One end of the stone is chipped and jagged. It was used as a pounder or hammerstone, held vertically in the hand to chop and crush hard material like nuts, seeds, or shells. The other end is worn smooth and rounded because of its use as a pestle to grind and crush soft organics like nut meats (mast), berries, other vegetal matter, and the ingredients to make pemmican, a combination of nut meat, animal fat, berries, and dried meat. This type of tool could also have been used to crush minerals such as hematite or red and yellow ochre as paints, although this particular tool shows no discoloration that would be evidence of such use.

The third use was as a grinder or roller held horizontally in two hands and used like a rolling pin to grind nut meat into flour, to flatten reeds for weaving, and to roll animal sinew or tendon into durable cordage for sewing and binding. The smooth surface of the tool was naturally weathered by exposure to water, and an Indigenous person then ground and shaped it along its length, likely by rubbing sand along it and by pecking at it with another hammerstone. The tool was likely proportional in size and heft to the individual and purpose for whom and which it was made.

FIGURE 1.9

A combination ground stone tool used as a pestle, hammerstone, and mano from Bay Terrace, Bayside, Queens. Bay Terrace was a site with evidence for multiple periods of occupation from the Middle Archaic through the Late Woodland period (7000–500 BP).
Qi#4 BTQ

It is difficult to date ground stone tools such as this one without knowing its depositional context—where it was discarded and what it was discarded with—because it is a type of tool that was used for millennia. Development in the 1940s in Bay Terrace exposed materials from the Middle to Late Archaic through the Late Woodland period

FIGURE 1.10

Transitional Archaic (4000–3000 BP). Two steatite bowl fragments collected from sites in Queens. *Top:* A lug-shaped handle on the exterior of a bowl and the interior face of the same bowl, showing carving scars on the lower left half. *Bottom:* Front and back of a mend hole, indicating this vessel had cracked and was repaired. An adjacent piece would have had a reciprocal hole, and the two pieces would have been bound together with sinew. The bowl pieces are too fragmentary to determine the overall shape of the original bowls. Qi#211890 KAZ and Qi#211889 KAZ

(7000–500 BP), but without better context, we do not know from which period the pestle and hammerstone came.

The Transitional Archaic marks the first appearance in the region's archaeological record of steatite (or soapstone) bowls (figure 1.10). Steatite is a broad category of soft stone with a high talc content, which makes it softer and more easily worked with stone tools into vessels.[44] These bowls are the oldest surviving containers used by Indigenous Peoples in the Northeast.[45] Their high talc content also makes them conduct and retain heat efficiently. As previously described, food in the Early and Middle Archaic was prepared by placing hot stones in water-filled hides, simmering and boiling whatever was inside. Such containers, however, could only be placed adjacent to the fire or they would combust.[46] Steatite vessels, in contrast, conduct heat efficiently, transferring it directly through to the contents without damage to the vessel. This meant steatite cooking vessels could be suspended directly over fires or buried in the coals and heated more consistently. This allowed for the preparation of more complex stews and braised foods than previously possible. It was a revolution in cooking and dining.

Analysis of steatite bowls from east of the Appalachian Mountains has determined that they come in three general sizes, small, medium, and large—measured by the sum of the length and width of the vessel—and in three depths, shallow, medium, and deep.[47] They were round or oval, and occasionally rectangular, square, and even triangular.[48] These size, depth, and shape differences afforded a variety of uses: food preparation, cooking, and serving. Residue analyses performed on steatite vessels found along the Seneca River in central New York State have shown that the vessels were used for processing a variety of food resources, including grass seeds, a legume (possibly wild bean), pine, animal flesh, and more.[49] In other words, these bowls were used as all-purpose vessels rather than specialized cooking tools.

Steatite vessels likely also served a range of social, political, and ideological purposes that would have varied from region to region. They have consistently been found as funerary offerings in various sizes: miniature or full-size, and whole or broken. The latter are thought to have been used to transport cremations or secondary interments to their burial.[50]

In present-day New York City, most steatite vessels have been found along the Long Island Sound into Queens and the Bronx and along the Hudson River. The vessels in the Repository's collection are probably from the Bronx, likely Pelham Bay, and from Long Island and Queens. They were collected by an avocational archaeologist who did not keep detailed notes.[51] The proximity of these vessels to rivers and the sound are likely a result of transportation routes from the quarries found in Massachusetts, western Connecticut, western Rhode Island, and southeastern Pennsylvania. There is a serpentine quarry—a relative of steatite—in Clove Lake, Staten Island, but the steatite artifacts found in other boroughs do not match the Staten Island serpentine.[52]

A sourcing study of steatite vessels in eastern Long Island identified two steatite quarries in Rhode Island as the source area.[53] Archaeologists have long hypothesized that steatite vessels were roughly shaped into round or oblong bowl forms at the quarry sites, making them easier to carry, and then transported along riverine and marine trade routes. Thus, those far from quarry sites, which were unevenly distributed in the Northeast, had access to the steatite.[54] Upon arriving at their final destination, steatite vessels were shaped and refined into their final circular, oval, or rectangular form as desired.

WOODLAND PERIOD (3000–500 BP)

After the Transitional Archaic came the Woodland era, a time in the Northeast marked by a series of social, economic, and technological changes. It was then that year-round villages emerged, supporting small-scale cultivation of squash, beans, and corn alongside seasonal procurement and hunting camps.[55] The Woodland era, spanning approximately two and a half thousand years, is divided by archaeologists, as earlier eras were, into Early (3000–1700 BP), Middle (1700–1000 BP), and Late (1000–500 BP) periods.

During the Woodland era, two connected changes emerged in settlement pattern and the adoption of small-scale farming. Woodland-era agriculture centered on the cultivation of maize, beans, and squash and brought with it the widespread production of pottery vessels for the first time.[56] Archaeologists theorize that the combination of farming and ceramic technology correlated with the emergence of permanent villages and a subsequent population boom, but the timing, nature, and extent of the transition to settled life and farming were regionally variable.[57] Social rituals also become more evident in the archaeological record, and stone smoking pipes provide the first evidence of ritual and/or social smoking. Many examples of elaborate human burials have been documented for this time period as well as the introduction of deliberate canine burials. Toward the end of the Woodland era, just before European incursion in the region, we can say that what is now the city was home to Munsee-speaking peoples.[58]

By 2000 BP, sea levels in the area of today's New York City had stabilized and were nearly at current levels.[59] A rich mixture of ecological and environmental habitats in the region made it a particularly viable and sustaining home for Woodland peoples. Some area forests had changed to mudflats and marshlands along the coast, providing around 350 square miles of oyster beds surrounding the five boroughs. Shellfish and crustaceans thrived: hard-shell and soft-shell clams, scallops, mussels, whelks, crabs, and lobster. New York Harbor housed seals, whales, porpoises, eel, flounder, sheepshead, blackfish, shad, and more. The rivers provided a predictable food source with seasonal runs of anadromous fish—inland spawning saltwater fish with nutritious fat reserves.[60] Indigenous Peoples supplemented coastal resources with inland hunting and gathering.[61] The region was rich with resources.

Not all Indigenous Peoples in the area adopted farming during the Woodland period. Archaeological evidence around New York Harbor suggests that coastal food abundance

Indigenous Pathways

Remnants of several paths established by the area's Indigenous inhabitants persist on New York's street grid. For one, imagine in your mind's eye that you are walking up St. Nicholas Avenue in Manhattan, cutting northward up the island on a diagonal from Central Park North to 169th Street, bearing right on Broadway, and continuing north toward the Bronx. Or, if you begin in Brooklyn, walk the length of Atlantic Avenue starting at the Brooklyn waterfront, go eastward into Queens where Atlantic transforms into Jamaica Avenue, and continue onward to the eastern tip of Long Island. If you are in the Bronx, the Boston Road will take you into New England. Return then to Staten Island and choose between Amboy Road along the ridge line or Richmond Avenue up over the hill to traverse the island.[64]

These well-known thoroughfares in each of the five boroughs began as Indigenous Peoples' footpaths before Europeans arrived. They circumnavigated marshlands and rock outcroppings. They connected villages and camps and indicated
the way to fishing and hunting grounds. These paths also connected Munsee-
speaking Lenape people to a broader landscape of relations and networks, including the Mohican and Kanien'kehaka (Mohawk) to the north and other Lenape or
Delaware communities located in New Jersey, Pennsylvania, eastern Long Island,
Westchester, and beyond. They facilitated the movement of goods and people to
interior regions the area's waterways could not access. Generations of use cut these
paths deeply into the landscape. The Europeans, upon their arrival, made use of
these tracks for their own purposes and connections. Wagons eventually widened
the trails and transformed them into roads. Current maps and satellite images
reveal that they are still evident, bisecting the neat geometry of the city grid or
tracing paths from east to west across boroughs preserved in asphalt (figure 1.11).

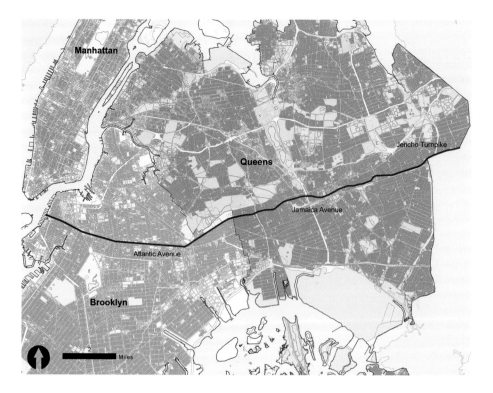

FIGURE 1.11
Atlantic Avenue cutting a path eastward across the borough of Brooklyn into Queens, where it becomes
Jamaica Avenue. The avenue continues eastward across the borough, transforming into the Jericho Turnpike
that tracks its way out to the eastern end of Long Island. This present-day route preserves an Indigenous
Peoples' pathway that existed for centuries, if not millennia, before Europeans arrived.
Image, Melanie Dieg, LPC.

may have been enough for some, who may simply have fished and traded with their farming neighbors for squash, beans, and corn.[62] Archaeobotanical evidence (micro and macro botanical remains) from harbor sites has shown, for example, that domesticated crops like maize are rare. Isotope analysis of human remains from Tottenville, Staten Island—which gives us a glimpse into the diets of early peoples by examining the isotopes that leave distinct chemical signatures on bones and teeth—shows that Indigenous Peoples on the island consumed marine foods and ate little maize.[63]

EARLY WOODLAND (3000–1700 BP)

The line dividing the Transitional Archaic from the Early Woodland period is blurry. Some archaeologists argue that the tool types of these periods overlap, making it hard to date sites by artifacts alone without context or scientific methods of dating such as radiocarbon. A brown jasper chipped stone tool (figure 1.12) excavated in the Bronx is an example of an artifact type that hardly changed for millennia, making it difficult to place in time. This handheld tool functioned as a knife and a scraper. The longitudinal sides are percussion-chipped, creating a bifacial (two-faced) cutting edge that would have been used to skin animals and cut hides or to cut and harvest plant materials. The short end of the tool functioned as a scraper, as indicated by the wear on the edge.

FIGURE 1.12
Brown jasper multipurpose tool (both sides pictured), excavated from Riverdale Park in the Bronx in 1989, dating to the Late Archaic or Early Woodland.
Qi#207031 RPAP

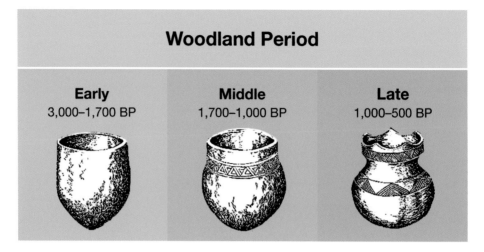

FIGURE 1.13
Basic changes in pottery style through the Woodland period. Over time, the plain, undecorated, pointed-bottom vessels of the Early Woodland gave way to the more rounded form in the Middle Woodland with incised-decorated collars. The rounded base vessels of the Late Woodland period had zones of distinct patterns and elaborately decorated collars applied to the vessel after the body was formed.
Image by Sarah Moses, LPC modelled on a figure in Public Archaeology Laboratory, New Discoveries at Old Place: The Story of Old Place Neck Site, Staten Island, New York.

One solid marker of the Early Woodland period is pottery. Pottery first appeared at this time, replacing the Transitional Archaic steatite vessels. As the Woodland period continued, the forms of pottery vessels and their surface modification and intentional decoration became more elaborate. These Early Woodland ceramics, which archaeologists call Vinette I pottery, were coil-made and paddled into shape with thick walls and very little if any surface decoration.[65] The vessels had pointed bottoms (figure 1.13, *left*) that were anchored between stones in a hearth or buried in a charcoal pit. Crushed steatite was sometimes added to the clay as a temper—an additive to prevent shrinkage and cracking during firing.[66] However, most of the clay had natural grit, sand, or shell inclusions, which served the same purpose.

MIDDLE WOODLAND (1700–1000 BP)

By the Middle Woodland period, ceramics had grown more elaborate and refined, a testament to more than a thousand years of experience making pottery. The vessel walls of Middle Woodland ceramics were thinner, and the overall body shape and base were more rounded than their Early Woodland counterparts (figure 1.13, *center*). Vessels no longer needed assistance to stand. The rims, collars, and shoulders were decorated with incised and stamped designs. The incised marks were made by a level continuous

FIGURE 1.14
Examples of three different decorative types of Middle Woodland ceramic vessels. Each is a rim sherd showing the exterior decoration. (A and B) Abbott Zoned Incised; (C) Wickham Punctate; (D and E) Bowman's Brook Stamped. The Wickham Punctate sherd (C) shows extensive blackening from use in an open fire.
(A) Qi: 211878 KAZ; (B) Qi: 211879 KAZ; (C) Qi#211880 KAZ; (D) Qi#211881 KAZ; (E) Qi#211882 KAZ

action with a smooth tool, whereas stamped designs were made by impressing differ-ent materials such as nets, cordage, fabric, or wooden sticks to make uniformly shaped holes (figure 1.14). In excavations from the Bronx, pottery was found with patterns from impressed corncobs (figure 1.15).

FIGURE 1.15
Middle Woodland ceramic vessel body sherd with decoration style known as corncob dentate. The small linear tripartite marks are where a corn cob was pressed into the wet ceramic before firing.
Schurtz Site, Bronx, NY Qi#229 SSB

Variations in use and form also emerge: jars are distinguished by a flared rim with narrow opening, while bowls are identified by their wide openings. The designs were independent of function and became more elaborate by the Late Woodland period. It is thought that the designs served several purposes: to set makers apart from one another, for aesthetics, and to signify cultural affiliation.[67] Archaeologists believe that potters were both men and women, but it was the women who passed down clan markings from generation to generation.[68]

Middle Woodland sites existed in many locales in New York State. Archaeologists have found them within today's New York City in both coastal and inland settings. Evidence for small semipermanent village communities has been found at Tottenville, Staten Island, in addition to a site in the Bronx called Throgs Neck, which avocational archaeologist Edward Kaeser first identified in the 1950s.[69] Also known as the Morris-Schurtz site, the Throgs Neck site was particularly interesting as it provided evidence for extensive trade networks during the Middle Woodland. Exotics found at the site—that is, artifact types and materials not local to New York City—include the surprising discovery of 510 plates of sheet mica.[70] Also found near the site was a reddish-purple argillite stone lanceolate (leaf-shaped) spear point known to archaeologists as a Fox Creek type. The form is local, but the argillite originated in New Jersey or Pennsylvania.

DOG BURIALS

Dogs are the only animals to have been domesticated in Indigenous America (although macaws and turkeys are known to have been domesticated in the American Southwest).[71] Dog burials have been documented in the Northeast and Midwest from the Archaic period onward and increase in frequency from the Middle to Late Woodland, archaeologically articulating the development of social rituals in this period. Some burials dating to the Middle Woodland period, found in Illinois, had the markings of great respect. The dogs were buried with clay figurines and copper beads, among other artifacts.[72]

Canine burials have been found in four of the city's five boroughs, and based on examples found in northern Manhattan, the Bronx, and Queens, their frequency increased in the Late Woodland period.[73] Dog burials found in the New York City area were often located near hearths, away from human burials. They were often buried within shell middens, which have contributed to their preservation. There does not appear to be a consistent pattern in these burials. Some were interred in groups, some singly, and some with what might be considered minor grave offerings. To date, none has been found with elaborate funerary goods. We do not know what meaning these burials had for the people who carefully interred them, but given the attention given to their placement, they must have had significance for those who consigned them to their graves.

Aakawaxung Munahanung (Island Protected from the Wind) Archaeological Site, Staten Island

The Aakawaxung Munahanung (Island Protected from the Wind) Archaeological Site was designated by the Landmarks Preservation Commission in 2021. It is the first NYC landmark specifically recognizing the many generations of Indigenous Peoples who lived in the region. Located in Tottenville at the southern-most point of Staten Island in the Conference House Park, it is the best-preserved archaeological site yet known in New York City that is associated with over 8,000 years of Indigenous occupation. At least nineteen archaeological projects were completed within the park, from excavations conducted by the American Museum of Natural History in 1893, others by the Landmarks Preservation Commission in 1980. These projects uncovered archaeological evidence of occupation dating from the Early Archaic period (9,500 to 7,000 years ago) to the Woodland period (1,500 to 500 years ago). The artifacts indicate that people hunted, fished, and gathered shellfish, nuts, and plants throughout this period and that a village was likely located at the site

FIGURE 1.16
Aakawaxung Munahanung (Island Protected from the Wind) Archaeological Site, also known as Wards Point, located in Conference House Park on the southern tip of Staten Island, looking northwest at the New Jersey coast across the Arthur Kill.
Photography by Kate Lemos McHale, LPC.

during the Woodland period.[74] Archaeologists have used multiple names for the site including Ward's Point. Significant historical archaeological resources associated with the seventeenth-century Conference House, also known as Billop House, have also been documented in the park as well. Conference House is a New York City landmark built circa 1675. Here, on September 11, 1776, there was an abortive attempt to seek a peaceful settlement of the Revolutionary War.[75] In 2021, it was the first Indigenous Peoples' site ever designated a New York City landmark.

The Aakawaxung Munahanung archaeological site name and definition resulted from consultation with the Delaware Nation, the Delaware Tribe of Indians, the Stockbridge-Munsee Community Band of Mohicans and LPC. Historical sources identified by anthropologist Robert Grumet noted that this name was first documented on July 10, 1657.[76] It likely referred to the whole of Staten Island as it did in a 1670 land deed that described "that Island lyeing & being in Hudsons Ryver, commonly callded Staten-Island & by ye Indians Aquehonga Manacknog."[77] It has also been posited that the name also referred to the village that was once located at the landmark site. The LPC consulted with the three Tribal Nations about the appropriateness of the name; they subsequently consulted Old Munsee language experts Jim Rementer and Ray Whritenour from the Lenape Talking Dictionary, who provided the correct spelling and concluded that Aakawaxung Munahanung meant "the island protected from the wind" when translated into English.[78]

LATE WOODLAND PERIOD (1000–500 BP)

In the Late Woodland period, today's city was home to a Delaware-speaking group of Eastern Algonquin peoples called the Munsee by the first European settlers; today many of these people are known as the Lenape ("the people").[79] The Munsee moved freely from western Long Island across the lower Hudson Valley and into New Jersey. Their borders were neither static nor well defined.[80]

The Munsee continued to seasonally exploit a range of environmental niches, moving between fishing, shellfish, and hunting and gathering grounds, but some also transitioned into permanent villages such as Shanscomacocke Village in Marine Park, Brooklyn, and the Keshaechquereren Village site in the Flatbush area of Brooklyn that were extant at the time of European colonization.[81] Archaeologists have identified other villages in the city at sites in Washington Heights–Inwood in Manhattan, Clason Point in the Bronx, Aqueduct in Queens, and Bowman's Brook and Aakawaxung Munahanung, in Staten Island.[82]

Chipped stone tools transformed just as pottery did. Contrary to the popular notion that all projectile points are arrowheads, many of the projectile points before the Late Woodland period were spear points. Bows and arrows were first used in the Late Woodland, which we know because the first true arrowheads appeared in this era.[83] These arrowheads include triangular points called Levanna and Madison and are found

FIGURE 1.17
A Late Woodland period triangular chert Levanna point found in Snug Harbor, Staten Island. The point would have been hafted to an arrow shaft, marking the emergence of bow and arrow technology in this period.
Qi#1680 SHMC

throughout the city, including a triangular gray-chert Levanna point excavated from the Snug Harbor site in Staten Island, now in the Repository's collection (figure 1.17)[84].

The Late Woodland ceramics are particularly distinctive in their shape and decoration. The rounded bottoms persist, but elaborate and frequently crenelated collars (figure 1.13, *right*; figure 1.18 D) were added to the top of vessels once the body had been formed. The necks of vessels become taller and narrower to accommodate these

FIGURE 1.18
Six different examples of Late Woodland decorated rim sherds from ceramic vessels. (A) Van Cortlandt Stamped, decorated with cord-wrapped stick pressed on the surface of the wet clay; (B) a punctate or impressed rim with regular impressions from the end of a reed or stick; (C) an incised and punctate rim combining tool impressions above linear and geometric designs; (D) shell-impressed sherd with a crenellated or raised-notch rim, decorated with the edge of a scallop shell; (E) Eastern Incised rim likely decorated with a fingernail; (F) a Chance Incised rim with distinctive horizontal marks above triangular marked collar.
(A) Qi# 211883 KAZ; (B) Qi# 211884 KAZ; (C) Qi# 211885 KAZ; (D) Qi# 211888 KAZ; (E) Qi# 211887 KAZ; (F) Qi# 211886 KAZ

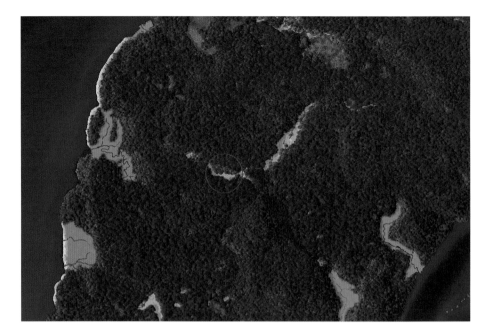

FIGURE 1.19
What Times Square looked like in 1609 when the first documented Europeans laid eyes on Mannahatta. It lay at the headwaters of a marshy stream, in stark contrast to today, home to wood ducks and hawks, snapping turtles and eastern painted turtles, muskrat, beaver, and vole—offering ecological richness and diversity enjoyed by Munsee-speaking Indigenous People who called the New York City area home. Graphic by Markley Boyer and Eric Sanderson, The Mannahatta Project, Wildlife Conservation Society.

distinctive collars. Decorative zonation—areas on the body, neck, collar, and rim with different patterns—are hallmarks of the Late Woodland period (figure 1.18 A, F). Archaeologists interpret this as an increase in the rights to use particular marks and configurations delineating matrilineal clan lineages. We see these patterns replicated in quills and beadwork of the period.[85]

The arrival of Europeans delineates the conclusion of the Woodland period. The end of the period was not a singular moment but an extended time of first encounters, trade, and interaction between Indigenous Peoples and European colonists. It ushered in an era of significant cultural, political, and ecological change (figure 1.19) throughout the region that affected the Munsee and Europeans differently. Whatever the difference in impact, both peoples' lifeways were dramatically altered, as was the landscape.

THE EARLY COLONIAL OR CONTACT PERIOD (500–250 BP OR 1450–1700 CE)

The Early Colonial period, also called the Contact period, marks the time when Indigenous and non-Indigenous people first encountered each other. Recent scholarship has transformed archaeological thinking to move beyond a single moment of contact.

Instead, contemporary archaeologists conceptualize this period as a process, a series of small- and large-scale historical encounters, and the subsequent entanglements between peoples of different cultures.[86] Until the early colonial period, archaeology, Indigenous Peoples' oral traditions, and ethnohistory are what we have to understand the lives of Indigenous Peoples. But the contact period brings the European written record to bear on the subject and adds a new resource for archaeologists to evaluate the archaeological and historical record. Like all texts, however, European histories are written with a cultural bias and perspective that must be contextualized and carefully considered.

In New York City, the Early Colonial period is when Indigenous Peoples, Europeans, and Africans—most of whom were enslaved—first encountered one another. This period is linked irretrievably to European colonialism and the geopolitical maneuvering of competing Indigenous Peoples and European colonial powers. Studies of this period seek to understand how each of these groups changed and were changed by the other, and how each of their worlds were reformulated as European imperialism gained control of the region. The complex cultural misunderstandings between Europeans and Indigenous Peoples have been described well as a "middle ground," an accommodation and system of meaning that developed between two groups so they could interact despite incomplete understandings of what the other wanted.[87]

European colonialism in the Americas, as elsewhere, began slowly. First it was traders and temporary visits, but soon those developed into lasting settlements that acquired Indigenous communities' lands, people, and possessions. This is not unique to New York or, indeed, to the Americas. European colonial interactions everywhere followed familiar pathways: resistance and domination, exploitation and commodification, and the modification of land, material goods, and resources.[88] Although the broad outlines of the story are nearly universal, the local particulars are various and sometimes unexpected. Most studies of this period have focused on European settlers rather than Indigenous people. It is important to recognize that Indigenous Peoples were not just passive reactors but were creative and innovative in response to colonialism. The archaeological record may help provide a fuller and less one-sided understanding of the early colonial period and is therefore important to continue to study.[89]

The Swannekens ("The Salty People")

When Europeans first arrived, Munsee speakers lived comfortably in what would become Manhattan and the other four boroughs. In warm seasons, they collected shellfish along rivers and shores; in winter, they moved into forests for warmth; if they farmed, they did so along rivers and flatlands. This way of life changed with the arrival of the first Dutch settlers in 1624. Some of the Munsee community names can still be found on our landscape, others no longer: the Manates and the Reckgawawanc of Manhattan, the Sinoway and Wecquaesgeeks in the Bronx, the Matinecooks in Flushing and the Rockaway in Newtown and Jamaica, Queens, the Canarsee in Brooklyn, and the Raritan, Hackensack, and Canarsee who jointly occupied Staten Island.[90] Their names

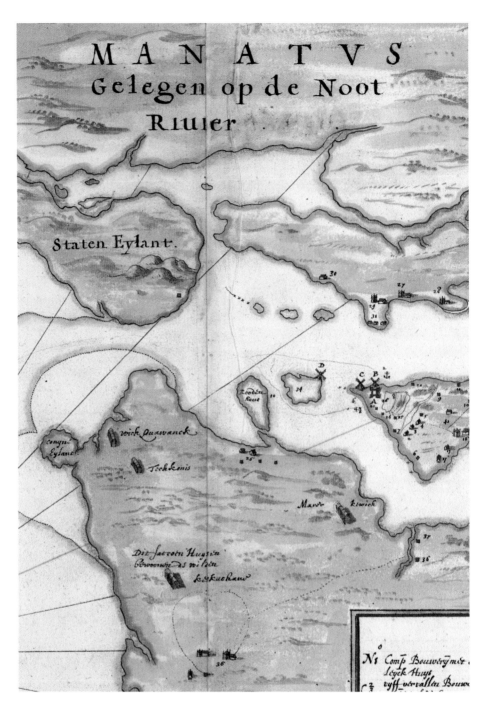

FIGURE 1.20

Detail of the Manatus Map of 1639 depicting Brooklyn, Staten Island, and the southern tip of Manhattan in the middle right. Governors' Island is in pink at the center with a windmill marked "D" and Red Hook to the left of it. The names of the first Dutch landholders are enumerated in the legend (partially visible, bottom right). Four Munsee longhouse settlements are illustrated in what is now Brooklyn, with their names recorded. Clockwise from the right, they are the Mareckewich (downtown Brooklyn), Keskaechqueren (Flatlands), Techkonis (Gravesend), and Wichquawanack (Bay Ridge). A pair of Dutch *bouwerji*, or farms, and a plantation are illustrated bottom left at number 36, owned by Wolfert Gerritse van Couwenhoven, after whom Gerritsen Beach is named.

Source: *Manatus Gelegen op de Noot River* (*Manhattan located on the North River*), Library of Congress.

come to us as documented in the records and accounts of early European settlers, such as the Manatus map originally drawn in 1639 that depicts Canarsee longhouse settlements in Brooklyn (figure 1.20). We know little of what the Munsee thought of the first arrivals, but we do know they called them *Swannekens* ("the salty people")—perhaps because they came from across the salty ocean, or perhaps because their actions left a bitter taste.[91]

The Munsee, like many other Indigenous Peoples who saw these strange-looking men in their harbors and on their land for the first time, were willing hosts. There was a brief period of contact when the impact that each culture made upon the other was small, when exchanges between the groups were thought of as gift giving. As noted, we do not know how the Indigenous Peoples viewed the Dutch, but the Dutch characterized the locals as *Wilden*, or "wild people."[92] Their written descriptions and portraits show Munsee men wearing a cloak (of duffle cloth or furs) over a hide breechclout. They often painted their faces, shaved some of their hair, and wore wampum ornaments and hide bags for pipes and other important possessions.[93]

Wampum

The word *wampum*, referring to an Indigenous Peoples shell bead, comes from the Algonquian language. It seems to have originated among the Iroquoian and Algonquian language groups in New York State and was used at least from the Middle Woodland period onward, although there is evidence that earlier, during the Archaic period, beads made from exotic (nonlocal) sources were traded.[94] True wampum is made from two shell species, both found along bodies of salt water: channeled whelk (*Busycon canaliculatum*, figure 1.21) provided white beads from the central column of the shell, and purple beads were obtained from the margins of the quahog (*Mercenaria mercenaria*).[95] The beads were tubular, well shaped, and of a consistent size.

FIGURE 1.21
Channeled whelk (Busycon canaliculatum) of the type used to make white wampum beads, excavated during the South Ferry Terminal project.
Qi#107630 SFT

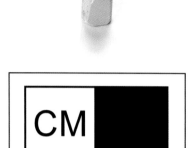

Stadt Huys Block (1987)

FIGURE 1.22
Tubular shell bead from a seventeenth-century or
early Colonial period deposit excavated from the
Stadt Huys Project in lower Manhattan. A European
saw and drill were likely used to manufacture these
beads.
Qi#203217 SFT

Wampum's seminal significance among the Haudenosaunee (Iroquois) dates dates to the founding of the Great League of Peace in the early twelfth century, but European contact assigned a variety of other roles to the beads.[96] They became a medium of currency in the beaver trade, and the Dutch used them as such in the mid-seventeenth century.[97] As European drills became available, they could produce wampum more easily (figure 1.22), and sometimes Europeans manufactured the beads.[98]

The long use of these beads suggests that they had symbolic meanings to Indigenous Peoples before they became currency within regional trade networks.[99] Wampum, woven into headbands and belts, was used to cement Indigenous treaties and marriages, was given to the bereaved, was used in important exchanges, and chronicled historic events using symbols woven into belts.[100]

Europeans began to use wampum simply as a currency of exchange, mostly for beaver skins. Initially they crafted it in upper New York State; but wampum making was soon transformed into semi-industrial production among coastal peoples, especially in winter months. The beads were strung into uniform lengths of about six feet. As Europeans began to control trade networks, they reset wampum values.[101] It has been suggested that a form of triangular trade developed between coastal wampum makers and the Dutch. The former made beads, which were exchanged for trade goods. The Dutch then used the wampum to secure pelts, which they sent to Europe.[102] Sites of wampum production are relatively easy to identify because of the high frequency of "blanks" and the tools used in wampum manufacture.[103] Ultimately, Europeans inserted themselves into the making of wampum, using better tools and displacing both the original meaning of the beads and their makers.

The Dutch did not appear to have much interest in the Munsee, except as providers of food and other assistance in the early days of the colony. They saw them as very different from themselves, almost a separate kind of being. The Dutch wanted land and offered goods in exchange. Initially, the Munsee were willing hosts, and Munsee culture was little affected.[104] Archaeobotanical studies of this period that have looked look at preserved plant remains, such as seeds, pollen, charcoal, and wood from early colonial sites in Lower Manhattan, suggest that most of the plants from the first half of the seventeenth century were dominated by indigenous squash, fruits, berries, and an assortment of food, medicinal, and craft plants, such as those for basket weaving and cordage.[105] The dominance of indigenous plant remains supports the idea that early Dutch colonists were dependent on a broader range of Indigenous Peoples' food sources than previously understood. But as the Dutch and others they brought with them, including enslaved and free Africans and indentured servants, began to reshape the region that would become the city, their incursion on Indigenous Peoples spiraled into cultural conflict escalating, at times, to warfare and massacres.[106]

The Europeans brought animals, farming practices, and concepts of land ownership that had a drastic impact on local Indigenous ecosystems.[107] The same archaeobotanical study that showed Dutch use of indigenous plant materials also indicated a sharp decrease in plant diversity as the seventeenth century progressed and European colonies became established settlements.[108] The indigenous plant diversity in Lower Manhattan underwent a 50 percent reduction by the end of the seventeenth century, increasing to an 80 percent decline by the early eighteenth century. After the first hundred years of settlement, only a handful of indigenous plants remained.

As colonial settlement expanded, farms were established. Farming meant two things. First, the land was in permanent demand and occupied by the Dutch. Fences were erected and European laws governing private property enacted, so the Munsee no longer had access to their hunting or fishing territories. Second, European domestic animals required particular conditions for survival. Forested areas were cleared for fields and pastures, streams were dammed for millponds, and wetlands were filled or drained. Indigenous ecosystems were permanently changed. The Munsee had to adapt, and one adaptation was to treat European domestic animals at large as fair game. The Dutch court records are full of complaints about Indigenous Peoples killing pigs that had wandered astray.[109] Apart from the temptation such creatures offered, they often caused damage; European pigs, for example, were eating Munsee gardens and plant resources such as acorns that were central to Indigenous Peoples' diets.

Indigenous Peoples Today

Indigenous Peoples still live in New York City. Some are descended from individuals who were here when the European colonists arrived, and others have come from across the Americas to live in what is now New York City. The descendants of the original Munsee now live among the Delaware Nation, the Delaware Tribe of Indians, the Stockbridge-Munsee Community Band of Mohicans, and the Shinnecock Nation, all of which are recognized by the U.S. federal government as Tribal Nations descended from those that once lived in what is now New York City.[110] New York State has also recognized these tribes, as well as the Unkechaug Nation.

The city's five boroughs are located on the ancestral homelands of these Tribal Nations. The Munsee ancestors of the contemporary Lenape people were separated by two dialects of the Eastern Algonquian language—Unami south of the Raritan River and Munsee to the north—and by family groups.[111] The Sinoway were in the east Bronx and the Wiechquaeskecks in the west Bronx and Manhattan. The Canarsee were in Brooklyn, with villages in southern Manhattan. The Rockaway and Matinecock were in Queens, and the Canarsee, Raritan, and Hackensack were on Staten Island. The Unkechaug and Shinnecock of Long Island had different ties that connected them culturally and by language to the Indigenous Peoples of southeastern Connecticut across the Long Island Sound to the north.[112]

During the seventeenth and early eighteenth centuries, the region's Indigenous communities faced increasing pressure from expanding colonial settlements hungry for land. These factors contributed to a rapidly changing ecosystem that affected Indigenous Peoples' food sources and other resources. Disease and armed conflict with Europeans further diminished the size of Indigenous communities. These forces combined and contributed to the displacement and reconfiguration of Tribal entities in the New York City region as they reestablished their villages farther away from European settlement. Some communities banded together to form new alliances among themselves, with their Unami kin, and with neighboring tribes like the Mahicans to the north and east. Land treaties brokered with Europeans provided temporary stability, until European expansion into new territories violated negotiated terms and displaced the Munsee farther north and west into Pennsylvania and Ohio. Today, descendants of the Munsee, including those who identify as Delaware or Mahican, live on Tribal land in Wisconsin, Kansas, Oklahoma, and Ontario, Canada.

Although Tribal Nations have been displaced from their ancestral homeland, federal legislation requires its agencies to consult those with hereditary ties to project locations for many development projects. Under these laws, agencies must consider the impact of their projects, consider alternatives, and then if an impact cannot be avoided, develop mitigation measures to address it and consult with Tribal Nations as well as other stakeholders throughout the process. It is also recommended that city projects with the potential to affect sites of Indigenous Peoples do the same.

Ultimately, the Dutch took Munsee lands, and Indigenous Peoples in the region were decimated by disease and driven from their established way of life. The Dutch sought beaver in trade, and the Munsee redirected their efforts to trapping, distorting their own economy to accommodate European demands. Predictably, the beaver harvest grew more and more difficult as the population were overexploited by the middle of the seventeenth century. Even reaching into larger portions of Haudenosaunee lands in northern and western New York was unsuccessful. At the same time, other Europeans, especially the French to the north in Canada, were vying to buy pelts from their Indigenous allies. The decline of the fur trade is closely tied to the loss of New Amsterdam to the British. The Dutch were purely concerned with commerce, but the British arrived to settle the land permanently.

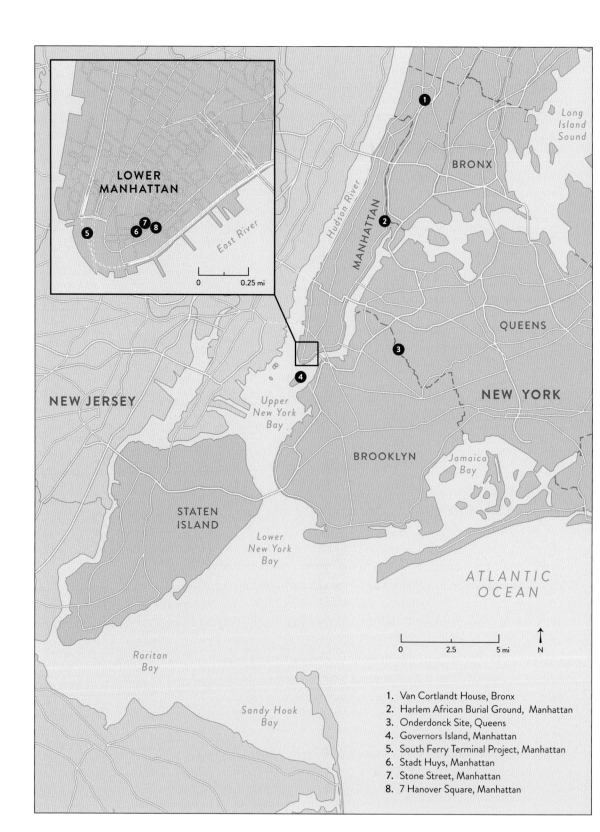

LOWER
MANHATTAN

East River

0   0.25 mi

Long
Island
Sound

BRONX

Hudson River

MANHATTAN

QUEENS

NEW YORK

NEW JERSEY

Upper
New York
Bay

BROOKLYN

Jamaica
Bay

STATEN
ISLAND

Lower
New York
Bay

ATLANTIC
OCEAN

0   2.5   5 mi   N

Raritan
Bay

Sandy Hook
Bay

1. Van Cortlandt House, Bronx
2. Harlem African Burial Ground, Manhattan
3. Onderdonck Site, Queens
4. Governors Island, Manhattan
5. South Ferry Terminal Project, Manhattan
6. Stadt Huys, Manhattan
7. Stone Street, Manhattan
8. 7 Hanover Square, Manhattan

2

DUTCH BEGINNINGS, 1624–1664

American children learn early on about the history of their country. To the extent that its origin stories look to European colonizers, neglecting previous Indigenous occupants, they tend to start with the British, settling in Jamestown and at Plymouth Rock early in the seventeenth century.[1] It seems that the British were the dominant players. But in reality, the Spanish were the earliest colonizers of the Americas, in the mid-sixteenth century, and Dutch colonies were almost as early as the British. The Dutch were the first European settlers by a long shot in what is now called New York, arriving in 1624.

When Henry Hudson famously sailed as a Dutch envoy in 1609 up the river that now bears his name, no one could have predicted the outcome of his expedition. Hudson, an Englishman in the service of the Dutch, was searching for a western passage to China. He continued exploring northward up the river as far as Albany, when the fear of shallow waters turned the boat back toward the Atlantic. The voyage of the *Halve Moon* (figure 2.1) alerted the Dutch to the commercial potential of the region in the burgeoning fur trade. It led the way to the establishment of Fort Orange, a trading post in present-day Albany in 1624, and New Amsterdam in the same year, two strategic footholds that anchored Dutch New Netherland, originally a much larger stretch of land claimed by the Dutch.[2] This first adventure suggested a promising situation to European colonizers—a land with many resources, a "land of milk and honey."[3] New Amsterdam was initially intended not to be permanent but to be simply a small settlement designed to extract furs. It seemed promising at its beginning, but as the number of beavers declined, the Dutch were unwilling to invest enough resources in the colony to protect it from an easy capture by the British. The Dutch had colonies in other parts of the world, including important ones in Batavia (Indonesia) and Brazil, both of which were more financially rewarding than their colony in New Amsterdam. Batavia yielded spices, among other things, and Brazil was a hub for the sugar trade.

FIGURE 2.1
Replica of *De Halve Maen* (*The Half Moon*), the Dutch East India Company (VOC) ship captained by Henry Hudson that sailed into New York Harbor in 1609 and into the land of the Munsee. The replica was built in Amsterdam in 1909 and given to the United States on the three hundredth anniversary of the ship's original voyage to New York.
New York City Department of Environmental Protection, DEP Archives, Digital Image ID p001206.

The archaeology of these years—the Early Colonial or Contact period—consists of two different kinds of sites. The first are those in which there are European artifacts presumably acquired through "down the line" trade, in which objects are passed from one Indigenous group to another, which may result in early European objects being found in places not yet colonized. A few sites in the region we now call New York City show indirect evidence of this contact—for instance, where glass beads and European goods are found at Indigenous sites such as Aakawaxung Munahanung (Ward's Point) on Staten Island.[4] The second site type includes those with evidence of both Indigenous and European peoples. There is no direct information from archaeological data that the Dutch were in New York before 1609, but it is possible, if unlikely, that some Europeans (such as French traders) may have made contact before Hudson's arrival.[5] However, New Amsterdam and Fort Orange in Albany show extensive direct contact between European and Indigenous Peoples after that date.

Although archaeologists have only discovered and excavated a handful of Dutch sites in New York City, there is good material evidence and enough early historic narratives to show us what life in New Amsterdam was like from the mid-seventeenth century onward. Archaeologists can identify evidence of town planning, some of which is still visible in Lower Manhattan, and we can see the Dutch focus on trade in the locations of their settlements in New Amsterdam and in Brooklyn, Queens, up the Hudson, and on Long Island. We can even see the interactions among groups—Indigenous Peoples, enslaved Africans, the Dutch, and other Europeans—in the archaeological record. Above all, archaeology reveals the strong desire of immigrants from the Netherlands to create homes that replicated their ways of life in Europe.

During the late sixteenth and early seventeenth centuries, the United Provinces (today known as the Netherlands) was at its economic and cultural peak. Trade, art, science, and the military were all functioning at a high level within the European sphere, during what historians sometimes call the Dutch Golden Age.[6] Trade, initiated by the Vereenigde Oost-Indische Compagnie (VOC), known as the Dutch East India Company, developed commerce in the East, especially Indonesia, in the very early seventeenth century and made the Dutch wealthy. It was also the era of the Great Masters—painters such as Rembrandt, Vermeer, and others.

The Golden Age began with Dutch independence. In 1568, the Protestant Dutch rebelled against the Catholic Hapsburg Empire and its head, King Philip II of Spain. Dutch colonial endeavors were in part a by-product of the rebellion. When it ended, the Dutch mercantile economy had a fleet of ships at its command and used them to explore the world.

After the long war of independence, the Dutch began to develop a distinctly commercial approach to the world around them. The government (States General) founded the West India Company (WIC), like the VOC an investor-owned joint-stock company, in 1621 to challenge and compete with the colonial enterprises (and empires) of the Portuguese, Spanish, and English in the Atlantic world. They saw the benefit of establishing far-flung bases before most other European countries. This brought them to the New World. Unlike later colonizers—especially the British—they were not interested in establishing permanent settlements. Instead, they hoped to establish hubs for trade with Indigenous Peoples through which they could harvest commodities such as beaver skins, especially after Hudson's expedition illuminated the potential benefits of such trade.

Two groups of non-Dutch people, Indigenous residents and enslaved Africans, were essential players in the history of the Dutch settlement. At first, Verhulst, the governor in 1625, and the settlers in New Amsterdam were directed to behave well toward the Indigenous groups, to be honest in dealing with them, and not to do them harm (figure 2.2).[7] These proscriptions were clearly not purely altruistic. The West India Company needed good relations with those who controlled the principal resource: furs. Therefore, land acquisition was to be peaceful, and any offenses against Native American people were to be punished.

Although the Dutch colony lasted only about half a century, its effects were vast. They brought several kinds of goods desired by Indigenous people. Some, such as

FIGURE 2.2

Detail from T'Fort Nieuw Amsterdam op de Manhatans, published by J. Hartger, Amsterdam, 1651, illustrating the interaction between Native Americans and Europeans, two distinctly different worlds. Note the foregrounding of Indigenous canoes of various types. It is unclear if their depictions are grounded in reality, although some historical accounts tell of the *Half Moon* being greeted by Indigenous Peoples in canoes "made of single hollowed trees" (Stiles 1867, 10).

The Miriam and Ira D. Wallach Division of Art, Prints and Photographs: Print Collection, New York Public Library.

glass beads, were thought to have spiritual properties. Others, such as duffel cloth and metal tools, were more practical.[8] And the beaver trade was strongly connected to wampum: "Wampum was the magnet which drew beaver out of interior forests."[9] The Munsee and local Algonquian groups had a mixed economy of hunting, small-scale farming, and the gathering of plants and shellfish, moving from one set of resources to another in a seasonal round. But the Dutch wanted beaver in great quantities, which the Munsee sought to provide. Soon the local beaver supply was exhausted, and the Europeans moved farther up the Hudson to trade with Mohawk groups. The distortion of the Munsee economy to accommodate European demands meant that, in their search for beaver, they neglected the harvesting of, and caring for, other resources. However, in spite of the impact on the economy, in some important ways, the effects of Dutch intrusion into Indigenous Peoples' lives were likely less extensive than the impact of Catholic colonizers like the Spanish and French in other settings.[10] The Protestant Dutch sent no missionaries, leaving Native Americans free to worship in their own religion. The persistence of religion is one of the most important elements in cultural continuity and survival.

At first, the West India Company (WIC) was granted a monopoly on collecting furs, notably beaver pelts, which were greatly prized in Europe and used to make felt hats (figure 2.3). Some in the Dutch government only valued trade. Others wanted a proper self-sufficient colony. However, New Amsterdam had relatively few settlers throughout the colony's existence, probably too few to sustain a thriving colony.[11]

FIGURE 2.3

Felted beaver fur was the preferred material for making hats in most of Europe from the sixteenth to the nineteenth century. In Johannes Vermeer's *Officer and a Laughing Girl*, painted circa 1657, the Dutch officer is wearing a wide-brimmed beaver felt hat that was the fashion of the time. Felting was a process in which the fur was separated from the skin and repeatedly heated and pounded, resulting in a compressed and thickened "felt." The natural qualities of beaver fur rendered beaver felt waterproof, strong, and malleable. Paintings by Dutch masters, such as this one, allow archaeologists to see what artifacts were in use in the homeland and are also vital for dating their use.

Copyright The Frick Collection.

This was likely because the conditions in the Netherlands were economically comfortable and tolerant of what was an ethnically and racially mixed population, so there was little incentive to move away. Probably a number of those who migrated to New Netherland expected to make some money and return home. Dreams of rapid riches rarely came to fruition, however, because of control from Holland that limited the furs that ordinary settlers could harvest.[12]

Managing the colony was difficult. A series of governors, some who were in control for as little as a year, experienced a variety of problems. Some of those who came to be in charge of the new settlement had little experience in governance and were chosen because of family connections. Others were unable to negotiate between authorities in Amsterdam and local conditions, especially with an ocean in between that took many weeks to cross. And even skilled managers would have had difficulties with creating an entirely new settlement, which needed new housing, food for settlers, and protection from potentially hostile neighbors, all of which had to be accomplished with a relatively small labor force, unfamiliar with the local terrain.

THE FIRST SETTLEMENT

In 1624, the first Dutch settled in what was to become New Amsterdam. Thirty Walloon families (from what is now Belgium), contracted to stay for six years, were the first group to arrive. The West India Company provided passage and supplies to entice settlement. A handful, mostly men, were sent to Noten Eylant, now Governors Island (a New York City historic district), along with a few soldiers, sailors, enslaved Africans, and employees of the West India Company.[13] The rest were dispersed to other strategically important places (Long Island Sound, the Connecticut River, and Fort Orange). By 1625, they had built a sawmill, probably wind-powered, on Governors Island. In 1998, archaeological testing uncovered the likely remains of this sawmill, although it was not in the place shown on the 1639 Manatus Map, which is our most detailed representation of this early period (figure 2.4).

The archaeology uncovered square or rectangular postholes from a circular structure with a thirty-five-foot diameter and handwrought nails, corresponding to its expected size and shape. There were clear indications of burning, suggesting that this was the sawmill of historical records, because records indicated that it had burned down in 1648.[14] This is a good example of how field archaeology in conjunction with historical records can show us the past. It demonstrates that the early map is reliable, though not entirely accurate as to the placement of the mill. It is important to recognize the significance of maps to colonial governments. They were used as tools of colonization and demonstrated to other European countries that they (in this case, the Dutch) had knowledge and some control of the terrain. They mapped what they were interested in, and what they thought was important. Since local settlers probably all knew where the sawmill was, it is not surprising that its location was not identified accurately.

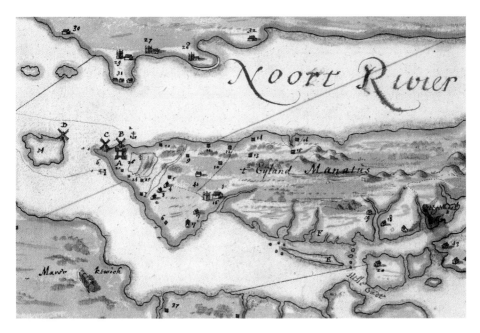

FIGURE 2.4
Detail of the 1639 Manatus Map depicting the wind-powered West India Company sawmill (letter "D"), which was used for cutting timbers for building materials and readying wood for export. Archaeologists located the windmill on the eastern, rather than the western, side of the island. The windmill was burned in 1648.
Image from the collections of the Library of Congress.

Even these early settlers were encouraged to bring enslaved people with them. The settlers were loaned land and farms by the West India Company and were allowed to trade with Indigenous Peoples.[15] But they agreed not to make any products (such as cloth) that would compete with Dutch manufactures.[16] There were more than a dozen enslaved Africans in this first settlement, probably from what we now know as Angola and the Democratic Republic of the Congo.[17] There are records of at least some of their names—Big Manuel, Little Anthony, Simon Congo, and Anthony Portuguese— although we do not know who chose these names. The Company made them build the colony's first structures on what is now Governors Island. By the end of 1625, the Company moved them to Manhattan and put them to work cutting brush and leveling hills, the first part of the long process of developing and settling the island. They cut timber, worked the mills, farmed the land, and did the heavy labor associated with the construction of the wharves and the loading and unloading of ships (figure 2.5).[18] Enslaved Africans lived in barracks outside the city wall.

In 1626, four ships with forty-five settlers, seeds, livestock, trees, tools, and trade goods arrived to add to the population. Thirteen years later, the Manatus map shows forty-five structures in the settlement (figure 2.4).[19] These houses and settlers were important to support the Dutch claim (against British interests) to the land surrounding

FIGURE 2.5

This 1640 engraving gives a glimpse of the enslaved African labor, customarily hidden, that built colonial New York City. The first Dutch settlement in New Amsterdam included more than a dozen Africans enslaved by the Dutch West India Company. The harbor and foreshore of the New Amsterdam settlement are observable in the distance.

Nieu Amsterdam. Cum Privilegio Ordinum Hollandiae et West-Frisae [*Copyright The States of Holland and West Frisia*]. I. N. Phelps Stokes Collection, New York Public Library.

the North River (the Hudson), with New Amsterdam to the south, and Fort Nassau/Orange (now Albany) anchoring the north end.[20] The West India Company originally had ambitious claims to a swath of land from the Delaware (which they called the South River), to the Hudson and beyond to Connecticut (figure 2.6), but they could not hold any of this area for any length of time. At forty years, New Amsterdam was their most persistent settlement.

Perhaps the most visible artifact of the Dutch period is the layout of the streets of Lower Manhattan south of Wall Street, which marked the original wall bounding the settlement. Dutch town planning was influenced by Italian, Spanish, and ultimately ancient Roman ideas of urban design, but these theories ran up against practical considerations. The fort, originally designed as polygonal, was apparently built as a square. We can see the influence of the Dutch homeland in the positioning of the town on a river, laid out by Crijn Fredericksz, who came to New Amsterdam in 1626 to plan the colony at the direction of the Company. The Company instructed Fredericksz to

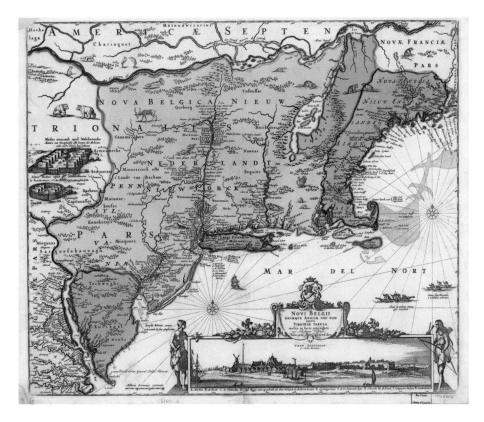

FIGURE 2.6

Novi Belgii Novaeque Angliae nec non partis Virginiae tabula multis in locis emendata, circa 1655, by Nicolaes Vissher. This plan was drawn for a Dutch audience, intending to attract Dutch settlers to New Netherland, and idealizes the comparative strength of the New Netherland colony (yellow) to New England's (in pink) at the time (see Cohen and Augustyn 1997, 32–33). The canoes, depicted in the lower view of Manhattan, are the same ones depicted in the Hartger map in figure 2.2, which suggests it was a stock image used by European cartographers who likely never saw the canoes for themselves.
I. N. Phelps Stokes Collection, New York Public Library.

create a strategic place that would safeguard its trading operations. His plan featured a fort with streets radiating from it following natural topography. The fort was near what is now the Alexander Hamilton U.S. Custom House, a New York City landmark.[21] He included the canal, a typically Dutch element, that lies under today's Broad Street (where the New York Stock Exchange, another New York City landmark, is located), and he did not impose a grid structure on the street layout. Fredericksz' urban plan has hardly changed over the past four centuries and is the only remaining above ground evidence of the Dutch settlement in Manhattan. The street plan itself is a New York City landmark, called the Street Plan of New Amsterdam and Colonial New York.[22] The Castello Plan, seen here, shows the layout of the town in 1660 (figure 2.7).

The Dutch did not settle only in Lower Manhattan. They also established a number of other strategically located small communities in a variety of locations. Fort Orange

FIGURE 2.7

Redraft of the Castello Plan, depicting 1660, from Stokes 1916, New York Public Library. The map shows what was New Amsterdam and is now part of Lower Manhattan; it is now the Street Plan of New Amsterdam and Colonial New York, a New York City landmark. The palisade on the right side of the plan runs along what is now Wall Street, and the canal is now Broad Street near the Stock Exchange. Note the low density of buildings and the many gardens.

John Wolcott Adam, Redraft of the Castello Plan, New Amsterdam as it appeared in 1660, engraved map, 1916. New-York Historical Society, 57812. Photography ©New-York Historical Society.

(Oranje), in the area of today's Albany, and the settlement of Breukelyn (Brooklyn) are probably the best known besides Haarlem. But there were also New Utrecht, Flatbush, Flatlands, Bushwick, and Maspeth, many of which survive as neighborhoods in the outer boroughs. The only known remains of Dutch Haarlem consist of traces of a burial ground.

Harlem Burial Ground

Nieuw Haarlem was a Dutch village founded in 1658 as a security buffer for New Amsterdam from northern invaders; it was also a farming outpost.[23] It was located between today's 124th and 126th streets alongside the Harlem River.[24] The initial settlement had a garrison with a few soldiers as well as Dutch and Walloon farmers, with households that included enslaved people. The Reformed

Low Dutch Church of Harlem was the center of the settlement. It had an associated segregated burial ground, likely in use from the late 1660s until the mid-nineteenth century, and in its later period people of African ancestry who were not associated with the church were also interred there. Historical documents indicate that the remains of those of European ancestry were disinterred and reinterred in Woodlawn Cemetery in 1869.[25] Burials of people of African ancestry—both enslaved and free—were left at the site in an area that today lies between 126th and 127th streets and First and Second avenues.[26] This block was subsequently redeveloped multiple times and has been, in order, an amusement park, a casino, a movie studio, and a bus depot. An archaeological survey completed in 2015 revealed that human remains that had been disturbed as a result of the past development are still present (figure 2.8).[27] The City of New York has been working with the Harlem African Burial Ground Task Force, including the Elmendorf Reformed Church (the descendant church of the Reformed Low Dutch Church of Harlem) and other community stakeholders, to appropriately document, memorialize, and commemorate the Harlem African Burial Ground.

FIGURE 2.8
Harlem African Burial Ground archaeological testing in 2015 inside the existing bus depot. Photograph by AKRF, Inc.

Governance and Land Ownership

Some of the governors of New Amsterdam are well known, and their names are taught in American history courses. The first of these, Peter Minuit, governed from 1626 to 1631 and famously bought (or so he thought) Manhattan Island in 1626 for sixty guilders' worth of goods (something like five thousand dollars today).[28] The Dutch thought they had purchased the land outright. The Munsee thought they were selling temporary rights to the land.[29] This fundamental misunderstanding was the source of much contention and conflict over the years. Indigenous Peoples in North America on the eve of colonial settlement held property collectively, although by somewhat differing rules depending upon their affiliations.[30] Individuals did not hold property. Regulations or conventions existed for the uses (shared or restricted to the family or kin group) of different types of resources: planting fields, clam banks, fishing ponds, berry-picking areas, and hunting grounds. A seventeenth-century court case related to a Dutch family—the Van Rensselaers—hints at the different cultural expectations of land transactions. For the Dutch, a transfer was a finite arrangement. After the purchase was made, the land belonged to the buyer. But for their Indigenous partners, it was not finite and was made to promote ongoing good relations between groups based on reciprocity and generosity. In this case, the Van Rensselaer estate land agent petitioned the Dutch court to recoup the costs he incurred when he fed, hosted, and gave gifts to groups of the Munsee who visited the estate often after the purchase, expecting to be treated generously. The Van Rensselaers refused to compensate the agent for these expenses. They regarded the expenses as unnecessary because, in their opinion, they owned the land.[31]

In the early years of the settlement, the West India Company had trouble attracting Europeans to the colony. So, in 1629, the Company announced the Patroonship Plan.[32] Under the new policy, the Company would establish estates in the Hudson Valley and provide enslaved Africans if the grantee brought fifty European immigrants to the colony.[33] This initiative drew about three hundred European settlers and about sixty enslaved Africans. But most of these endeavors failed, and the Europeans left. The only profitable patroonship, which lasted into the 1650s, was established by Kiliaen Van Rensselaer, a Dutch diamond and pearl merchant from Amsterdam.

Forced Import of Africans

After the West India Company captured Elmina on the southern coast of modern Ghana in 1637, the Dutch sent even more enslaved Africans to all their colonies, including New Netherland. Elmina or Mina, as it is popularly known, was simultaneously a mercantile trading post, a dungeon for African captives held for transport into enslavement, and a defensive fortress (figure 2.9). It was built by the Portuguese

FIGURE 2.9
Castelo de São Jorge da Mina in Elmina, Ghana. Fortress, trading post, and prison, Elmina was captured by the Dutch in 1637 and became a center of Dutch slave export to the Americas.
Photograph by Matthew C. Reilly.

in 1482 to facilitate and protect their trade interests in West Africa. Elmina was captured by the Dutch in 1637 and became a center for the export of enslaved people to their colonies in Brazil, the Caribbean, and North America. An estimated thirty thousand captives passed yearly through Elmina's infamous "door of no return" for transport across the Atlantic. All told, the Atlantic slave trade, involving most European countries (the Portuguese, the British, the Spanish, the French, the Dutch, and the Danish), is thought to have transported between 12 million and 15.4 million Africans into bondage.[34]

The Dutch initially allowed elements of personal freedom and autonomy for enslaved Africans while still holding people in bondage. In 1636, the local Dutch clergyman, Dominie Evarardus Bogardus, sought a schoolmaster to teach all of the children of the settlement, including children of African ancestry. He encouraged everyone to attend religious services regardless of birth. He also performed wedding and baptismal services for people of African descent, treating the enslaved as humans. However, these limited measures were soon rolled back; in 1655, the Dutch Reformed Church changed its policy and would no longer baptize children of African descent.[35] More fundamentally, there is no known evidence that any Dutch person challenged the institution of slavery in the colony.

KIEFT'S REIGN

In 1638, Willem Kieft arrived as the newly appointed governor, although he lacked experience in governance. He saw himself as a member of the elite, and he was arrogant toward colonists and Indigenous Peoples alike. He found the settlement in a dilapidated state: the fort needed repair, and the animals owned by the West India Company were lost. He attempted at once to establish some governance, and he promoted town planning, free trade, and expansionism.[36]

The New Amsterdam settlement depended upon African men as a buffer to protect the community from hostile Munsee because their dwellings were on the outskirts of the colony and so were most likely to be attacked first.[37] In the summer of 1643, Kieft granted half-freedom and some land to eleven men of African ancestry and their wives along both sides of what is now Third Avenue in the Bowery (figure 2.10), north of where the European settlers lived in Lower Manhattan. Their wives remained enslaved and, critically, so did their children. While these African men were no longer forced to take orders on a daily basis, they were not free. They had to make annual payments or return to bondage. Even while not fully enslaved, they were obliged to work for the Company when so directed.[38] Twenty years later, just before the British takeover, these and other enslaved men under the control of the West India Company were emancipated.[39]

Around this time, the West India Company again changed its policy, relaxing its fur trade monopoly as an incentive to settlers, for many of the earliest colonists had left New Amsterdam to go home.[40] Other groups began to immigrate: traders and merchants, farmers and craftsmen, enough to create a small town with all those needed to conduct life in the community. There were many kinds of artisans and workers, merchants, ship masters and sailors, tailors, bakers, and carpenters. Contracts from the West India Company reveal several housing types planned in the colony: ordinary houses as well as housebarns (in which farmers, their workers, animals, and equipment lived under one roof) were built of wood, while churches were made of stone. Houses, a form of material culture, also revealed the distinctive influence of Dutch architecture, urban and rural. In urban New Amsterdam, Dutch houses were built with the narrow gable end facing the street (figure 2.11); there was a tax advantage because houses were taxed by linear rods (the Dutch unit of measurement) on the street front.[41]

Kieft is probably best known for inciting a series of terrible wars with the Munsee, Raritans, and Wecquaesgeek.[42] The origins of these wars may be traceable to a "contribution" he and the settlers required of the local Indigenous groups. They demanded corn, furs, or wampum in recognition of the "benefits" (such as the construction of the fort) the Munsee derived from the Company's efforts in New Amsterdam.[43] But from the Munsee perspective, as recorded by David Peietersz de Vries, a Captain in the colony:

> they had from ancestor to ancestor lived there and it was their fatherland . . . [Kieft] must be a very [mean fellow] who came here to live on their land, and they had not called him here, and he now intended to force them to give their corn for free.[44]

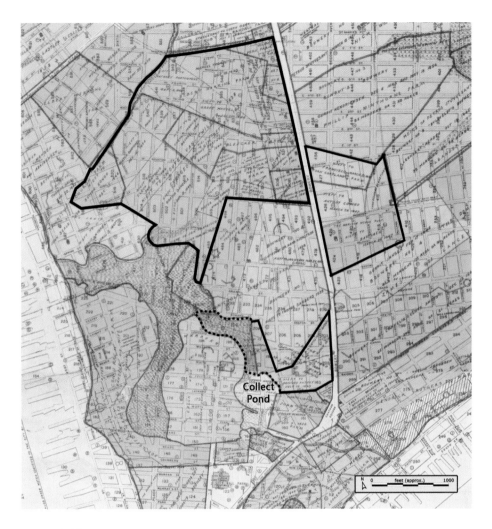

FIGURE 2.10
The approximate location of land issued to African men and women by the Dutch in 1634 is outlined in black, superimposed on a Lower Manhattan street grid (circa 1835). The land grants formed a loose arc to the north of the freshwater Collect pond, buffering the Dutch settlement from Native American attacks from the north. The African farms were eventually reconveyed to Europeans.

Outline of African land patents adapted from *New York African Burial Ground (ABG) Archaeology Final Report*, Volume 1, Chapter 2, Documentary Evidence on the Origin and use of the African Burial Ground, p. 46, citing *The Iconography of Manhattan Island* by I. N. Phelps Stokes, 1915–1928, Volume 6: Plates 84B-a and 84B-b. Base map from I. N. Phelps Stokes Collection, New York Public Library. Image by Angela Garra Zhinin.

Kieft was known to attack Indigenous Peoples, sometimes on the slimmest of provocations. An example in 1640 is typical of escalating Dutch battles. A group of Raritan Indians on Staten Island were accused of killing pigs. When they refused to make reparations, troops were sent, and "the expedition turned into a bloodbath." The local Indigenous Peoples were shocked by Dutch warfare, in which whole groups were annihilated, including women and children. One particularly brutal massacre in

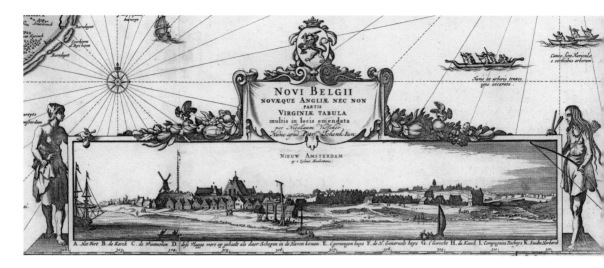

FIGURE 2.11
One of the earliest images of New Amsterdam, depicting the settlement in 1651. The steep gable-end houses are indicative of Dutch urban architecture. Detail from Nicolaes Visscher, *Novi Belgii Novaeque Angliae* (see also figure 2.6).
Library of Congress, Geography and Map Division. Printed in 1685.

the winter of 1643 killed more than 120 Munsee.[45]This first Dutch-Munsee war lasted until 1645, into the administration of the next and last governor of New Amsterdam, Petrus Stuyvesant (see below).

DUTCH MATERIAL CULTURE: OVERVIEW

The archaeology of the remains of Dutch households at the Stadt Huys Block, the 7 Hanover Square Block, the South Ferry Terminal, and elsewhere revealed the extent to which Dutch immigrants brought with them the material culture of their homeland.[46] From the most basic materials like bricks to decorative tiles and furnishings, immigrants went to great lengths to import a familiar material culture. House style, décor, glassware, and dishware in New Amsterdam and Fort Orange all replicate the comfortable and elegant settings of home across the ocean.

There is little evidence of the influence of Indigenous material culture on Dutch households—unlike in other settler colonies, established by Catholic countries such as Spain or France, where Europeans formed joint households with Indigenous women who then created material settings that reflected a mixture of cultures. Dutch men rarely established such living arrangements, and thus their kitchens and living spaces were predominantly European.[47]

No urban architecture survives from New Amsterdam. However, a handful of Dutch-style dwellings dating from the late seventeenth century and early eighteenth century survive in what is now New York City, particularly in Brooklyn, Queens, and Staten Island; all of them are designated landmarks.[48] It should be noted that these farmhouses are distinctly rural in their design, so only archaeology and documents can tell us about the built environment in the urban context of New Amsterdam. A number of traits define the town as distinctively Dutch. Perhaps most significant was the physical structure of the town, centered around a few roads, the fort, and a canal (located along what is now Broad Street). The harbor was established on the East River, as it was mistakenly believed that it would not freeze.

The first Dutch colonists of New Amsterdam carried with them a cultural understanding of architecture. However, recent scholarship has highlighted that what we know as "Dutch" architecture is largely a product of scholarly interpretations formed in the late nineteenth and early twentieth centuries, based on buildings constructed after the English assumed control of the colony—in some cases, one hundred years after.[49] In the initial period of settlement, the documentary record (colonial building contracts in New Netherland) indicates that buildings reflected a Dutch prototype, but soon the colonial enterprise shaped the expression of Dutch building practices. For one thing, these first settlers were not only Dutch; there were also Walloon settlers (from what is now Belgium), English, and enslaved Africans. Thus, most of the architecture built in New Netherland was not purely Dutch but combined several influences. In addition, the building materials in the New World were different. Fieldstone, for one, was readily available in New York, in contrast to the Netherlands. And there were not as many or as skilled craftsmen in the New World as in the Old, resulting in "vernacular" or interpreted building forms.[50] Within this variability, however, the archaeological and documentary record illustrates the transmission and persistence of Dutch material culture within New Netherland well into the eighteenth century.

Tiles, Bricks, and Houses

Several Lower Manhattan archaeological sites, including the South Ferry, 7 Hanover Square, and Stadt Huys excavations, have uncovered the hallmarks of New Amsterdam architecture: the distinctive S-shaped pantile or roof tile (figure 2.12 *top*), a Flemish invention; the distinctive yellow brick predominately used for foundation walls (figure 2.12 *bottom*, *left* and flooring and the heavy redware floor tiles glazed in green and black (figure 2.12 *bottom*, *right*).[51] The serpentine roofing tiles were laid in overlapping rows so the downturn of one tile met the upturn of the adjacent tile. This created a trough to channel rainwater down and off the roof. The tiles were also fireproof, which was a real help in an urban environment where fire was a persistent threat. In 1648, Director General Stuyvesant enacted city ordinances requiring the use of nonflammable materials in new buildings.[52] Visscher's 1651 depiction of Manhattan's wooden skyline (figure 2.11) shows just how flammable Stuyvesant's New Amsterdam was. Slate roofing tiles, a regionally available material that was similarly fire retardant, gradually replaced the pantiles on the New York roofs.

FIGURE 2.12

Building materials imported from the Netherlands: (*top*) the face (*left*) and profile (*right*) of a pantile, or roof tile; (*bottom*) a "yellow" Dutch brick (*left*) and a redware floor tile (*right*). The pantile lug, visible top right, anchored the tile to the roof. The worn surface of the green-glazed tile speaks to the practical nature of tiles in high-traffic areas of the house—easy to clean and durable. The yellow brick, with mortar still adhering to its surface, has become synonymous with the Dutch, although the different regions in the Netherlands produced different sizes and colors of brick.
Qi#104004 SFT, Qi#202500 SHB, and Qi#206622 7HS

Houses are very important components of a material culture assemblage. Methods of construction, materials used, the house layout, and even how components are attached to one another all vary from one culture to another. As the initial settlement developed and expanded, the housing became more substantial as local sources for building materials came into use. Wood construction predominated in New Amsterdam until the mid-seventeenth century. As noted previously, the first sawmill was in operation on Noten Eylant (Governors Island) by 1627, and two more were established on Manhattan by 1639. The ready abundance of wood, however, did not curtail the urban Dutch preference for building in brick. For those who could afford it, brick was imported. It was not until mid-century that the first brick kiln was established in New Netherland to satisfy local demand.[53]

Different towns and areas in the Netherlands produced different sizes and colors of bricks, including yellow and red. Imported brick imparted a distinctly Dutch flavor to New Amsterdam that was captured by seventeenth- and eighteenth-century visitors to the city. In 1697, when Dr. Benjamin Bullivant of Boston visited the city, he took note of the dissonance between the British architecture of Boston and the Dutch-inspired New York:

[the] auncient buildings were very meane, but most of theyr new buildings are magnificent enough, ye fronts of red and yellow (or flanders) brick Lookeing very prettily, some of them are 6 stories high & built with a Gable end to ye front & so by Consequence make Very narrow garratts. the 3d story is usually a warehouse, and over it a Crane for hawleing up goods. the Lower part is comonly Very substantiall & neate . . . The windows are high & large, as are the stories, ten or 12 foot ye first . . . most bricked houses have ye date of the yeare on them, contrived of Iron cramps to hold in ye timber to the walls.[54]

The urban Dutch-style buildings described by Bullivant persisted well into the eighteenth century. A drawing by Swiss naturalist Pierre Eugene du Simitière, who visited New York in 1767, captures Bullivant's description (figure 2.13) and illustrates the steep-roof urban construction. The narrow stone building pictured has a pantile roof and brick façade, with the gable end facing the street. The date of construction "contrived of iron cramps" is visible between the third and fourth floors. Bullivant goes on to describe the interior of the Dutch-style dwellings, commenting specifically on the characteristically Netherlandic use of ceramic tiles within the dwelling, citing the presence of "Dutch tyles on each side of the fire place, carried very High," in addition to the practice of tiling the sides of the staircase and the bottom of windows.[55]

Archaeologists have recovered two types of tiles used on the interiors of Dutch dwellings in urban New Amsterdam. The first is a heavy, thick redware floor tile, either unglazed or covered in a buff-slip lead glazed in green (figure 2.12 bottom, *right*) or black. They were easy to clean, durable, and aesthetically appealing, especially when laid in a contrasting checkerboard pattern as often depicted in Dutch still-life paintings of the period.[56] In 1704, recording her trip from her native Boston to New York, Sarah Kemble Knight wrote of New York interiors, whose hearths "were laid with the finest tile that I ever see, and the stair cases laid all with white tile which is ever clean, and so are the walls of the Kitchen which had a brick floor." The ease of cleaning a tiled kitchen is a legacy carried into present-day kitchen design. Kemble also noted the exteriors of the buildings sometimes employed a checkerboard pattern: "the bricks in some of the houses are of divers coullers and laid in checkers, being glazed look very agreeable."[57] Here, function and aesthetics went hand in hand.

FIGURE 2.13
A Dutch-style house in Manhattan, drawn circa 1767 by Swiss naturalist Pierre Eugene du Simitière.
The five-story house pictured here, dated 1689, illustrates the continuity of Dutch building practices even
twenty-five years after New Amsterdam became a British colony.
Library Company of Philadelphia, as illustrated in Van den Hurk 2006, Yi2 1412.Q.9.

The second type of tile—to which Kemble and Bullivant both refer—is the tin-glazed wall tile that lined the baseboards, stairways, kitchen walls, and hearths of Dutch dwellings. (A glaze containing tin rather than lead was used for Dutch pottery for more than two hundred years.) These are found frequently at archaeological sites in Lower Manhattan. They were either covered in an opaque white tin glaze, as Kemble describes, or hand-painted in rich cobalt and manganese (blue or purple) over the opaque white. The painted tiles displayed an array of everyday scenes, flowers, sailing ships, soldiers, or children's games.[58] One important kind of tile, frequently imbedded on the wall surrounding a fireplace, showed biblical scenes (figure 2.14). It is thought that these religious-themed tiles were used to educate the young through storytelling.

FIGURE 2.14 ›
Hand-painted Dutch tin-glazed earthenware wall tiles depicting biblical excerpts known as Histories.
These tiles were used in fireplace surrounds and on interior walls in a Dutch tradition. (*Top*) This tile was
found during the South Ferry Terminal project (Manhattan) and is thought to depict the story of 1 Kings
13, which tells of a prophet who disobeys the word of God and is killed by a lion, or that of St. Jerome who
was also attacked by a lion. (*Bottom*) This tile was found during the Van Cortlandt project (the Bronx) and
depicts the sale of Joseph into slavery by his brothers. Fireplace tiles remained popular in New York City
until around the 1750s (see Leslie E. Gerhauser, "Hart Tyles and Histories: Dutch Bible Tiles in Eighteenth-
Century New York," in *Soldiers, Cities, and Landscapes: Papers in Honor of Charles L. Fisher*, ed. Penelope
Ballard Drooker and John P. Hart, 87–105 (Albany: University of the State of New York, 2010).
Qi#111556 SFT and Qi#209661 VCP

CM South Ferry (2012)

CM Van Cortlandt Park (1992)

Material Culture Tells Time

Many of the objects from these sites are what archaeologists call time markers, allowing them to date an entire deposit, or a layer (stratum) within it, by relatively few artifacts. Time markers are styles, designs, colors, and manufacturing techniques that occurred in a specific period of time; thus, their presence in the archaeological record allows archaeologists to date the artifacts roughly to that time period. Particular corner details on tin-glazed wall tiles, for example, were used only in specific eras. Ox-head corners, such as the one in figure 2.14 (*top*), appeared in the early eighteenth century; spider-head corners are from the first to the third quarter of the eighteenth century (figure 2.14 *bottom*).[59] Other temporal markers are clay pipes, found frequently at Dutch sites. The shape of the bowl and the designs on it are often time-sensitive (figure 2.15). A manufacturer's mark on the bottom of the pipe can also tell us the date it was made (figure 2.16), but even a broken pipe stem without a stamp gives us clues to its time. The bore hole (through which the smoke flows) became smaller through the sixteenth and seventeenth centuries as technology improved.

Pottery is an especially useful artifact in the archaeological record. Ceramic types and designs provide manufacturing date ranges and can sometimes reveal trading relationships, as when a Dutch site contains French pipes. Their fragility also means that ceramics often broke and were thrown out, so there are many of them to be found. The most common ceramics from New Amsterdam were tin-glazed earthenware (used for dishes, cups, serving pieces, and accessories) and redware, made of red

Stadt Huys Block (1987)

FIGURE 2.15

A Walter Raleigh smoking-pipe stem, also known as the Jonah pipe, depicting a scaly sea creature with an open mouth and sharp teeth. They were popular among sailors circa 1630–1640 and then fell out of fashion. Their narrow window of manufacture makes them very useful dating markers that can indicate an early colonial occupation. The maker of this pipe is unknown, but there is an apocryphal tale about Sir Walter— best known as an explorer and courtier of Elizabeth I who popularized tobacco in England—falling into the sea, but because he smelled so strongly of tobacco, fish refused to eat him.
Qi#201406 SHB

FIGURE 2.16

"EB" mark stamped on the heel of a clay smoking pipe. Edward Bird was an English pipe maker who settled in the Netherlands and married Aeltje Govaert, a Dutch woman. They produced pipes stamped with EB on the heel until Bird died in 1655. At that time, their son, Evert, continued the business. Around 1672, the mark was sold to another Dutch family, who continued to use it. The "EB" pipes are the most abundant of the initial-marked pipes found in seventeenth-century New York City archaeological deposits and have been recovered from archaeological projects in Amsterdam and England (Dallal 1995, in Cantwell and Wall 2001, 320, n. 7).

Qi#205121 7HS

clays (used for cooking, storage, and serving), but archaeologists have also found small quantities of other European types and even some Chinese porcelain. Tin-glazed wares were made over a long period (1571–1800) in England and Holland, but archaeologists can date them by whether they had lead glaze on the exterior surface as

Pipe Makers' Marks

White ball clay pipes for smoking tobacco were made in the Netherlands and England beginning in the seventeenth century. Marks identifying the makers were stamped on the bottom of the flat heel spur at the base of the bowl where it intersects with the stem (figure 2.17). These marks provide important dating information and can establish the place of manufacture. The impressions, however, can be ephemeral and difficult to discern. Often photographs, the primary means of recording information about archaeological finds, cannot capture the level of detail necessary. It is in these instances that archaeological drawings are commissioned. The series of three pipe makers' marks illustrated in figure 2.18 show the fine detail captured with pen, ink, and a skilled hand.

FIGURE 2.17

White ball clay smoking pipe likely made in southwest England circa 1660–1680. The flat "heel spur" at the base of the bowl where it intersects with the stem is stamped with a mark identifying the maker as the Gauntlet family (see figure 2.18a), although it may be a seventeenth-century forgery copying the popular Gauntlet family brand.

Qi#115750 SFT

A   B   C

FIGURE 2.18
Seventeenth-century pipe makers' marks. (A) The hand-shaped mark of the Gauntlet family from West Country, England, circa 1660–1680; this mark was widely pirated, and it is likely this example is actually a copy of a Gauntlet family pipe. Qi#115750 SFT. (B) A crowned "HG" mark for Hendrik Gerdes, a seventeenth-century Dutch pipe maker from Amsterdam. Qi#207032 SHB. (C) An unattributed mark called a Tudor Rose that was likely used by an English pipe maker living in the Netherlands during the seventeenth century. Qi#207034 SHB. Drawn by Alaina Wibberly.

well as tin glaze on the interior, and by specific decorative motifs. Earlier pieces used more color—yellows, blues, and greens (figure 2.19)—than later dishes that trended blue, and specific designs, like the Wan Li border that imitates Chinese porcelains (figure 2.20), the tulip, seen on tiles after the 1630s.

FIGURE 2.19
Dutch-manufactured tin-glazed earthenware salt dish excavated during the 7 Hanover Square project. This is an atypical example of a salt dish, many of which had more delicate bases. The salt would have filled the top recess, where diners would pinch with their forefinger and thumb the desired quantity to flavor their meal. Salt was the important seasoning and at that time was not easily accessible. Salt dishes were made in a variety of materials, depending on the household's wealth, ranging from silver and pewter to wood and clay. Qi#206609 7HS

FIGURE 2.20
Wan-Li style decorative border on a tin-glazed
plate sherd excavated from beneath a seventeenth-
century barrel at the Stadt Huys site. The Dutch-
made vessel was decorated to imitate Chinese
porcelain.
Qi#202056 SHB

Stadt Huys Block (1987)

Cm

These wares also provide important information on settlers' homes and how they chose to set their tables. Redware and other utilitarian ceramics are more difficult to date than decorated wares, because their manufacture did not change for many years. Some recent research in identifying clay sources can establish the place of manufacture and differentiate pottery made in the Netherlands from pottery made in New York (figure 2.21).

THE STADT HUYS BLOCK SITE

The Stadt Huys Block site, located on what was then the waterfront on Pearl Street and the first large excavation in New York City, in 1979–1980, revealed foundations and deposits from the Lovelace Tavern or King's Tavern that stood from around 1670 to 1706.[60] Archaeologists found locally made Dutch earthenware jugs, clay smoking pipes, imported French wine bottles, and several types of drinking glasses—what seventeenth-century tavern in New Amsterdam would be complete without glass *roemers*? Fragments of these distinctive transparent pale green goblets that once held beer and wine were found among the remains of the tavern (figure 2.22) and else-where on the site. Manufactured in the Netherlands and Germany, copying an ancient Roman form (hence the name *roemer*), these delicate glasses seem an unlikely fixture in a rowdy tavern. Roemers have distinctive cylindrical stems studded with decorative "prunts," applied globs of glass in various designs, meant perhaps to enable the drinker to hold onto the glass. They also had a flared conical foot made by coiling molten glass. Generally, only fragments of roemers are found archaeologically. The laughing girl in

FIGURE 2.21

Dutch-style cook pot, or *kookpot*, found during the 7 Hanover Square excavations. This simple, common, three-legged pot came in a variety of sizes and was used in the Netherlands from the thirteenth century onward and in New Netherland for cooking and serving. Other utilitarian redware vessels were used, but these *kookpotten* with their everted rim and handles were so characteristic that they mark Dutch households wherever they are found. This one likely broke before it was used and was discarded, because it does not show any evidence at its base of having come in contact with the coals of a cook fire (Janowitz and Schaefer 2021). Qi#206620 7HS

Vermeer's 1657 *Officer and a Laughing Girl* (figure 2.3) holds a roemer. They became popular in England and were copied by English glassmakers from the late eighteenth century into the nineteenth, carrying the Anglicized name *rummer*.

Archaeologists also found an unusual artifact just below the tavern deposits containing pipe stems and ceramics: a slate pencil (figure 2.23). The material found with it dates to the English period (1691), but it was found on land belonging to Wellen Abramsen van de Border, a Dutchman. Pencils of this type were used for school

FIGURE 2.22

(*left*) Glass *roemer* fragments excavated during the Stadt Huys project associated with seventeenth-century deposits in Stone Street. *Roemers*, or *römers*, were large drinking glasses used for beer or wine that were popular in the Netherlands (and Rhineland) from the fifteenth through the seventeenth centuries. Seen here are decorative "prunts" (*left*, *top*, and *center*) and a flared conical foot (*left*, *bottom*) made by coiling molten glass. Prunts come in designs such as "raspberry" (pictured *top row left*) and on the glass held by the drunken Dutch drummer. The prunts pictured in the middle left are pointed or barbed prunts, followed by a rounded and smooth variety of prunt. (*right*) *Dronken tamboer met roemer en toorts* (drunken drummer with roemer and torch) by Jacob Gole after Cornelis Dusart, Amsterdam, 1695–1724. Rijksmuseum.
Top: Qi#201541 SHB, Qi#204131 SHB, Qi#201728 SHB; Middle: Qi#204422 SHB, Qi#204370 SHB, Qi#204275 SHB; Bottom Qi#202584 SHB, Qi#204424 SHB, Qi#204134 SHB

learning, for navigation, for keeping accounts, or for art and drafting. What is appealing about this pencil, which would have been fitted into a holder, is that it had been sharpened at the tip, likely with a knife, as students using ordinary lead pencils have done for centuries.

FIGURE 2.23

Seventeenth-century slate pencil nib excavated from the Stadt Huys block belonging to Wellen Abramsen van de Border. Much used, the tip was sharpened, likely with a knife, until the pencil was too short for continued use or was lost to its user. Illustrations from the era show pencils like this attached to a writing slate or book with a cord tied around the carved and indented band on the left. Qi#202118 SHB

FIGURE 2.24
Wyckoff House, Flatlands, Brooklyn built circa 1652.
Photograph taken by LPC in 1965 at designation.

Because only a small handful of Dutch deposits have been found in New York excavations, many aspects of life in New Amsterdam are not reflected materially, especially in regard to its economy and politics. We are lucky, in fact, that any archaeological sites had remains from the Dutch period, given the small number of Dutch settlers, as seen in the Castello Plan (figure 2.7), and subsequent intense land use. Every building lot was built upon several times up through the modern period, so it is not surprising that there are no standing structures remaining from what was once New Amsterdam. Fortunately, there are some outside Manhattan, but within the bounds of today's New York City.

SURVIVING DUTCH HOUSES AND STRUCTURES

The Pieter Claessen Wyckoff House in Flatlands, Brooklyn (figure 2.24), was the very first site to be designated a New York City landmark after the city's landmarks law was enacted in 1965. The designation report states that it is the oldest building in New York

City and State and specifically mentions its archaeological importance because it still stands on its original site.[61] It is now a house museum owned by the New York City Department of Parks and Recreation.

The Wyckoff House is one of the few remaining Dutch buildings in New York State built in this period. The oldest surviving section of the house was built around 1652; additions were constructed between 1740 and 1820. It is a wooden one-story farmhouse with a very steep roof, an example of the Flemish Medieval Survival and Dutch Colonial styles of architecture. Pieter Claessen (who added the name Wyckoff when the colony was taken by the English), emigrated from Holland in 1636. Wyckoff and his descendants owned this home for many generations, although no material of Dutch origin was found during archaeological excavations at the site. However, the archaeology confirmed that Canarsie Lane, on which the house stood, had been moved from one side of the house to the other in the early nineteenth century, thus changing the house's orientation. What had been the front of the house was now the back, requiring a change in the entryway and other modifications. Moreover, while the location of the Wyckoff House had remained unchanged since its construction, archaeological excavation has shown that its relationship to the surrounding streets has been highly modified. Now sitting on a slope below street level, it was originally sited on a small mound above the marshy landscape. Later landfilling raised the level of the surrounding streets, giving the house lot its present concave position.

The city is home to a few other early Dutch farmhouses, all New York City landmarks, including the Adrian and Ann Wyckoff Onderdonck house in Queens. A small structure on the grounds dates from 1660, although the house itself was built in the third quarter of the eighteenth century and reconstructed from 1980 to 1982 after a major fire in 1975. The site was designated a landmark in 1995, based in part upon its archaeological potential, and today it is a house museum. No Dutch materials were recovered in the archaeological research done at the site.

Another survival from the colonial period is in Gravesend, Brooklyn, an English settlement, which was established in 1645 by Lady Moody, a baroness who had left England and later Massachusetts after she was persecuted for Anabaptist beliefs. It was one of the earliest planned communities in the nation, and the earliest founded by a woman. One can see the original square plan of the settlement still existing in the modern street plan (figure 2.25). The village was divided into four quadrants by Gravesend Road (now MacDonald Avenue), which ran north-south, and Gravesend Neck Road, which ran east-west. Each quadrant had space for ten houses, whose fields ran radially out from the settlement. Gravesend was the only English settlement among the six early settlements of what became Kings County. It had a palisade wall and, in the center of one of the quadrants, a village cemetery, a New York City landmark. Archaeological excavations revealed that, in the early nineteenth century, the cemetery was used for picnics and, in the early twentieth century, occasionally for garbage disposal. No eighteenth-century artifacts were recovered.

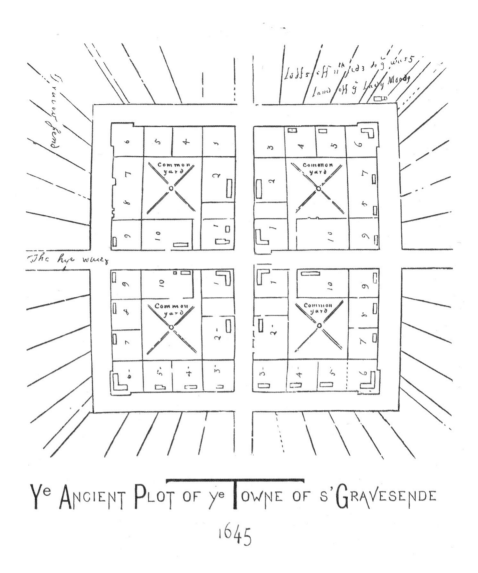

FIGURE 2.25

The square town plan of Lady Deborah Moody's Gravesend, the first settlement founded by a woman in the Americas, that now encompasses parts of Bensonhurst, Coney Island, Brighton Beach, and Sheepshead Bay in Brooklyn. Residents of Gravesend were able to practice their preferred religion without interference under Lady Moody's mandate.

Stiles 1884, 114.

Finally, there are several burial grounds in the city that are said to contain seventeenth-century graves, including the grave of Governor Peter Stuyvesant, who was interred in what is now St Mark's-in-the-Bowery Church (a New York City landmark), which is reputedly built on top of his "Bouwerie Chapel."[62]

PETER STUYVESANT

Peter Stuyvesant was governor of New Amsterdam from 1647 until 1664, making him the longest-ruling and most significant governor of the colony. He did a great deal to organize and regularize New Amsterdam, and his efforts led to the Netherlands States General formally recognizing it as a town in 1650. Being a town instead of simply a colony meant that New Amsterdam enjoyed a measure of self-governance that other colonies did not. This was good for the residents, as the West India Company had been losing interest in the colony as it became more expensive and less profitable.

In 1653, Holland approved the city charter, granting the town the right to govern itself and creating a system of courts that were locally run and no longer administered from Holland.[63] Some historians mark the date of this charter as the beginning of the city's history. Stuyvesant established a new town body, the Nine Men. This group included three representatives each from the town merchants, the burghers (or citizens), and the farmers, with rules about the length of terms and succession procedures.[64] The governor also established a civil court and defined new governmental offices: a *schout*, two *burgomasters*, and five *schepens*, following the principles of government in the Netherlands.[65] Legitimate traders (great and small burghers) were protected by paying a fee, which kept out unlicensed traders, who were devaluing wampum by accepting loose beads. Wampum beads, as described in chapter 1, were meant to be used in strings of standard lengths when traded.

Stuyvesant regulated taxes, markets, weights, and measures. He created tax lists that reflected income classes, suggesting clear stratifications in New Amsterdam society. There was no regular, periodic, nor apparently consistent basis for taxation. Taxes were assessed for any significant improvement needed by the settlement. There is an interesting account of a supposedly voluntary tax in 1655, assessed on "traders, skippers, merchants, factors and burghers." If any refused to participate, burgomasters were authorized to "assess a reasonable contribution toward the construction of a plank wall 5–6 feet high to repair and strengthen it against the Indians."[67]

The wall was coming to be increasingly important as during Stuyvesant's administration there were two Dutch-Indigenous wars—the Peach War and the Esopus War—leading to a heightened sense of insecurity. Both flared up in the 1640s with the decline of the beaver population, and they reflected different cultural understandings between Europeans and Indigenous Peoples. The Munsee believed that trading partners should continue to support one another and share what they had, whereas Europeans hoped to extract maximum return for minimum investment. Other trade goods were still important, but beaver pelts were the most profitable.

In addition, Stuyvesant faced pressure from the Dutch government, which was coming to be unhappy with the expenses of maintaining the town, as it was not agriculturally successful and considerable food and other necessities had to be imported.[68] Dutch settlers could provide some of their own food, keeping a domestic animal or two in their kitchen gardens. Other foods were obtained in markets, beginning in 1654, and there was some small-scale local hunting in the early days of the colony. Animal bone, representing the remains of meals, offers a more nuanced view of the interaction between Dutch and Indigenous peoples than the documentary record does; it reveals a diet (especially in the early period) that included songbirds, small animals such as squirrels, some deer, and a great deal of fish and shellfish. Deer (not frequent in Manhattan) was usually acquired by trade with native hunters.

In the period between 1624 and 1700, which encompasses the entire Dutch colonial settlement, the ratio of wild to domestic species was 54 percent. That figure vacillated a bit between 1701 and 1760 but declined drastically to 1.5 percent after 1760,[69] indicating that hunting had largely disappeared and the transition to domestic animals for food was virtually complete.

An important attribute of New Amsterdam, as opposed to other settler colonies, was its diverse social composition and mixture of peoples, which echoed that of the Netherlands. Half of New Amsterdam's people came from European countries other than Holland, and they brought many religions with them. This culturally diverse population was crucial in determining the nature of New York after the Dutch were no longer in control (see chapter 3). The Netherlands was famous for its tolerance of other religions and cultures.[70] For instance, in 1657, the Flushing Remonstrance petitioned the governor to stop persecuting Quakers, whose Meeting House is seen here (figure 2.26). None of the signatories were themselves Quaker.

FIGURE 2.26
Friends Meeting House in Flushing, Queens (a designated New York City landmark), built in 1694 with additions 1716–1719. It is the oldest house of worship still standing within New York City. View looking northeast in 1936.
Library of Congress, Prints & Photographs Division, HABS, HABS NY, 41-FLUSH, 1–14.

Dutch culture also differed from that of British and other European societies in its unusually permissive attitude toward women's participation in the economy, empowering them in a way that was distinctive. Many women worked. They served as traders, owned small businesses, and ran taverns. They also had the same inheritance rights as their brothers. Under Dutch/Roman law, a woman was entitled to half of her husband's estate.[71] A marriage was a partnership, similar to a joint venture. After the British took over the colony, women of Dutch origin retreated from—or could no longer pursue—economic activities, and their economic rights diminished. In the eighteenth-century cemeteries of Brooklyn and Queens, the gravestones of Dutch women retain their birth family names. This is not the case in British cemeteries like Trinity Church and Graveyard, a New York City landmark.

In the late 1650s, Stuyvesant was facing mounting pressure from the British, whose presence in the surrounding areas had grown much larger than that of the Dutch. By 1660, there were ten British colonists for every Dutch one in the region.[72] British colonists from the start were more interested in acquiring, settling, and farming the land than were the Dutch.[73] As more settlers sought land, conflict arose with the Munsee. This pressure prevented the Munsee from using resources as they had been accustomed to when they had had unfettered access to large tracts of ecologically distinctive subregions. This pressure broke out into violence more than once. The land itself was changing. The Munsee had used it only seasonally and less intensely than farming required, and the settlers now divided and fenced the land through which the Munsee once traveled freely.[74]

Although there was no battle for the city, Stuyvesant surrendered to the British in 1664, recognizing their superior numbers and power. By then, the West India Company was little interested in New Amsterdam. It had originally focused on Brazil as its most significant American colony, but then sugar trade profits declined around 1654, and New Amsterdam became more important to trade networks.[75] But this value, too, fell away when trade declined because of fluctuations in the beaver supply and price. The Company was unwilling to offer much protection against the British invasion. It should be noted that the Dutch retook the settlement from the British in 1673 and briefly renamed it New Orange (figure 2.27). However, in 1674, it reverted to British control and to the name New York.

The first English governor, Colonel Nicolls, promised that the residents would be free to live as they had lived, and New Amsterdam remained largely Dutch in many ways. The people stayed put, and, in the short term, Dutch officials remained in place. The patroon system became the manor system.[76] After a year, many Dutch officials were replaced with English ones, but the Dutch language, religion, and practice remained. Even into the nineteenth century, some churchgoers attended Sunday services conducted in Dutch.[77]

Dutch traits also persisted in homes into the nineteenth century.[78] Some scholars suggest that "Dutchness" persisted as a foil to "Englishness" and that some Dutch characteristics in the New World were exaggerated to show this cultural affiliation and were more marked than in the Old World.[79] The most common traits remained in material

NEW-YORK.
in 1673.

Conquered and named New Orange.

[*Explained* 1843.]

—Capsey, or dividing point of the Hudson and East Rivers [now State street.]
.—Albany sloops.
.—Flagg-staff.
.—The Fort—a square—4 bastions—42 cannon.
.—Goal.
.—Governor's house [100 feet long, 50 wide, 24 high.] [1st row of houses outside the fort, along Pearl, between Battery and Whitehall. The second along Capsey, now State street.]

S.—Stuyvesant's house [near junction of State and Whitehall streets.]
2.—Public Wharf.
3.—Public Dock or Harbor [lower part of Whitehall street.]
4.—Marketfield [whence a lane to Broad street, now Marketfield street.]
G.—Public Storehouses [on *Winckel*, now Stone street.]
H.—The Weigh, or Balance.
I.—*Heeren-gracht*, Gentlemen's Canal [now Broad street.]
K.—Stadt-Huys [City Hall on High street, now S. W. corner Coenties slip lane and Pearl street.]

R 1.—Redoubt [or half-moon Fortification, head of Coenties slip.] [K to 7, or High street, as it curved into Smith, now Pearl to William, was the *Cingel* or Encircling street.]
R 2.—Redoubt [head of Old slip.]
7.—Smith [now William street.]
8.—Smith street lane.
9.—Burgers' or Citizens' path [Pearl, along Hanover square to Wall street.]
L.—Lutheran Church

10.—Moat, earthen wall or breastwork a[Wall street.]
R 3.—Redoubt [now head of Coffee Hou[
M.—Water Gate and Block-house [near Wall and Pearl streets.]
O.—City Gate [head of Wall in Broadway[
P.—Way to the fresh water [Collect.]
Q.—Wind-mill [between Cortland and [Broadway.]
11.—Maagde-paetje [Maiden Lane.]
N.—*Smidt's-valley* [foot of Maiden lane.]
T.—East River.

FIGURE 2.27
A view of New York, or New Orange, in 1673, when it was briefly back under Dutch control, as interpreted by historians in 1843.
Library of Congress Prints and Photographs Division.

culture and domestic life, including foodways (such as cookies, pancakes, and coleslaw), pottery (tin-glazed earthenware), and home décor (tin-glazed wall tiles, floor and roof tiles). The influence of Dutch material culture on New Yorkers persists and has become iconic: the use of blue and white on tiles and other wares and the designs on both European and Chinese ceramics (which, it could be argued, have influenced each other) have persisted from the seventeenth century until today.

In the end, New Amsterdam as a Dutch colony was hobbled by persistent troubles: the conflicts between European and Indigenous Peoples, infrequent imports, a disordered economy that meant the Dutch struggled for existence despite the bounty of the land, and the stinginess of the West India Company unwilling to spend on the maintenance of the colony.[80] But the influence of Dutch culture and its colonists still lends a flavor to contemporary New York, especially in Lower Manhattan's layout and in its mixture of peoples, derived in part from Dutch openness. Archaeological findings emphasize the degree to which Dutch colonists longed for their homeland and tried to replicate it through familiar material culture.

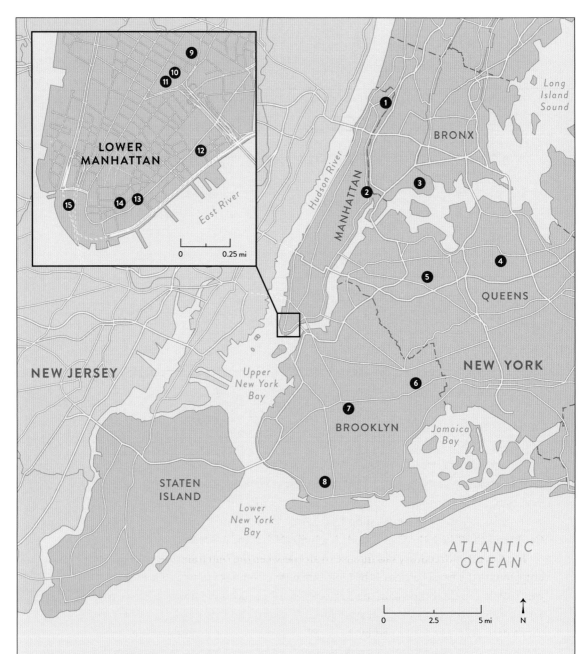

LOWER MANHATTAN

Hudson River

East River

0   0.25 mi

MANHATTAN

BRONX

QUEENS

NEW YORK

Long Island Sound

Upper New York Bay

NEW JERSEY

STATEN ISLAND

BROOKLYN

Jamaica Bay

Lower New York Bay

ATLANTIC OCEAN

0   2.5   5 mi   N

1. Inwood African Burial Ground, Manhattan
2. Harlem African Burial Ground, Manhattan
3. Hunts Point Burial Ground, Bronx
4. Old Towne Flushing Burial Ground, Queens
5. Elmhurst African Burial Ground, Queens
6. Sankofa Park, Brooklyn
7. Flatbush African Burial Ground, Brooklyn
8. Gravesend Cemetery, Brooklyn

9. African Burial Ground, Manhattan
10. Tweed Courthouse, Manhattan
11. City Hall Park, Manhattan
12. Beekman St Reconstruction, Manhattan
13. 7 Hanover Square, Manhattan
14. Stadt Huys, Manhattan
15. South Ferry Terminal Project, Manhattan

3

THE BRITISH COLONIAL CITY AND
THE NASCENT REPUBLIC, 1664–1800

Britain launched its empire with its first settler colony in North America at James-town, Virginia, in 1609, followed by one in Massachusetts in 1620. New York was taken from the Dutch in 1664, and by the end of the seventeenth century, English communities had been settled in many parts of northeastern North America. These colonies were distinctive in that, unlike the Dutch New Netherlands, they were designed to replace an Indigenous population with a new colonial British population that would take control of the land and resources. In establishing its empire, Britain was deliberate in selecting places to colonize, prizing natural resources. Its colonies were rich with timber, fur, agricultural products, and iron ore, which were exported to Great Britain and other markets. The colonies were also markets in which Britain could sell its own finished goods, such as iron tools, kettles, and woven materials. The British directed the new colony's economy to serve imperial ends and employed whatever political means were necessary to do so—including force. After colonizing North America and the Caribbean, the British Empire expanded to India, Africa, and Australia.

The seventeenth century saw intense rivalry between the Dutch and the English that erupted into the naval battles of the First Dutch War from 1652 to 1654. It also spurred construction of the Dutch palisade fortification in the location known today as Wall Street, meant to keep out British and Indigenous invaders from the north. New York City's development was shaped by its dual Dutch and British origins and immigrant populations, a relentless drive to trade, and an associated willingness to transform the island to serve these purposes.

British control of New York required wresting the colony from the Dutch, who had settled it in 1625. In August 1664, Dutch governor Peter Stuyvesant surrendered New Amsterdam in a bloodless capitulation to the British. At first, little changed except the city's name, in honor of the Duke of York, who would become King James II in 1685. The twenty-three Articles of Capitulation, signed at Stuyvesant's farm (or *bouwerie*), stipulated that if the Dutch residents of New Amsterdam took an oath to be loyal to King Charles II of Great Britain, they would not lose their property or be required to abandon their religion or language.[1] Initially, although there were few new British settlers, it soon became obvious to the Dutch elite that there were economic and social advantages to becoming at least partially British. Some Dutch Anglicized their names and joined the Episcopal Church. Charles Bridges, an Englishman in the colony, changed his name twice: first to Van Brugge when living in New Amsterdam and then back to Bridges when the British captured the city.[2] Many British men married Dutch women, so among the top echelon there was a mixture of British and Dutch. The population as a whole, however, remained mostly Dutch for years.

THE BRITISH SETTLEMENT

New Amsterdam began as a port city and remained one as New York. The waterfront was prime real estate, and the city organized itself along social and economic lines. Merchant warehouses lay along the river. Broadway was the elite avenue for the houses of both British and Dutch residents, as noted by Noah Webster, who visited in 1786 and described it as "agreeable and pleasant, high and wide."[3] The west side housed the poorest New Yorkers and many of the Dutch. Residents of the east side were a mixture of merchants and mariners.[4] And in each neighborhood or ward, as they were called by 1683, there were multiple institutions including churches, markets, and taverns. The city remained a compact place for many years. The Castello Plan (figure 3.1) captures the size and shape of the Dutch town; the British city grew slowly, initially expanding above the wall in the central and eastern portions of the settlement area shown. By 1728, the city had nearly doubled in area and the population was approximately 8,600.[5] Even in the early nineteenth century, the majority of the residents lived to the south of what is today Fourteenth Street.

During the early years of the colony, political upheavals in Great Britain affected New Yorkers. The Glorious Revolution of 1688 replaced a Catholic English king with a Protestant (German) prince. That revolution resonated in New York and involved both churches and political philosophies. There were militant factions among the majority Dutch population who remembered the recent British takeover. In 1689, the colony lacked an effective governor, and a wealthy man, Jacob Leisler, who was anti-British and devoted to Dutch Protestantism, declared himself governor.[6] He was backed by the working men of the city and believed he would be supported by the new Protestant king. He was not. In 1692, Benjamin Fletcher was appointed governor and given the task of creating order after the Leisler Rebellion. Fletcher is credited with improving the colony's defenses, essential during this period of high tension between the British and French governments.[7] To New Yorkers of the day, however, politics in the home country were never as pressing as the turmoil of the local economy. Local concerns were primarily those elements of the city that affected trade: the maintenance of piers and streets, the provision of water, and the security of the settlement.[8] Archaeologists working in

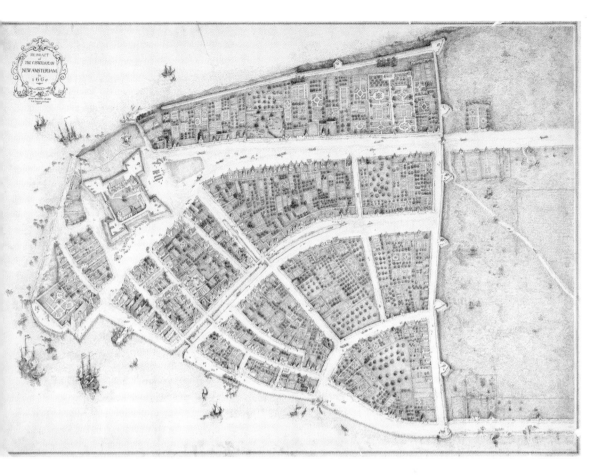

FIGURE 3.1
Redraft of the Castello Plan, depicting New Amsterdam in 1660, a few years before the British took control of the city. The map shows what was then New Amsterdam and is now part of Lower Manhattan.
John Wolcott Adam, Redraft of the Castello Plan, 1916. Lionel Pincus and Princess Firyal Map Division, New York Public Library. New York Public Library Digital Collections.

the Lower Manhattan of today find remnants of these issues: town and street design, landfilling (the making of new land), drinking wells, and privies, which apart from their primary function were also used to dispose of trash. What was once considered trash includes many objects valued by archaeologists.

The Excavator's Perspective: The Stadt Huys Project

Pearl and Broad streets in the financial district of Lower Manhattan lay on land that was prime waterfront real estate in the late seventeenth century. Between 1979 and 1980, a team of more than twenty archaeologists, led by Diana Wall and me (figure 3.2) and including Meta Janowitz, Eugene Boesch,

FIGURE 3.2
Dr. Nan A. Rothschild during the Stadt Huys excavation in 1979 to 1980 in Lower Manhattan.
Photograph from The Stadt Huys Project, NYC Archaeological Repository.

and Arnold Pickman, were able to excavate there for more than a year. The project was the first large dig in New York City, and we did not know if we would find anything intact. But we found a great deal, more than one ton of artifacts! The team included a large number of women, and as having women at construction sites or doing urban archaeology at all were both so new, we were initially uncertain about whether the workmen on the site would be comfortable working with us. However, we all got along extremely well. They were very helpful, even allowing one of the crew to ride in the backhoe bucket to take photos.

We were hoping to find the remains of the Dutch Town Hall, the *Stadt Huys*. The town hall had been converted from a tavern (called the *Stadt Herberg*) into a municipal government building when the Dutch first incorporated the Town of New Amsterdam in 1653. Taverns were the logical places to house city headquarters in early cities: they were the only large secular buildings around. We did not find the Stadt Huys. Instead, we found something else. It was in the wrong place to be the Stadt Huys, but its artifacts—broken clay pipes and fragments of wine bottles—still signaled a tavern. However, ceramics were much less frequent than in other parts of the site. City taverns, unlike

rural inns, did not always house travelers, so meals and therefore dishes were proportionally less frequent in relation to glassware and pipes than in rural taverns. When we first identified the tavern, we petitioned the Landmarks Preservation Commission to override the developer's objections and allow us more time to excavate. It was a very stormy meeting because the developer wanted to proceed without any additional archaeology; the lawyer for the developers followed me out onto the street shouting "you'll never work again!" However, we were granted more time and also given permission to create an exhibition of important features from the site on the plaza of the new building, which is still there (85 Broad Street, formerly the Goldman Sachs headquarters). With the additional time, we opened and investigated more test pits, and the artifacts and documentary research made it clear that we were digging in the basement of what had originally been called the King's House, also known as the Lovelace Tavern.
—Dr. Nan A. Rothschild

LOVELACE TAVERN

In the Colonial era, taverns were much more than bars that offered alcoholic drinks. They were meeting places where news was disseminated and discussed and also served as places where mail was collected and distributed and where travelers could eat and spend a night. The Lovelace Tavern was owned by New York's second British governor, Sir Francis Lovelace, and existed from 1670 to 1706. When the original Dutch Stadt Huys fell into decay and was deemed unsafe by the Common Council in 1697, the adjacent tavern became the city's temporary town hall until 1701 or 1702.[9]

> "Whereby his Majesty subjects might be endangered should the Courte of Judicature be longer held there, itt is therefore Resolved yt the Courts of this City and Common Council doe sitt att the House of George Rescarrick [Lovelace Tavern] Adjoyning ye Citty Hall until the 13th day of October, Next."
> —Minutes of the Common Council, November 13, 1697

At Lovelace, archaeologists uncovered objects that were indicative of the tavern as a social place. Locals would gather here to exchange information, drink, play games, and pass the time, as was true of other urban taverns.[10] There were thousands of artifacts including gaming pieces, clay smoking pipes (figure 3.3), glass shards from bottles and

FIGURE 3.3
Gaming piece and ball clay smoking pipe excavated from the Stadt Huys Block site. Expedient gaming pieces, such as this one refashioned from a tin-glazed earthenware vessel, were used for games of chance. The preservation of this nearly complete pipe stem is unusual. Pipe smoking—equivalent to the cigarettes of the day—and gambling were signatures of relaxation and sociability among tavern patrons in New York City in the Colonial era. Qi# 204008 SHB and Qi# 202774 SHB

drinking glasses, and in one corner of the basement, a series of intact but empty glass onion bottles (figure 3.4) inside the remains of a barrel. These barrels were probably containers for wine shipped from Europe; regular customers of the tavern could leave their bottles and have them filled and ready. There were some plates and other ceramic dishes, including serving jugs (figure 3.5), and there were bones from the relatively few meals consumed in the tavern. The patrons ate pork, chicken, and beef, as well as goose, turkey, and passenger pigeon. Finally, some surprising and fragile materials were recovered, including eggshells and remnants of some matting that had been on the floor of a section of the tavern.

GOVERNOR FLETCHER'S WINE

Benjamin Fletcher, governor of New York from 1692 to 1697, liked his wine. Wine was shipped from Europe to colonial New York in barrels or casks. Once in New York, the casks would be decanted because opening them allowed for the introduction of air,

FIGURE 3.4

Top, A wooden barrel delineated by the dark circle in the soil found in the basement of Lovelace Tavern at the Stadt Huys site. The barrel contained intact glass wine bottles like the one seen emerging from the soil at the bottom center of the barrel and in the bottom image. These bottles were a mid-seventeenth-century invention and were called onion bottles because of their distinctive shape. The form harkens back to an earlier type seen in Dutch and Western European paintings of the sixteenth and seventeenth centuries.
Qi# 202734 SHB.
Photograph, the Stadt Huys Project, NYC Archaeological Repository.

which could quickly spoil the wine. The wine would be transferred either into ceramic jugs for immediate consumption, as might be the case where large amounts of drinking could be expected such as in a tavern, or into glass bottles for storage. Glass bottles were handblown and expensive in the seventeenth century. Their onion shape made them impractical as shipping containers over long distances, but their dark green color protected the wine from light oxidation and the thick walls were durable and reduced breakage for local transport.

Stadt Huys Block (1987)

Cm

FIGURE 3.5

One of five lead-glazed red earthenware jugs excavated from the basement of the Lovelace Tavern, Stadt Huys Block site. Dating from between 1670 and 1706, these jugs were likely used to serve tavern patrons wine or beer decanted from barrels. They were modeled on European tin-glazed earthenware forms. When they were initially analyzed, they were thought to have been imported from the Netherlands, but subsequent analysis of the clay indicated that they were locally made.

Qi#202773 SHB

Bottles were sometimes embossed with small blobs of glass on the neck or shoulder. The designs on the glass, which were often initials, family crests, or other insignia, identified the owner of the bottle, who may have been an individual or a retailer. This was important from a practical standpoint, as the bottles could be sent out of the household to be filled and then returned to the owner. They were also a marker of the wealth, worldliness, and connoisseurship of the owners. Very few members of New York society could afford these bottles.[11] The glass wine bottle seal in figure 3.6 was discovered adjacent to the eighteenth-century battery fortification in what is now Battery Park in Lower Manhattan during the construction of a new subway tunnel. The seal marks it as the property of Governor Fletcher.[12] Aside from restoring order after the Leisler Rebellion, Fletcher is credited with improving the defense of the colony, essential during this period of high tension between the British and French governments. He also chartered Trinity Church, the seat of New York's Anglican church, and established the first printing press in New York.[13]

Despite these accomplishments, Fletcher is now largely known for consorting with pirates, an offense for which he was recalled to London. Whether this was because the government wished to make an example of Fletcher to curtail piracy in New York's economy or because of the lobbying efforts of New Yorkers who disliked Fletcher's rule—or a combination of both—we do not know.[14]

FIGURE 3.6
Wine bottle seal with the coat of arms of Benjamin Fletcher, English governor of New York City from 1692 to 1697. The arms depict a shield with a "fluery," or flowery cross, between four scallop shells.
Qi#102889 SFT

TRINITY CHURCH AND GRAVEYARD

Trinity Church was the seat of New York's Anglican Church and the British colony's officially sanctioned church. It, along with its graveyard, is located at Broadway and Wall streets in Lower Manhattan. The current church, completed in 1846, is the third building at this site. The surrounding burial ground, however, is much older and contains many Colonial-era graves, including that of Mary Dalzell (figure 3.7). Her inscription, as well as the lack of a "maiden" name, marks Mary Dalzell as the wife of James Dalzell, probably of Scottish ancestry. Contemporary Dutch gravestones such as those in Gravesend, New Utrecht, and Flatbush burial grounds in Brooklyn and the Reformed Church in Port Richmond, Staten Island (all New York City landmarks), are frequently written in Dutch and give the wife's family name as well as that of the husband. The commonly used eighteenth-century slate and brownstone grave markers last much longer than the white limestone (or "marble") stones of the nineteenth century, which have become unreadable over time, eroded by acid rain. As can be seen in this example, historical cemetery markers are a prime source for archaeologists: they can reveal demographics and religious beliefs, as well as linguistic and art-historical traditions.

SLAVERY IN EIGHTEENTH-CENTURY NEW YORK

The practice of enslaving Africans, which had been established in New Amsterdam by the Dutch, intensified under British control of the colony. As the city grew, the number of enslaved African people increased dramatically. One suggestion is that the numbers were so large because children born to enslaved people did not survive; the conditions were too harsh.[15] Enslavers are known to have picked up captives along the coast of West Africa: some enslaved people also came from Madagascar, but the majority came from West and West Central Africa.[16] By 1737, almost one in five New Yorkers was Black, and nearly all of them were enslaved.[17] There were frequent sales of enslaved men and women in a market on what is now Wall Street known as the Meal Market, because it was also the place where much of the city's grain, corn, and meal were sold. The market was the site at other times for the "rental" of Indigenous and enslaved African labor on a daily or other basis.[18]

   With the increase in slavery came security concerns about potential slave uprisings. The city government passed repressive laws regulating the movement of enslaved people in the city that restricted their gathering in groups of three or more, even at funerals.[19] Great violence was used to put down uprisings when they occurred. For example, on March 25, 1712, between twenty-five and fifty people of African ancestry rebelled, killing nine white colonists. The city government responded by taking more than seventy enslaved people into custody, twenty-five of whom were subsequently executed, including three who were burned at the stake.[20]

FIGURE 3.7

The 1764 headstone of twenty-eight-year-old Mary Dalzell in the Trinity Church graveyard. Her inscription reads: "Adieu my dearest Babe and tender Husband dear, the time of my departure is now drawing near, and when I am laid low in the silent Grave where the Monarch is equal with the Slave Weep not my friends, I hope to be at rest to be with Jesus Crist is the best." The chubby-faced winged cherub is a typical mid-eighteenth-century gravestone motif. Photograph by Amanda Sutphin, LPC

The existence of slavery, providing a pool of unpaid labor, also contributed to racial resentment from working-class and poor whites. When, as mid-century neared, the economy slowed, white working-class men blamed unfair competition from skilled and enslaved Black tradesmen, whose work was often cheaper than that of their white counterparts, for their declining financial prospects. The situation was exacerbated in 1741 when record snowfall and cold temperatures nearly exhausted the city's supply of food and fuel. The poorest were in danger of starving, if they didn't freeze to death first.[21] As the freeze gave way to spring in March and April, a series of ten fires burned across the city in just three weeks.[22] Although there was no evidence that the fires had been set by enslaved Africans, a grand jury accused them of trying to burn down the city and overthrow the government (figure 3.8). A Salemesque witch hunt ensued, and by June more than two hundred people, primarily of African ancestry, were arrested.[23] Ultimately, eighteen Black people were hanged, and thirteen were burned at the stake. Fifty additional enslaved Black people were found guilty, expelled from New York, and deported to the harsh plantation economies of Surinam, Madeira, Hispaniola, and Curaçao. It will probably never be known whether a conspiracy actually existed, but as a result of the 1741 proceedings, white working-class men filled the labor void at least temporarily.[24]

THE AFRICAN BURIAL GROUND

The African Burial Ground was the place of interment for people of African ancestry from at least 1712, when its existence was first noted in writing, until 1795, when the land under which it lay was platted for development. The burial ground was likely founded around 1697 when Trinity Church banned the interment of people of African ancestry—both enslaved and free—within its cemetery (which we take to mean that it was permitted before this date).[25] In 1755, the burial ground was located outside of the city's second wooden palisade, adjacent to the present-day Chambers Street, which was constructed after the earlier palisade at present-day Wall Street (figure 3.9).

DISCOVERY OF THE AFRICAN BURIAL GROUND

The African Burial Ground was discovered by archaeologists in 1991 during the construction of a new federal building. As required by the National Historic Preservation Act, the potential impact of the project on archaeological resources had to be considered by the General Services Administration (GSA), the federal agency that was building the project. Historical sources, including the 1755 Maerschalck Plan shown in figure 3.9, indicated that the burial ground had been within the project area, and initial archaeological testing confirmed that burials were still intact. However,

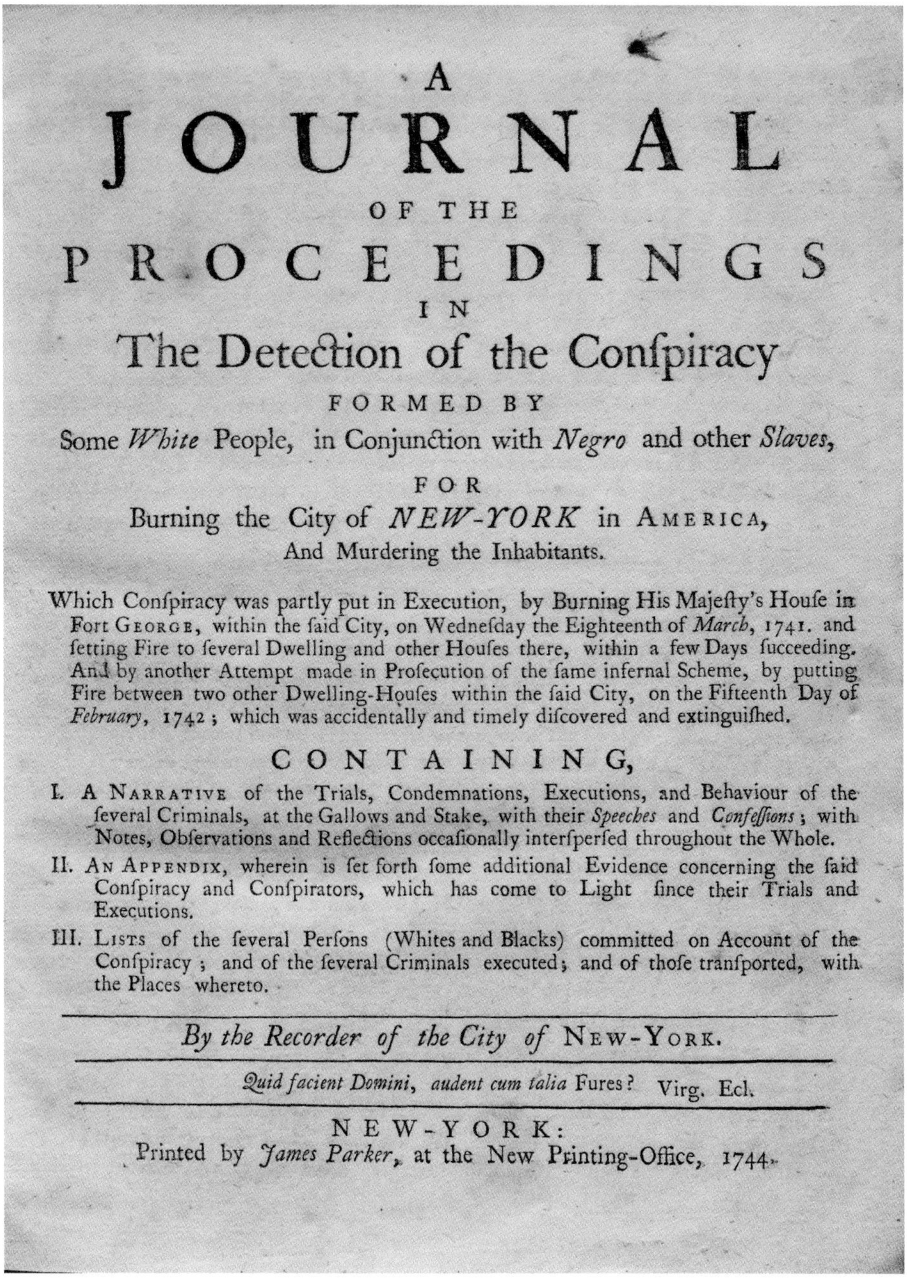

A
JOURNAL
OF THE
PROCEEDINGS
IN
The Detection of the Conspiracy
FORMED BY
Some *White* People, in Conjunction with *Negro* and other *Slaves*,

FOR
Burning the City of *NEW-YORK* in AMERICA,
And Murdering the Inhabitants.

Which Conspiracy was partly put in Execution, by Burning His Majesty's House in Fort GEORGE, within the said City, on Wednesday the Eighteenth of *March*, 1741. and setting Fire to several Dwelling and other Houses there, within a few Days succeeding. And by another Attempt made in Prosecution of the same infernal Scheme, by putting Fire between two other Dwelling-Houses within the said City, on the Fifteenth Day of *February*, 1742 ; which was accidentally and timely discovered and extinguished.

CONTAINING,

I. A NARRATIVE of the Trials, Condemnations, Executions, and Behaviour of the several Criminals, at the Gallows and Stake, with their *Speeches* and *Confessions* ; with Notes, Observations and Reflections occasionally interspersed throughout the Whole.

II. AN APPENDIX, wherein is set forth some additional Evidence concerning the said Conspiracy and Conspirators, which has come to Light since their Trials and Executions.

III. LISTS of the several Persons (Whites and Blacks) committed on Account of the Conspiracy ; and of the several Criminals executed; and of those transported, with the Places whereto.

By the Recorder of the City of NEW-YORK.

Quid facient Domini, audent cum talia Fures ? Virg. Ecl.

NEW-YORK:
Printed by *James Parker*, at the New Printing-Office, 1744.

FIGURE 3.8

New York City Supreme Court Justice Daniel Horsmanden's accounting of the 1741 slave "conspiracy." The Gilder Lehrman Institute of American History (GLC04205.01).

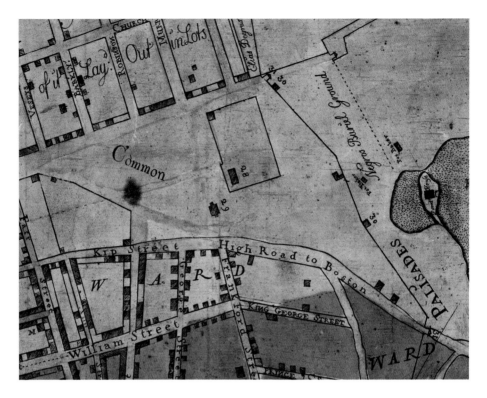

FIGURE 3.9
Detail from the 1755 Maerschalck Plan of the City of New York. Note the "Negros Burial Ground" to the north
of the Common (to the right in this drawing, in script). The Common is now City Hall Park. Note also the
palisade, a wooden stockade fence, which ran along today's Chambers Street.
Library of Congress, Geography and Map Division.

rather than stopping the construction project to fully assess what had been found
and consult with all stakeholders about what should happen, as was required, GSA
chose to proceed with the project as initially designed. As expected, archaeological
excavation for the project encountered burials. More than four hundred burials were
carefully disinterred. Public protests led by Black New Yorkers, including the city's
first Black mayor, David Dinkins, demanded that GSA stop work because it was des-
ecrating their ancestors' remains. These protests finally resulted in several actions
mandated by Congressman Gus Savage (D, IL), chairman of the House Subcommit-
tee on Public Buildings and Grounds, after a hearing. The mandate was to ensure that
(1) the project was redesigned so that burials that were still in situ were protected in
place; (2) the discovery would be analyzed by Black archaeologists led by Dr. Michael
Blakey, then at Howard University; (3) disturbed remains would be reinterred and
memorialized on site; and (4) an interpretive center would be created. A ceremony

to reinter those burials that had been removed was held on October 4, 2003. A portion of the burial ground was made a national monument in 2007 and is now open to the public.

The entire burial ground was designated by the Landmarks Preservation Commission (which had been involved with the federal project) in 1993 as the African Burial Ground and the Commons Historic District. Because it was designated for its archaeological significance, the LPC regulates all subsurface work within the district to ensure that any burials or remains that are still within this area will be appropriately addressed. The designation also includes City Hall Park, which was once the settlement's Commons. It was designated in part because

> it is a tangible reminder of African life in colonial times . . . And today symbolizes both the oppression under which enslaved peoples lived in America, and their ability to persist in honoring their African heritage while forging a new culture. It is also significant that many of those buried at the site probably helped materially in the building of the city which throughout the eighteenth century refused to formally acknowledge their final resting place.[26]

This project remains one of the largest archaeological excavations of a Colonial African burial ground. Analyzing these remains gave an unprecedented view of the origins of enslaved people as well as the physical conditions under which they lived, worked, and died. Bioanthropologists examined the burials exhumed from the African Burial Ground to determine the sex, age, and health of the buried individuals. They also analyzed the isotopic and elemental chemistry of the teeth—a distinct composition created by the food that individuals ate and the water they drank during their lifetime. Water from different regions of the world produces different patterns of elements and isotopes, so these signatures are evidence of where people were born and lived. The anthropologists determined that most of the adult skeletons represented people who had been born in Africa but captured, enslaved, and brought to New York, where they lived and died. Most of the skeletons of the children, in contrast, showed that they had been born in New York. The skeletal population revealed high levels of infant and child mortality; in general, the skeletons indicated high rates of malnutrition, injury, infection, and, as seen in enlarged muscle attachments to bone, overwork.[27]

There was homogeneity in the burial practices. Some burials showed traces of African cultural traditions, such as filed teeth and beads worn around the waist. The bodies were buried in coffins, the head oriented to the west—a traditional Christian orientation so that on Judgment Day the dead could sit up to face the rising sun in the east; the body was supine, and the interments were individual rather than grouped. The most common artifacts within the coffins were wound wire straight pins (figure 3.10).[28] During this time in New York, the dead were often covered in a pinned shroud and then

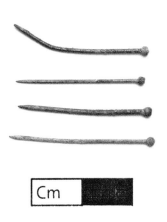

FIGURE 3.10
Shroud pins, City Hall Park. Wound-wire straight pins like these were common multipurpose implements in the eighteenth and nineteenth centuries. City Hall Park once included several historical burial grounds, including two associated with the 1735–1736 Almshouse where City Hall now stands (Landmarks Preservation Commission 1993, 344). These pins were found in the area of the Almshouse's burial ground during an archaeological excavation associated with the reconstruction of City Hall Park in 1998, which is why they are presumed to be shroud pins (Brooklyn College Archaeological Research Center 2008, 325–365). Qi# 8376 CHP, Qi#8595 CHP, Qi#8563 CHP, Qi#213308 CHP

placed in a wooden coffin, which may have been stacked with other coffins within the grave. The pins were brass, a copper alloy, but sometimes covered in a white metal to imitate silver. The copper in the pins reacts with the moisture in the soil and the oxidation often leaves verdigris—green staining—on the surrounding area, including the bones.[29] We do not know what the shrouds were made of because they decomposed, but at the time the British government mandated that burial shrouds be made from wool, an effort to protect their wool trade.[30] The site remains one of the most significant in New York City.

African Burial Grounds in New York City

The African Burial Ground National Monument site is the city's largest African burial ground. Its rediscovery has stimulated additional work to understand the lives of enslaved people and free Black people and to memorialize and commemorate their lives. Other burial sites of people of African descent have been located within the city, including the Harlem African Burial Ground in East Harlem (see figure 3.11); Inwood African Burial Ground in Upper Manhattan; the Hunts Point Slave Burial Ground in Drake Park in the Bronx; Sankofa Park African Burial Ground in East New York; Flatbush African Burial Ground in Flatbush, Brooklyn; Olde Towne of Flushing Burial Ground in Flushing, Queens; and the Elmhurst African Burial Ground in Elmhurst, Queens. Although these projects differ from eachother, all of them include significant community input and reflect the importance and sacredness of these sites to many members of the Black community.

FIGURE 3.11
From left to right: Sharon Wilkins; Reverend Dr. Patricia A. Singletary, Elmendorf Reformed Church Pastor; and Melissa Mark-Viverito, New York City Council Speaker from 2014 to 2017. Reverend Singletary is shown blessing the human remains that were found during archaeological testing on site at the Harlem African Burial Ground, September 24, 2015.
Photograph by John McCarten, New York City Council Photographer.

FEEDING EIGHTEENTH-CENTURY NEW YORK

Feeding the growing population was a challenge. By the eighteenth century, the kitchen gardens and orchards that had populated the Lower Manhattan of the Castello Plan in 1660 (figure 3.1) had given way to the real estate demands of an expanding city. This made it more difficult for urban residents to feed themselves. To meet their needs, twice-weekly markets brought meat and fish, fruit and vegetables from the farms of upper Manhattan, Brooklyn, and other agricultural places.[31] Some early "receipt books" record the diet of elite families such as the Van Rensselaers, while printed cookbooks such as Englishwoman Hannah Glasse's *The Art of Cookery Made Plain and Simple*, first published in 1747 and extremely popular on both sides of the Atlantic, give some indication of the diets of the upper and middle classes.[32] For example:

> To Roast a turkey the genteel way.
>   First cut it down the back, and with a sharp penknife bone it, then make your source-meat thus: take a large fowl, or a pound of veal, as much grated bread, half

a pound of sewet [suet] cut and beat very fine, a little beaten mace, two cloves, half a nutmeg grated, about a large tea-spoonful of lemon-peel, and the yolks of two eggs; mix all together, with a little pepper and salt, fill up the places where the bones came out, and fill the body, that it may look just as it did before, sew up the back, and roast it. You may have oyster sauce, sellery [celery] sauce, or just as you please; but good gravy in the dish, and garnish with lemon is as good as anything. Be sure to leave the pinions on.[33]

The analysis of faunal remains—animal bones—from samples excavated from two large-scale excavations in Lower Manhattan during the early 1980s, at the Stadt Huys Block and 7 Hanover Square, showed broad changes over time in the diet of everyday New Yorkers. In particular, there was a noticeable shift in proteins—mammals, fish, including mollusks, and birds—consumed from the time of initial settlement to the outbreak of the Revolutionary War. Unfortunately, little food other than bone, shell, and some seeds are found in archaeological deposits because organic materials do not preserve well. Travelers' accounts and menus left from this period indicate that New Yorkers ate their vegetables, but meat, fish, and game were the preferred foods. The wild deer, rabbit, and squirrel that graced the tables of the earliest European colonists were gradually replaced by domesticated mammals. Beef, followed by lamb and mutton, and then pork, were the largest source of protein for New Yorkers between 1624 and 1700. They also ate fair amounts of fish, shellfish, especially oysters, and birds.[34]

As the eighteenth century progressed, the faunal analysis showed, New Yorkers turned to larger amounts of cheaper chicken and fish. By 1761, colonists ate as much fish protein as mammal. Residents of lower Manhattan went from locally fished sheepshead and striped bass to deepwater cod, sea bass, and scup. The deep-sea fishing industry had grown in the 1760s with the introduction of well-smacks, ships with water-holding tanks that could transport live fish over a greater distance.[35] But it is also likely that over-fishing and the landfilling of the estuarine habitat of the sheepshead and striped bass depleted their populations and forced the shift to deepwater fish. Native species like Black Drum and Sheepshead fish, for example—for which Sheepshead Bay in Brooklyn is named—live in brackish inshore areas where they dine primarily on shellfish, for which their distinctive teeth are adapted (figure 3.12).[36]

"Above New York they find innumerable quantities of excellent oysters, and there are a few places which have oysters of so great a size: they are pickled and sent to the West Indies and other places."
—Peter Kalm, *Travels Into North America* (1771), 237.

The construction of wharfs along Manhattan's shoreline beginning in the seventeenth century buried intertidal oyster beds. This and the polluted runoff from the growing city reduced the oxygen levels of the city's coastal waters, choking the oyster

FIGURE 3.12
The pharyngeal plate, or jaw, of a fish with distinctive teeth used for grinding shellfish excavated during the South Ferry Terminal Project.
Qi#198193 SFT

beds and all the creatures who depended on them. This was not lost on colonial New Yorkers. A Finnish naturalist visiting the city in June 1749 wrote in his diary: "Several gentlemen and merchants, between fifty and sixty years of age, asserted, that during their life they had plainly found several kinds of fish decrease in number every year; and that they could not get near so many fish now as they could formerly."[37]

Oysters, before their decline, were central to the diet of eighteenth-century New York. Their abundance and great size (figure 3.13) meant they were popular among New Yorkers of all social classes by the end of the century.[38] New York oysters, preserved in butter or pickled in vinegar to stay shelf stable even in hot climates, were a key export to the Caribbean and throughout the Atlantic well into the nineteenth century.[39]

The relative size of the shells in archaeological excavations is often a good clue to the sites' dates. The shells grow by adding a layer of material each year, so counting layers gives an indication of their age. As a result of overharvesting and changes to New York's waterways over time, oysters were harvested at younger and younger ages, so sites with small shells indicate younger oysters—in the sense both that the oysters lived fewer years and that the sites with smaller shells are more recent. Excavations in Lower Manhattan have left the New York Archaeological Repository with several hundred boxes of shells. In Colonial times, they were used to make lime mortar and in some cases to pave streets (Pearl Street in Manhattan and Shell Road in Brooklyn, for example).

FIGURE 3.13
Two large eighteenth-century oyster shells excavated during the South Ferry Terminal Project, with between 20 and 25–27 growth breaks that, like tree rings, indicate that the oysters lived for between twenty and thirty years before they were harvested. Qi#103926 SFT

FIGURE 3.14
Eighteenth-century coffee beans and coconut shell excavated during the South Ferry Project. These were not locally grown but products of the Atlantic and global trade.
Qi#103534 SFT and Qi#108320 SFT

Transatlantic trade brought food from all over the world into New York kitchens. Beginning in the fifteenth century, Europeans brought coconuts—native to islands of Southeast Asia and the Indian Ocean—to Brazil and the Caribbean, where they flourished.[40] From there they made their way into Atlantic circulation and to eighteenth-century New York (figure 3.14). We do not know how common a sight the coconut was in city markets, but coconut recipes, including those for Cokernut Tarts and Cokernut Pudding, indicate that coconuts found their way into the cookery of elite New Yorkers by 1780.[41]

A taste for coffee—first cultivated in Ethiopia and then Yemen in the Middle Ages—had spread to Europe and its colonies by the late seventeenth century and was under cultivation in the Caribbean colonies by the eighteenth century.[42] New York was fully established as a centralized market for coffee by 1674, supplying the other North American colonies. In 1730, Jamaica became the first of Britain's Caribbean colonies to grow coffee.

New York's first coffeehouse, the King's Arms, a mark of the city's Anglicization, was established in 1696 and offered the city's elite men an alternative to the taverns preferred by the lower classes to conduct their business. Coffeehouses were quickly integrated into the mercantile fabric of the city.[43] The Exchange Coffee House, established in 1729 at the foot of Broad Street, became the locus of real estate transactions. The Merchants' Coffee House, a tavern at the intersection of Wall and Water (then Queen) streets that converted to a coffeehouse in 1737, was the favorite of the city's merchants and traders who frequented the nearby Meal Market. The market, mentioned previously, opened in 1711 and lasted until 1762; it was given the name Meal Market in 1726.

Archaeologists would later excavate a large deposit of burned coffee beans in the landfill deposits of Lower Manhattan at White Hall Slip, part of the South Ferry Project excavations (see figure 3.14)—a testament to the city's coffee consumption. These dumps were used to infill and convert the slip from water to land. The charred beans lost to a fire or perhaps overzealous roasting would have been a disappointing and expensive loss to the merchant.[44]

Trade dominated the British colonial endeavor. New York settlers wanted English or European imports: ceramics, glassware, objects for the home, and tools. The Crown, in turn, demanded that flour, corn, pork, beef, and farm products be produced by New York and then exported predominantly to the British and Spanish Caribbean, both to support the military during European wars and to feed enslaved workers who grew sugar on Caribbean plantations.[45] Sugar was central to British tables.

THE BEGINNINGS OF NEW YORK CITY REAL ESTATE DEVELOPMENT: THE WATERFRONT EXPANDS

Although New Amsterdam and New York were founded on trade, the most dramatic changes to the settlement in the seventeenth century involved the beginnings of urban expansion and the physical transformation and privatization of the Manhattan landscape. The Dongan Charter of 1686, named after Thomas Dongan, another important early governor, created "water lots"—parcels of water sold by the city to private individuals who would fill them in with anything at their disposal.[46] The water lots close to shore were often filled with soil from leveled hills and domestic refuse; those farther out employed wooden cribwork (figure 3.15) packed with rocks, dead animals, household and industrial waste, and sometimes unwanted old ships that were sunk to make land. The first lots were sold to merchants and to those in the shipping trades. These water lots served two main purposes: they generated funds for the city, and they enabled the construction of deeper-water docks so that larger ships could tie up and unload. They drastically altered the shape of the island and began the process of defining land as a

FIGURE 3.15
Horizontal log cribbing from Whitehall Slip unearthed during the South Ferry Excavation.
Photograph by AKRF, Inc, URS Corp., and Linda Stone; Courtesy of the Metropolitan Transportation
Authority.

commodity, having cash value rather than use value.[47] The Dongan Charter also established that "all the waste, vacant, unpatented and unappropriated lands lying and being
within the city of New York and on Manhattan Island aforesaid extending and reaching
to the low water mark" belonged to the city.[48]

A second city charter was established in 1727 by Governor John Montgomerie, a
Scottish-born member of Parliament who was appointed governor of New York by
King George II. It too claimed all remaining unoccupied and common land for the
city. Land was scarce because expansion had reached the limits set out in the Dongan Charter; in addition, a bad storm in 1723 had destroyed many docks, so new ones
were needed.[49] While Montgomerie was governor, from 1727 to 1731, the charter
made way for further expansion into the Hudson and East River. By the mid-eighteenth century, the water lots of Pearl Street, Front Street, and South Street had been
filled in, and the "made land" of Lower Manhattan included Greenwich and Washington streets on the West Side, broadening out the shape of the island. Both land
and water were now dedicated to commercial use, and New York exports exceeded
those of Boston and Philadelphia for the first time.[50] In 2012, Hurricane Sandy
flooded much of the land granted and developed by the Montgomerie charter back

to the approximate line of the 1650 shore, likely because these areas of fill remained at a lower elevation.[51]

The 7 Hanover Square site was the first large archaeological site to be excavated on a landfill block.[52] It represented the earliest generation of such landfilling and lay between Pearl and Water streets, where the water was relatively shallow. The excavations uncovered thousands of artifacts and features from the Colonial period to the nineteenth century. Associated research shows that families of different national origins lived side by side. Robert Livingston (the elder), Scottish by birth, moved to Holland and then New Amsterdam in 1674. He married Alida Schuyler, of Dutch ancestry, and became a wealthy trader with an estate in Albany and a large house in New York City. Robert and Alida were the great-grandparents of Robert R. Livingston (known as "the Chancellor"), ambassador to France, who was one of the five authors of the Declaration of Independence. They are also the ancestors of both presidents George Bush. Their house was adjacent to the more modest dwellings of Dutch families. The Livingston household included enslaved people and indentured servants.

The following indenture agreement from 1742 was likely made between Robert and Alida Livingston's son, also named Robert Livingston, and John Reid.

THIS Indenture Witnesseth, that John Reid of freedhold in the County of Monnmouth Jersey by and with the Consent of his father John Reid of Sd place hath put himself, and by these Presents doth voluntarily, and of his own free Will and Accord put himself an Apprentice to Robert Livingston Jun of New York with him to live, and (after the Manner of an Apprentice) to Serve from the first Day of Novembr : Anno Domini, One Thousand Seven Hundred and Forty two till the full Term of five years be compleat and ended. During all which Term the said Apprentice his said Master faithfully shall serve, his Secrets keep, his lawfull Commands gladly every where obey: he shall do no Damage to His said Master nor see to be done by others without letting or giving Notice to his said master he shall not waste his said Masters Goods, nor lend them unlawfully to any, he shall not commit Fornication, nor contract Matrimony within the said Term. At Cards, Dice or any other unlawful Game, he shall not play, whereby his said Master may have Damage with his own Goods, nor the Goods of others within the said Term, without Lisence [*sic*] from his said Master, he shall neither buy not [*sic*] sell, he shall not absent himself Day nor Night from his said Masters Service without his Leave, nor haunt Ale-Houses, Taverns or Play-Houses; but in all Things as a faithful Apprentice he shall behave himself to his said Master and all his during the said Term. And the said Master during the said Term shall by the best Means or Method that he can, Teach or cause the said Apprentice to be Taught the Art and Mystery of a Marchent [*sic*] And also shall find an provide unto the said Apprentice sufficient meat Drink and Lodging

For the true Perfomance of all and every the said Covenants and Agreements, either of the said Parties bind themselves unto the other by these Presents. In Witness whereof they have hereunto interchangeably put their Hands and Seals this first Day of November in the Sixteenth Year of His Majesty's Reign Annoq; [*sic*] Domini, One Thousand Seven Hundred and Forty Two, (signatures)[53]

SIMEON SOUMAINE'S WORKSHOP

Among the discoveries made during the 7 Hanover Square excavations was a trash midden—a bounded and discrete refuse deposit—found in the basement of a seventeenth-century dwelling that fronted on Pearl Street.[54] The midden contained nearly one thousand ceramic crucible fragments (figure 3.16). Crucibles are specialized vessels designed to withstand extremely high temperatures to contain molten metal.[55] A number of the crucible fragments were blackened on the exterior, exhibiting traces of intense firing, and some contained blackened residue on the interior. Using x-ray fluorescence (XRF), a noninvasive elemental analysis tool, archaeologists analyzed a fragment of a crucible containing this residue.

Historical records indicate that Huguenot craftsman Simeon Soumaine lived and worked on the 7 Hanover Square block from about 1709 until his death around 1750.[56] Soumaine was an accomplished silversmith whose silverwork is today part of the Colonial silver collections at the Metropolitan Museum of Art and elsewhere (figure 3.17). The XRF analysis determined that the residue in the crucible was silver, further validating the association of the artifact deposit with Soumaine's workshop (figure 3.18).

The Soumaine family was among the many thousands of Protestant Huguenots who were expelled from Catholic France between 1680 and 1690. They fled to Germany, Holland, and England, as well as to the American colonies. The Huguenot families dominated the textile and metalworking industries in France and took their expertise with them, to the detriment of France. The Soumaine family first went to London before immigrating to New York in 1685.[57] By 1709, Soumaine established his workshop and dwelling on the block of 7 Hanover Square. Soumaine and his wife, Mary, had many children—six of whom died in the smallpox epidemic of 1730 and were buried in Trinity Churchyard.

Also, resident at the Pearl Street house were three indentured servants or apprentices, each serving a seven-year indenture to Soumaine, and Tom, an enslaved man who was expelled from New York as a result of the conspiracy of 1741 described previously. Two of Soumaine's three apprentices—Elias Boudinot and Elias Pelletreau—were Huguenots as well, sent by Huguenot families to train in the craft of silversmithing from one of their own.[58]

FIGURE 3.16

Triangular-mouthed stoneware crucibles associated with the workshop of silversmith Simeon
Soumaine. The one on the left appears to have never been used. Crucibles and similar manufacturing
materials are often found in archaeological excavations. The completed silver products are rarely found
archaeologically because they were usually either melted down or kept as heirlooms and today may be
found in museums.

Qi#209648 7HS, Qi#209646 7 HS, and Qi#209761 7HS

FIGURE 3.17

Simeon Soumaine tea caddy set, circa 1720. The service includes two octagonal tea caddies, on the right and left, and a sugar box, center. The vessels are engraved with the seal of the Bayard family, who were large sugar producers. At this time, tea and sugar were indicators of wealth and gentility, emphasized here by the use of the costly silver containers.

Image copyright © The Metropolitan Museum of Art. Image Source: Art Resource. From left to right: 64.249. Sa, b; 2015.93.2a, b; 2015.93.la, b. Overall: 4 5/16 × 2 11/16 × 2 1/4 in. (11 × 6.8 × 5.7 cm); 5 oz. 15 dwt. (178 g); Body: 3 1/16 in. (9.4 cm); 5 oz. 1 dwt. (156.6 g); Cover: 1 3/8 × 1 1/4 in. (3.5 × 3.2 cm); 14 dwt. (21.4 g). Gift of E. M. Newlin, 1964; Purchase, Nancy Dunn Revocable Trust Gift, 2015 (64.249.Sa, b; 2015.93.la, b-.2a, b).

FIGURE 3.18

Circular graphite crucible with traces of melted silver adhering to the bottom of the vessel. From the silver workshop of Huguenot Simeon Soumaine who lived and worked on the 7 Hanover Square block from 1709 to 1750. Qi#209698 7HS

LOCAL POTTERY PRODUCTION

The city's local pottery industry was similarly rooted in family networks and a centuries-old craft tradition brought from the Westerwald region of Germany, the center of stoneware production in Europe, to New York at the turn of the eighteenth century. New York offered experienced craftsmen the chance to practice their trade in a bourgeoning marketplace for goods. This opportunity was seized by German stoneware potters Johann Willem Crolius and Johannes Remmey, who immigrated to New York City in the early eighteenth century.[59] The two men established themselves as potters by 1730, and both married into the Corsilus family, another German family which had begun working as potters in late seventeenth-century Manhattan producing stoneware for the local New York market (figure 3.19).

Their potteries were situated on Pot Baker Hill on the outskirts of eighteenth-century Manhattan between the collect pond and the Commons, north of today's City Hall. The potteries were deliberately located away from the prime residential areas, along with other industries such as tanneries that produced noxious by-products and needed open space to work.[60] The potteries were located close to the African Burial Ground, also relegated to the city's periphery. Two kilns, or Pot Bakers, proximate to the potteries of the three families, are depicted on either side of the "Negro Burial Ground" on the 1755 Maerschalck Plan shown in figure 3.9.

Archaeologists working on the African Burial Ground project and excavations at City Hall and Tweed Courthouse have found manufacturing evidence of Crolius and Remmey potteries.[61] These finds include ceramic wasters, vessels that broke during firing and were disposed of, and kiln furniture used to stack the vessels for firing (figure 3.20). These particular artifacts have provided valuable insight into the manufacturing process employed by the New York potters, along with the types of vessels they manufactured for the New York market. We have also gained an understanding of the decorative types used by the Crolius and Remmey families through time as they prospered through three generations into the nineteenth century. The recovery of stoneware fragments directly associated with the Crolius and Remmey potteries has also provided archaeologists the opportunity to experiment with clay sourcing, a key element in determining the place of manufacture of stonewares found in New York City.

It is generally difficult to distinguish a New York–manufactured stoneware from a German-made stoneware based on appearance alone because they are so similar, having both been made in the same craft tradition. A team of archaeologists from Brooklyn College set out to resolve this problem and to test the analytical capacity of x-ray fluorescence (XRF) in determining the place of manufacture. They compared the elemental composition of the clay from stonewares known to have been manufactured in Germany to those excavated from City Hall thought to have been locally manufactured. They discovered that the New York stonewares consistently returned a higher ratio of rubidium to strontium (Rb/Sr) than those made in Germany.[62] The higher levels of rubidium in New York stoneware can be explained by

FIGURE 3.19

Local, New York–made stoneware vessels: (*top left*) handled cup; (*top right*) barber's bowl from the Crolius
or Remmey pottery; (*bottom*) two pieces of a wide-mouth storage jar made by one of the aforementioned
two potters. The vessels were excavated during the City Hall Park (2008) and South Ferry Project (2012) in
Lower Manhattan, not far from the potteries themselves.
Qi# 56681 CHP, Qi# 98629 CHP; Qi#110798 SFT

the residual mica found in the New York–area clay produced by the weathering of
Manhattan's micaceous schist bedrock. This is the same stone that can be seen in
the walls of St. Paul's Chapel and Graveyard, a New York City landmark by City
Hall Park. This study proved both that New York–made stonewares have an elemental fingerprint different from their German counterparts and that XRF analysis provides a reliable and nondestructive means of distinguishing between places
of manufacture.

The Soumaine silver crucibles and the Crolius and Remmey stonewares mark the
emergence of local production of goods in New York City. These industries built upon

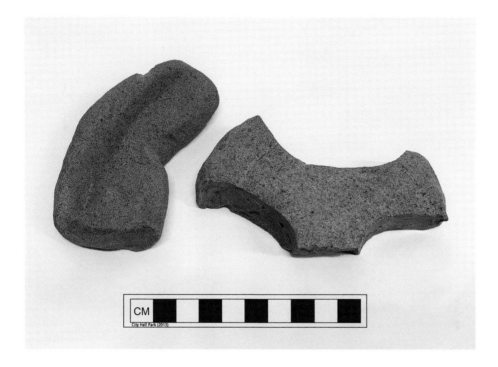

FIGURE 3.20
Stoneware kiln furniture (pads) from the Crolius or Remmey potteries excavated from City Hall Park in 2010. The pads were used to separate stacked vessels in the kiln for firing. The orange outline of a vessel rim is visible on the left, and a mug imprint can be seen on the right. The piece on the right represents two arms of a tri-armed flat pad whose cutouts allowed the salt vapor to circulate to the interior of the vessels while stacked. When salt is thrown into a sufficiently hot kiln, a chemical reaction creates a glaze that is glossy and has an orange-peel-like texture.
Qi# 123072 CHP and Qi#123073 CHP

the skills of French and German immigrants and took advantage of the new markets and resources the city provided. These immigrants were of a higher status than the majority of those who worked with their hands—bricklayers, masons, seamen—and who did not have shops. Cartmen also count as working men, although having horses put them on a slightly higher footing than the others.

THE GROWTH OF THE CITY

The Lyne-Bradford Plan of 1730 was the first map of New York to be printed in the city (figure 3.21).[63] Drawn by surveyor James Lyne and printed by William Bradford (founder of the city's first newspaper, the *New-York Gazette*), the map shows that the British had nearly doubled the city's area, expanding north of the original palisade (located at today's Wall Street), mainly to the east of Broadway. However, New York

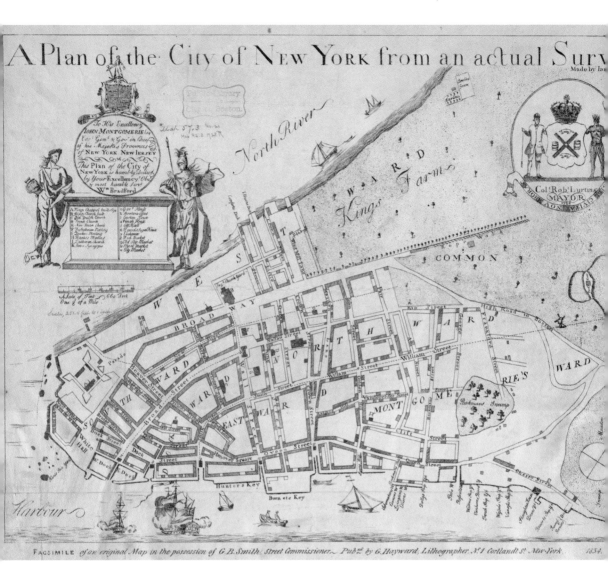

FIGURE 3.21
The City of New York from an Actual Survey by James Lyne, 1730 (printed in 1731). Note the fort in the South Ward, the slips for oceangoing trade on the East River, the Rope Walk (for making ships' hawsers and other ropes) on Broadway, and the High Road to Boston (on the east side of the Common).
Norman B. Leventhal Map Center Collection, Boston Public Library.

remained a small settlement that one could easily walk across in an hour. Churches and taverns sat at the center of social life. Prayer, drink, and trade united and divided New Yorkers.

In comparison to other colonial cities such as Boston and Philadelphia, which were comprised mainly of groups of similar people fleeing persecution, New York included a greater mix of people of different ethnicities and religions. In addition to Dutch and

British, many early settlers, like Simeon Soumaine, were Huguenot Protestants. The diverse population is reflected in the many churches and congregations that the immigrants established. The Lyne-Bradford Plan shows seven religious institutions: the Anglican Trinity Church, the New or Middle Dutch Church, the French Church, the Presbyterian Meeting House, the Quaker Meeting House, the Baptist Meeting House, and Shearith Israel.[64]

The growth of New York's population picked up speed through immigration in the eighteenth century. After the Huguenots came the Palatine Germans, Protestants who fled from rural southwestern Germany after Catholic France began attacking them in 1688 and later when devastating famine and typhoid epidemics ravaged their people. The Palatines immigrated en masse, first to New York City in 1709 and then to the Hudson Valley and Pennsylvania.[65] The Scots and Scots-Irish followed: fifteen thousand to the North American colonies between 1720 and 1730. Along with them came as many as eighty thousand Irish Catholics as well as other Germans.[66] By 1760, fifteen thousand immigrants came to the city each year, mostly from the British Isles: Ireland, Scotland, London, and Yorkshire. Many came indentured to tradesmen or artisans. Others came hoping for work in the New World's flourishing economy. Immigrants to the growing town tended to live in clusters of people from their home country, or even their hometown, as seen in church, tax, and census records.

From the beginning, New York's ethnic diversity shaped its social and political structure. It also spurred religious conflict and transformed the nature of leadership within the community. Ethnicity and class intersected as the city grew and influenced social geography and urban life—an influence that continues today. As the city's ethnic makeup varied from other cities, so did its political hierarchy. Elsewhere, the wealthiest were the most powerful. While New York did have an affluent, politically powerful elite, it also had a strong, politically active group of artisans, tavern keepers, sea captains, and cartmen who counterbalanced the wealthy elite.[67] (A cartman owned a cart and often a horse and used them to transport household and commercial goods and trash around Manhattan.)[68]

The 1720s were defined by conflict between two principal elite groups. On the one side were mercantile interests like the Delancey, Philipse, and Schuyler families, most of whom were Anglican. On the other side were the wealthy landed folk, like the Livingstons, Van Rensselaers, and Beekmans, who were Presbyterian.[69] Besides their opposing religious and economic interests, these factions were also on opposite sides in the emerging French-British conflict, which centered in part on control of North American land and resources.[70] This constant infighting weakened British rule and perhaps made New York more tumultuous than other colonial cities such as Boston or Philadelphia, where wealth and political power were synonymous.

Divisions within the city's social fabric were exacerbated by new methods of production, which prefigured industrialization. Before the nineteenth century, goods were produced in craft workshops like the Soumaines', in which apprentices lived in the household and were given food, shelter, and domestic services in exchange for their labor.[71] (As well as apprentices, these households also included enslaved workers.) The domestic unit was equivalent to the productive unit. But the early stages of industrialization upended this, separating the home and the workplace, creating the beginnings of class-based neighborhoods. We can distinguish these neighborhoods by the different architectural styles that characterized them.[72] The Church Farm or Kings Farm housed artisans and laborers (carpenters, masons, and cartmen) in small wooden houses on land leased out by Trinity Church in the western part of the city between Broadway and the Hudson River (see Kings Farm at top right in figure 3.21). The middle and upper classes lived in brick Georgian residences to the east and north of Broadway.[73] Between these areas lay the city Commons (also shown in figure 3.21); this was not, however, land held in common as was the case in England and in New England villages. Sole ownership of the Common was held by the city under the Montgomerie Charter, and its use was strictly regulated by the Common Council.[74]

THE ALMSHOUSE: MUNICIPAL CARE FOR THE POOR

The Commons held the Almshouse, a refuge and workhouse for the needy built between 1735 and 1736. It was the first municipal institution in New York specifically constructed and operated for the indigent (figure 3.22). The Almshouse itself represents a change in the treatment of the poor. Before 1641, care of the poor was the responsibility of the church, which provided food and necessities to the indigent of their parish.[75] By 1734, as the population rose, land for small gardens and orchards decreased, and hundreds of men were without work, care of the poor was a burden to the community.[76] The Almshouse was created by the Council to house the poorest and teach them a simple trade. The Common Council Minutes of 1736 list furnishings of the Almshouse meant for this purpose, including a spinning wheel.[77]

According to the 1736 Minutes of the Common Council, occupants of the Almshouse included people who

> shall be sent or committed thither and able to labor; and also all disorderly persons, parents of Bastard children, Beggars, Servants running away or otherwise misbehaving themselves, Tresspassers, Rogues, Vagabounds, poor persons refusing to work . . . all such sturdy beggars as go wandering and begging about the streets, and asking Alms.[78]

Button production was one of the tasks of the Almshouse, although the Common Council minutes do not mention the tools for button making. It may be that such tools were so simple they would have been beneath notice. Bone button waste from City Hall Park excavations indicates that buttons of all sizes were made there in the eighteenth century (figure 3.23). The bones could have come from the stockyards to the north of what

FIGURE 3.22

Detail of the David Grim City Plan (1742) depicting the city's almshouse, or poor house, as it looked then. The municipal entity housed the city's poorest and provided instruction in various trades. Lionel Pincus and Princess Firyal Map Division, The New York Public Library. New York Public Library Digital Collections.

FIGURE 3.23

Stages of bone button manufacture excavated from archaeological projects at City Hall and Tweed Courthouse. The top rows and bottom left illustrate manufacturing waste; the two semifinished button blanks, bottom right, were probably intended for a waistcoat and coat, like those worn by the Rapalje sons, which would have been covered with textile to match the suit (figure 3.24). Qi# 11286 CHP, Qi#9249 CHP, Qi#7445 CHP, Qi#11235 CHP, Qi# 9262 CHP, Qi# 9262 CHP.

is now Chambers Street or from the food refuse in the trash pits of the Commons. In the eighteenth century, buttons were almost exclusively menswear: fasteners and ornamentation for coats, waistcoats, and breeches.[79] We can see this in eighteenth-century portraits of the wealthy. Buttons at the knee, down the waistcoat, or on the coat sleeves show the cost of the clothing and the wealth of the portrait's subject (figure 3.24). The buttons still found on men's suit or jacket sleeves are modern remnants of their eighteenth-century profusion.

Buttons, button cores, and the refuse from making buttons are the most common bone artifacts found in New York sites of the eighteenth century. Cheap buttons were made from the leg bones of large animals, usually cattle, and were cut from the bone with a rotating compass-like drill that left a hole in the middle.[80] They were of different sizes depending on the garment for which they were intended. Small buttons, up to twelve millimeters in diameter, were used for underwear and shirts. Medium buttons, from twelve to eighteen millimeters, fastened waistcoats and breeches. Large buttons, over eighteen millimeters, adorned coats such as those displayed in figure 3.24.[81] Exterior buttons on clothing consisted of bone button cores covered in fabric or stamped copper-alloy metal that would have shone gold, whereas buttons on underwear and shirts were often used without further modification.

Wooden buttons were made by cabinetmakers. Buttons of precious stones or shell were made by jewelers. Cloth-covered or metal buttons were made by button makers or dry-goods merchants, or else they were made at home.[82] The production of bone buttons left easily identifiable waste in the archaeological record: thin fragments of animal leg bones with round cutouts (figure 3.23) are clear signs that buttons were made on site or close by in homes or shops that may have dumped trash there.

Only a few of the actual buttons or button cores found at City Hall Park seem to represent completed products. Those that may be complete are the cheapest kind of button. Almost all button cores or blanks excavated from City Hall are thin bone disks (figure 3.23, bottom right) that would have been covered with textile or a thin sheet of stamped copper alloy as a final step. Many lack the four holes that would identify them as finished sew-through buttons (figure 3.25).

There were also British barracks in City Hall Park, so it is strange how few military buttons have been recovered. The buttons in figure 3.23 are also missing traces of thread wrapping or covering material. They may have come from an initial stage of button making, at least for larger buttons for outer garments, providing cores to merchants who then sold them to tailors or modified them to the customers' specification.[83] Diderot's *Encyclopedie* illustrated both men and women making buttons using a simple bow drill or a spinning wheel to power the button drill (figure 3.26). The refuse from the Almshouse production and some unfinished button cores wound up in the many trash pits in the Commons, evidence both of the poorest of New Yorkers and of a new civic approach to their welfare.

By the mid-eighteenth century the city had become an economic success, in spite of the hardship of many of its inhabitants.[84] In New York, as in New England, this was

FIGURE 3.24

John Durand, *The Rapalje Children*, 1768. Born into a wealthy Manhattan mercantile family, the Rapalje children wear clothing that illustrates their position in society. The boys' waistcoat buttons are covered in cloth to match their vests, while their larger, outer coat buttons are made from brass. Their sister, Helena, displays no buttons, as was customary for female clothing in the eighteenth century.

Oil on canvas, 58 1/4 × 47 1/4 in. Gift of Mrs. Eliza J. Watson in memory of her husband, John Jay Watson. New-York Historical Society, 1946.201. Photography ©New-York Historical Society

FIGURE 3.25
Four-hole bone button excavated from City Hall
Park (1989). The center hole was created by the
drill point used to manufacture the button. The
concentric circles were made by a drill bit with
at least two teeth on either side of the point
resembling Diderot's "Fig.1" in figure 3.26.
Qi#9269 CHP

Cm

marked by the push for the domestic production of imported products, from homespun textiles to iron kettles, pots, and plows manufactured at the Peter Curtenius & Co. New-York Air Furnace, or iron foundry, established in 1767 on the Hudson River. This success is also seen in the archaeological record in the diversity of items from far-flung places—coffee from Africa, coconuts from Southeast Asia by way of the Caribbean, blue and white porcelain from China, and shoes and smoking pipes from the Netherlands. Perhaps the most essential trading good, however, was sugar.

SUGAR IN NEW YORK CITY

Though far from the sugar plantations, New York was a city built on sugar and slavery. Sugar was a crucial empirewide commodity. The working class in Britain lived on tea with sugar, bread, and jam. The upper class used sugar in elaborate desserts like gingerbread houses, fancy cakes and confections, candy hearts and the like.[85] In *American Cookery*, the first cookbook published in America, Amelia Simmons instructed home cooks to use "three quarters of a pound sugar" when making bread or orange puddings and a full "one pound of fine sugar" in their lemon puddings and tarts.[86] One pound of sugar is the equivalent of 2¼ cups and is about twice as much sugar as modern recipes typically use for such desserts.

Fueled by endless enslaved labor, sugar plantations in the eighteenth-century Caribbean grew, milled, and boiled sugarcane, transforming it into raw sugar and molasses. The raw, partially refined sugar was sent to European and North American cities to be refined. Sugar became so profitable and was in such demand that West Indian planters converted all available land to cane production and relied on the North American

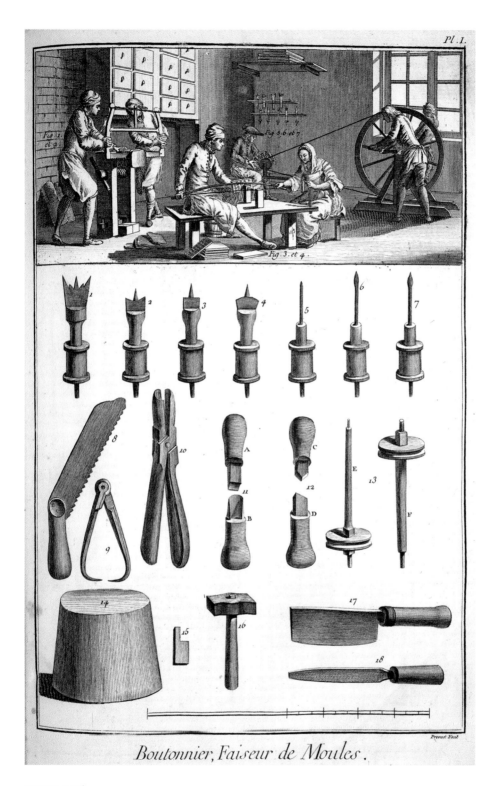

Pl. I.

Fig. 1. et 2.

Fig. 5. 6. et 7.

Fig. 3. et 4.

Prevost Fecit

Boutonnier, Faiseur de Moules.

FIGURE 3.26

Button making as depicted in Diderot's *Encyclopedie*, 1765. The drill bits (top row) were powered by the men turning the large wheel (back right). Smaller holes in the buttons were made by the workers sitting in the foreground. Note that turning the wheel was hard work (no shirt on the turner) and that both men and women participated in this work.

Encyclopédie, ou dictionnaire raisonné des sciences, des arts et des métiers, etc., eds. Denis Diderot and Jean le Rond d'Alembert. University of Chicago: ARTFL Encyclopédie Project (Spring 2021 Edition), Robert Morrissey and Glenn Roe (eds), http://encyclopedie.uchicago.edu.

colonies and Europe to export to them the necessities of daily life such as food, clothing and construction supplies.[87] New York merchants involved in this trade received rum, molasses, and their own raw sugar in exchange, although the majority was sent to Great Britain. Ironically, refined loaf sugar was brought back to the Caribbean as well. Heavy import duties on refined sugar imposed by England discouraged the island producers from refining the raw sugar.

The sugar trade lasted through the eighteenth century, requiring the hard labor of more and more enslaved African people. It also required ever increasing numbers of ships and barrels, as well as more flour, pork, tallow candles, butter, and refined loaf sugar for the Caribbean.[88] City merchants and grocers were directly tied to this trade and widely advertised the sale of sugar in newspapers and with signs outside their shops (figure 3.27).

Nicholas Bayard (1698–1765) and his wife Elizabeth Rynder (1704–1755) were connected to New York's colonial elite families, counting Peter Stuyvesant and Jacob Leisler among their direct relations. They owned Bayard Farm, located north of the Collect Pond, marked today by Bayard Street in Chinatown. Elizabeth Street, Hester Street, and Ann Street (now Grand) were named after their daughters.

In 1730, a merchant named Nicholas Bayard advertised in the *New-York Gazette* the completion of his sugar "refining house" on Wall Street in Lower Manhattan adjacent to City Hall (figure 3.28). He extolled the virtues of the artisan he had procured from

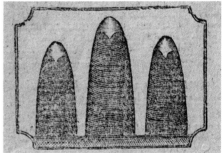

FIGURE 3.27

Eighteenth-century commercial signs of (*left*) Smith Richards, New York City grocer and confectioner, whose wares were advertised "at the sign of the tea canister and two sugar loaves" and (*right*) George Webster, Grocer, whose goods could be found "at the sign of the three sugar loaves." These images appeared in eighteenth-century New York city newspapers and mirrored signs that hung from Richard's and Webster's storefronts aiding customers who could not read.

(*Rivington's New-York Gazetteer*, September 9, 1773, page 4, 2nd column; *New-York Journal*, December 10, 1772, page 6).

Courtesy of the American Antiquarian Society.

PUblick Notice is hereby given, That *Nicholas Bayard* of the City of New-York has erected a Refining House for Refining all forts of Sugar and Sugar-Candy, and has procured from Europe an experienced Artift in that Myftery At which Refining House all Perfons in City and Country may be fupplied by Whole-fale and Re-tale, with both double and ǹngle Refined Loaf-Sugar, as alfo Powder and Shop-Sugars, and Sugar-Candy, at Rea-fonable Rates.

Europe versed in the magic art of sugar refining and declared his venture ready to sup-ply the city and country with a variety of refined sugars. The mystery to which Bayard referred was the process of converting raw or muscovado sugar from the Caribbean into pure white sugar, the desired quality for the table.[89]

In the eighteenth century, before the mechanization of sugar refining, raw sugar was boiled in enormous cauldrons to release impurities. Once cooled, it was packed into unglazed earthenware ceramic molds (Figure 3.29, *center*). The molds were then inverted into redware syrup jars (Figure 3.29, *left*) and clayed, a process in which a clay slip—a mixture of white clay and water—was poured over the sugar in the molds.[90]

The paired vessels were then dried in heated rooms for at least five days (figure 3.30). The water from the clay percolated slowly down through the sugar separating and forcing out residual molasses and impurities, which drained through the tip at the narrow end into the syrup jars below. The syrup jars were glazed on the interior to con-tain the liquid molasses, whereas the sugar molds were unglazed to allow moisture to evaporate.

After drying, the mold was tapped to release the cone-shaped sugar loaf, and the hard clay cap was removed.[91] The loaves were then wrapped in blue paper for sale,[92] or else the clay application was repeated to produce the "double-refined sugar loaf-sugar" Bayard advertised. The residue of the clay slip can be seen in the interior of the sugar mold frag-ment excavated from the Battery wall (figure 3.29, *right*.) The extracted molasses was distilled into rum or used as a sweetener in its own right.

Bayard's sugar house, as it became known, was the first of many sugar refineries established in Lower Manhattan and Brooklyn. Sugar refining quickly became one of the city's most lucrative industries. By the outbreak of the American Revolution, there were five sugar refining houses south of today's Chambers Street. By the nineteenth century, New York City had become the dominant center of sugar refining in the coun-try. Its position as a leading port, its capacity to finance the import of large quantities of raw sugar, the availability of cheap anthracite coal, and its access to cheap unskilled immigrant labor made this possible.[93] By 1860, there were fourteen sugar refineries operating in the city, producing half the nation's supply of refined sugar.[94] At the turn of the twentieth century, New York's Havemeyer family controlled 98 percent of the sugar production in the United States. By 1920, Havemeyers & Elder Filter, Pan & Fin-ishing House (later known as the American Sugar Refining Company and the Domino Sugar Refinery), located along the Brooklyn waterfront (a New York City landmark),

FIGURE 3.29

This curiously shaped conical sugar mold and syrup jar fragments were excavated in 2005 from the landfill deposited to make land around 1800 in Whitehall Slip, now Whitehall Street: (*left*) interior-glazed syrup jar fragment; (*center*) bottom portion of cone-shaped sugar mold; (*right*) interior of sugar mold showing residue of the white clay slip used to refine muscovado sugar. The fragmented jar and cone seen here are similar to those illustrated by Diderot in figure 3.30.
Qi#102548 SFT, Qi#102541 SFT, and Qi#108596 SFT

FIGURE 3.30

Heated curing house for sugar refinement illustrated in the 1772 sugar refining engravings from Diderot. Pl. VI, [plate 6] *OEconomie Rustique, Affinerie des Sucres*.
City of Vancouver Archives.

could produce as much as twelve hundred tons of refined sugar each day, dominating the American market.[95]

Sugar, and its celebrated by-product rum—or brandy—popularized the drinking of punch by everyone from sailors to the upper crust in seventeenth- and eighteenth-century New York, whose ornate punch bowls encouraged celebration (figure 3.31). The other required ingredients could be any mixture of lemon or lime juice, water, and spice—and even milk. Milk in punch counteracted the high acidity of the citrus and, once curdled and strained, clarified the milk punches and made them shelf stable and very popular into the mid-nineteenth century.

Mary Rockett's Milk Punch

1711

To make Milk Punch. Infuse the rinds of 8 Lemons in a Gallon of Brandy 48 hours then add 5 Quarts of Water and 2 pounds of loaf sugar then squize [sic] the juices of all the lemons to these Ingredients add 2 Quarts of new milk Scald hot stirring the whole till is crudles [sic] grate in 2 nutmegs let the whole infuse 1 Hour then refine through a flannel Bag. Yield: 36 cups or 12 750-mililiter bottles.[96]

FIGURE 3.31
Late-seventeenth- to early-eighteenth-century tin-glazed earthenware punch bowl from the 7 Hanover Square excavation that would have served up a heady combination of rum or brandy, citrus, and spice—in other words, punch.
Qi#210390 7HS

The West Indian market became the bedrock of the city's economy by 1720. By then, more than half of the ships entering and leaving New York Harbor were engaged in the West India trade. The success of North American sugar refineries and rum manufacturing prompted the British Parliament to enact the Molasses Act of 1733, which guaranteed West Indian planters a monopoly of the North American market.[97] The subsequent Sugar Act of 1764 raised taxes on many imported items, including coffee, wine, and printed calico textiles.[98] The acts were designed to regulate the sugar trade by discouraging the importation of cheaper sugar and molasses from the French and Dutch West Indies and, in the process, raise tax revenue for the Crown. The New England colonists reacted by increasing the smuggling of molasses, and the Molasses Act taxes were rarely collected. These acts distressed New York's merchants and generated petitions to all political entities in Great Britain, including the king, asking him to stop squeezing the colonists for money. The fomenting discontent would eventually boil over into revolution.[99]

THE BEGINNINGS OF WAR IN NEW YORK

The revolution that would end Britain's rule of the colony was not the city's first experience with international conflict. In 1740, a series of Anglo-French and Anglo-Spanish wars brought New Yorkers into the global conflict, not as fighters but as manufacturers. For about twenty-five years, the city prospered during these wars, provisioning goods for the military, especially clothing, shoes, and food. Merchants and artisans hired more workers, residents built more houses, and shipbuilders built more ships. However, there was concern that the wars could come to New York, and the city was readied defensively as a result. At the same time, the British levied an increase on New Yorkers to support British military operations internationally, the first of a series of taxes that would soon prove onerous and grounds for a rebellion of their own.[100]

DEFENSIVE FORTIFICATIONS

In 2005 and 2006, four foundation segments of a fortification were found in Battery Park in Lower Manhattan by archaeologists as part of a construction project. After extensive historical research, the archaeologists determined that the fortification had been constructed in two phases, one in 1741 and the second in 1755–56; they would have been related to emerging concerns about protecting the city. The construction campaigns were to reinforce fortifications originally created by the Dutch to command the East and Harlem rivers and rebuilt multiple times. In 1741, the fort and adjacent battery walls mounted with cannons to defend the city were strengthened in response to increasing concern that Great Britain's growing hostilities with France might lead to a French invasion of New York. In 1754, the concerns about France and Great Britain going to war were realized when the French and Indian War (the North American arm of the European conflict known as the Seven Years War) began. In 1755, New York's military defenses were further bolstered in response along the Lower Manhattan waterfront.[101]

GIS Use in Archaeology

The archaeologists at Battery Park used geographic information systems (GIS) in each step of their analysis. GIS applications are computer tools that manage and analyze geographic data. The software was initially developed by Dr. Roger Tomlinson in 1960 and came into much broader use in the 1990s.[102]

GIS is customarily used on projects before the archaeologists begin any fieldwork to analyze the archaeological potential of the project area. In the case of Battery Park, South Ferry Terminal Project archaeologists began by overlaying a series of historic maps from the seventeenth to twentieth centuries onto the modern street grid. Here, portions of the proposed subway tunnel overlapped with, among other locations, some mid-eighteenth-century fortifications (see figure 3.32).[103] The use of GIS for this work is challenging: often the scale and orientation of historic maps does not correspond to modern cartographic standards. However, the fortifications were found exactly where they had been predicted to be. The final archaeological report used GIS to overlay the locations of what had been found against historic maps and against the current conditions, as shown in figure 3.32.[104] This was the first large-scale project in New York City to successfully use GIS through multiple phases of work.

The close of the Seven Years War in 1763 brought a depression to the New York City economy and stirred unrest among its workers. A complex interplay of forces was at work here. The demand for exports dropped off at the end of the war; the British Crown tightened its grip over colonial trade; and the gap between the rich and poor had yawned ever wider. "The rich grew mighty by 'pernicious trade' that led to the experience and ruin of the people at large.'"[105]

In 1765 the Stamp Act, originating in Boston, taxed paper and paper products produced in the colonies. The funds were meant to support the British Army and recoup the costs of a war fought in part to protect the colonies. The day the Stamp Act took effect, there were many demonstrations in New York (as well as Boston).[106] More British troops were sent to the city to quell protests.[107] New Yorkers favoring independence joined those from Boston and Philadelphia, forming the Continental Congress.

The Revolution shattered New York, turning it into a battlefield. Fires destroyed more than a third of the city. The loss of the Battle of Brooklyn on August 27, 1776, might have dashed the Continental Army's hopes if Washington had not managed a retreat across the river to Manhattan under the cover of darkness. Pursuing them, the British took control of New York and drove the retreating Continentals through New Jersey

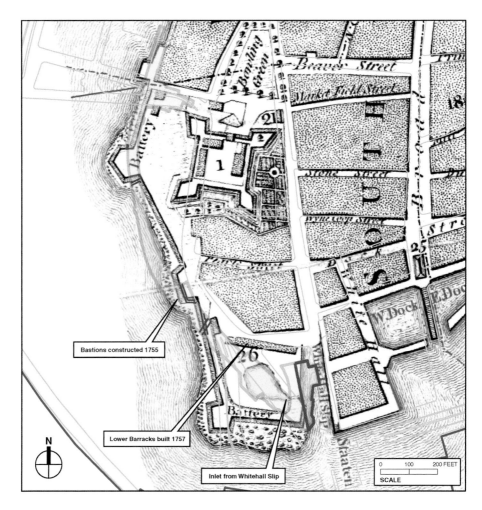

FIGURE 3.32
Outline of contemporary street grid showing the 1755 fortifications that were archaeologically documented
by overlaying the 1776 Ratzer Map depicting New York in 1766–67.
Image from AKRF, URS, and Stone 2012, figure 4.15.

and Pennsylvania.[108] The British occupied the city for the rest of the war as a barracks
and army headquarters.[109] Many patriots moved away, while those loyal to the Crown
returned to the city. However, the city was deeply divided, as the regimental buttons
from South Ferry excavations testify (figure 3.33). Whether by war or evacuation, the
population of New York was devastated.

The confusing and chaotic period between British control and the emerging American nation provided an opportunity for escape for enslaved people. Many took refuge in
the city once it was controlled by the British.[110] During this time, enslaved people could
live with their families within British lines, but at the end of the war, they had to flee
to Canada or to Indigenous Peoples' settlements farther north to avoid being enslaved

FIGURE 3.33
New York at War. American and British enlisted men's patterned buttons from the South Ferry excavations: (*left*) pewter Continental Army "USA" button, ca. 1778–1782; (*right*) English Thirty-First Foot Regiment button, ca. 1779–1784. Relatively few military artifacts have been found in archaeological excavations in New York. Qi#106393 SFT and Qi#106389 SFT

again.[111] Historian Paul Gilje considers the Revolutionary period the largest slave revolt of the eighteenth century.[112] Some estimates suggest that between 80,000 to 100,000 people escaped enslavement throughout the thirteen colonies, representing about one-fifth of all enslaved people.[113]

New York City remained the British headquarters for most of the war, which ended with the signing of the Treaty of Paris in 1783. Governor Clinton hosted a public dinner in celebration of the war's end that included thirteen formal toasts in honor of Washington and his officers at Fraunces Tavern, 54 Pearl Street in Lower Manhattan (a New York City landmark). The last of the British soldiers left the city on November 25, which became known as Evacuation Day. For years afterward, New Yorkers celebrated the day with parades and military displays.[114]

AFTER THE REVOLUTION: THE NASCENT REPUBLIC

The relatively short period from 1783 to the early nineteenth century was, perhaps, more significant than the Revolution in the formal creation of the new nation. It was chaotic, marked by conflict and adventure. There was no clear path or model of a state based on Enlightenment principles (rationality, individuality, and a belief in science), in Europe or elsewhere. The goal had been to defeat the British, but then what? The entity that was now America was a jumble of colonies, each with its own history, orientation, ethnic composition, and desires. The lines of cleavage within the United States included gentlemen versus common folk, party affiliation (Tories—allied with the British—versus Whigs at the outset), agrarian versus mercantile occupations, coast versus interior, urban versus rural, race, and others. The republic, in theory, was egalitarian, but in a society that was still largely based on land ownership and supported by slavery, land was not available to all. The mix of peoples included a component of enslaved people (20 percent of the whole)[115] and Indigenous groups of uncertain legal and social status.

During this time, many events were centered in New York City, where the Congress of the Confederation convened in 1785, meeting at City Hall, then at Broad Street's northern end, where George Washington was sworn in as the first president in April 1789 (figure 3.34). This is now Federal Hall National Memorial (a New York City landmark, the current building was completed in 1842). The city remained the virtual capital until 1790, when it was relocated to Philadelphia. The Constitution created the federal government of today, with a bicameral legislation, an elected president, and a court system. A Bill of Rights was added at the insistence of those who opposed the federal system. Property ownership was required in order to vote; women and enslaved people were not eligible.

After the Revolution, as New York City began to rebuild and reshape itself, its distinctive heritage reemerged. It had begun, like other American cities, as a settler colony but one of unique ethnic composition, which structured its classes and politics. It was also distinguished by the politically active artisans and small merchants, many of humble origins, who were involved before the Revolution, some of whom were elected to the first legislature.[116] Politics had not yet been invented as a profession, but officeholders came to be seen as having the middling sort of occupation.[117]

As the new nation was being established, thousands of immigrants arrived in (or returned to) the city; some became significant in its leadership. Conflicts among New Yorkers along party lines threatened to disenfranchise any who had supported the British, but Alexander Hamilton (a Whig himself), intervened, suggesting that the new country needed all its citizens. He also noted that such an act was opposed to the republican principles basic to the Revolution, in which all would share in the new government.[118] A subsequent election in 1785 moved the Congress somewhat to the right, and restored the Tories to citizenship status.

Overseas trade commenced immediately, as a vital part of the new country's economy. The first bank (now Bank of New York) was created, even before the Congress of the Confederation convened, by a group of merchants eager to take advantage of a new opportunity. Other financial issues were crucial—in particular, the fact that the new nation had enormous debts from the war, and no way to pay. The Congress created by the newly approved Constitution created a number of agencies that exist today, with

FEDERAL HALL
The Seat of CONGRESS
Printed & Sold by A Doolittle New Haven 1790

Peter Lacour delin.

A Doolittle Sculp.

Re-engraved on copper

by Sidney L. Smith

The Society of Iconophiles
NEW YORK
1899

FIGURE 3.34
President George Washington taking his oath of office on the second floor of Federal Hall (this building is no longer standing).
Image engraved by Amos Doolittle, Library of Congress Prints and Photographs Division.

broad powers to control trade and markets and set standard weights and measures; it created a navy, a post office, the mint to create paper money and coins, and courts. The mint was particularly important, as currency was very difficult to procure. The Talbot, Allum, & Lee one-cent token shown in figure 3.35 illustrates one solution created by a New York firm to provide its patrons with a form of specie. Once the Congress had assumed and consolidated war debts, New York City garnered great wealth through the sale of stock in the new Bank of the United States, located in the city.[119]

America as we know it was influenced by a number of individuals who exercised power to a degree not possible today. George Washington, of course, was an important symbol. He was sworn in as president in April 1789 and served two terms. Alexander Hamilton may have been the only individual who had a coherent vision of the new form of government that was needed, and he was influential in many elements of the new Constitution, although he had initially proposed that a president would serve a term for life.[120] Other individuals such as James Madison, John Jay, and Thomas Jefferson were influential in shaping the new country. Hamilton and Jefferson brokered a deal in 1789 that mollified southern states by locating the new political capital of the government in Washington, DC,[121] resulting in the country's having two capitals, one economic (New York) and one political.

The new nation lacked an identity—not surprising because prior to the Revolution it was not an entity. George Washington played a larger-than-life role as a symbolic figurehead (figure 3.36) as well as president, and ceramics from this era show the development of expressions of national identification, often found particularly in elite households (figure 3.37). These have been recovered archaeologically, although they are not numerous. Some porcelain tea sets used symbols that later emerged as emblems of the new country: eagles, arrows, stars, and stripes were particularly common.[122] However, it is significant that these motifs were drawn on ceramics imported from England and China; we do not see American motifs on locally made stonewares and redwares,

FIGURE 3.35
American one-cent token commissioned in 1794 by William Talbot, William Allum, and James Lee, partners in an East India trading company located at 241 Water Street in New York City. Manufactured by Peter Kempson's mint, Birmingham, England. Obverse: Liberty & Commerce. 1794. Reverse: Talbot Allum & Lee. One Cent. New York. Edge: Payable at the store. Excavated in City Hall Park. Qi#2386 CHP

FIGURE 3.36
Transfer printed pearlware tankard depicting George Washington on a horse. Found during the City Hall Park 2011 Excavations. Qi#124364 CHP

FIGURE 3.37
Black-overglaze printed image of Columbia, a figure commonly used to represent America after the Revolution, found on a shell-edged pearlware soup plate excavated from present-day Beekman Street in Lower Manhattan. Further honoring the nascent republic, the eagle with the stars-and-stripes shields in the foreground at her feet bears the country's motto *e pluribus unum* (out of many, one), while the pyramid-shaped tomb behind her to the right reads "Sacred to the memory of Washington." Image courtesy of Diane George. Qi# 212350 BSP

suggesting that Americans had neither a sense of their cultural and political unity nor a clearly developed set of material objects that expressed their identity at this time. This would change in the nineteenth century.

While there was much political activity and upheaval in the city toward the end of the eighteenth century, changes were occurring in other spheres of life that were to become fully realized in radical experiments in the nineteenth century. The basic concept of family life was changing, at least for middle-class and elite families. Women were now thought to be needed at home, while homes became physically separate from workplaces, partitioning the domains of women and men.[123] The city was growing, spatially and in population. It had become the largest manufacturing center in the nation even before the Revolution. The lack of waterpower and the cost of real estate, however, led to the abandonment of large-scale manufacturing in the nineteenth century as the opening of the Erie Canal gave primacy to the city's merchants and financiers.[124] The first waves of yellow fever began at the turn of the century, sending frightened middle- and upper-class residents to the better air "up north," where they established neighborhoods in today's Greenwich Village.[125] These changes heralding the new republic are reflected in archaeological sites and artifacts of the late eighteenth century, foreshadowing the more momentous development of the city in the next hundred years.

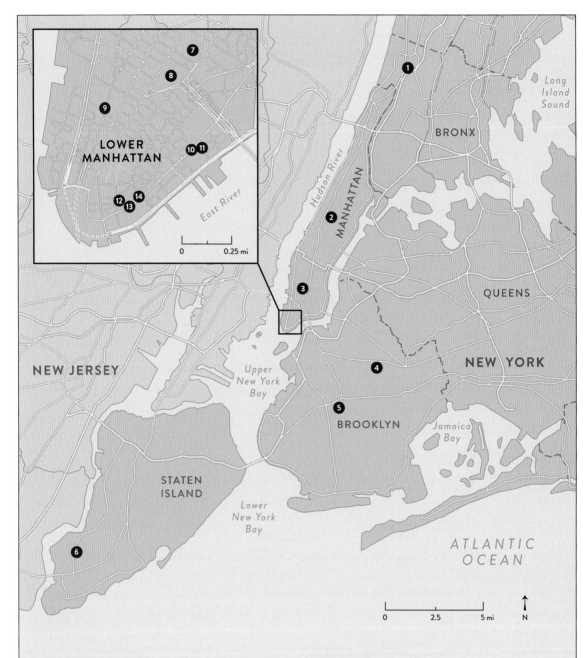

1. Van Cortlandt House, Bronx
2. Seneca Village, Manhattan
3. Washington Square Park, Manhattan
4. Weeksville, Brooklyn
5. Erasmus Hall High School, Brooklyn
6. Sandy Ground, Staten Island
7. African Burial Ground, Manhattan
8. City Hall Park, Manhattan
9. World Trade Center Ship, Manhattan
10. Fulton Street and Peck Slip Reconstruction, Manhattan
11. Beekman St Reconstruction, Manhattan
12. Stadt Huys, Manhattan
13. Coenties Slip, Manhattan
14. 7 Hanover Square, Manhattan

4

GROWING PAINS, 1800–1840

As the nineteenth century dawned in the new republic, New York had a drinking problem. Not beer, not rum, not hard cider—all of which the city had in abundance—but water. This was not a new problem. The Common Council had passed laws as far back as 1696 to protect the quality of the water supply.[1] But by 1800, there was not enough healthy drinking water for the growing population, which had almost tripled in twenty years—from thirty-three thousand in 1790 to nearly one hundred thousand by 1810.[2] There were wells available in each neighborhood, but their contents left much to be desired. The "clear and pure" water remarked on by Adriaen van der Donck in his 1649 account of life in New Netherland was a dim memory.[3] The wells stank from offal—runoff from the streets and cesspools—and domestic and industrial garbage that piled up as the city grew. Cleaner water could be retrieved from the Collect, the pond where Foley Square now stands, but by 1800 this too was polluted and nearly undrinkable. Taverns, with their alternative drinks, thrived.

New Yorkers also needed water to fight fire, although here the problem lay in its distribution rather than its potability. Fires, always a problem in a city of wood-framed buildings heated by wood and coal stoves, were hard to put out with only the water from the local well. Volunteers with leather buckets and hoses drawing water from the sometimes frozen river tried their hardest, but disastrous fires leveled great swathes of the city in 1776 and again in 1835. The Great Fire of 1835 consumed the financial area of the East Side, destroying approximately seven hundred buildings over thirteen acres, from Coenties Slip in the south to Maiden Lane in the north and from the waterfront to William Street in the west. The area around Hanover Square was among those destroyed, and archaeological excavations of this site in 1981 revealed the fury of the fire.

"Gunny Bags—10,000, for sale . . . 52 Water Street," announced the advertisement placed by George A. Gannett, consignment merchant, in the *New York Journal of Commerce* on December 1, 1835. Fifteen days later, Gannett's stock of burlap bags went up

FIGURE 4.1
Gunny, or burlap bag, burned in the Great Fire of 1835 and excavated from 7 Hanover Square. Closeup to the right shows the open weave of the coarse gunny fabric preserved as carbon, preventing its decay.
Qi#210246 7HS

in flames, a casualty of the Great Fire. Gunny bags, or burlap, were historically made of natural fibers such as jute or hemp. Almost 150 years later, archaeologists excavating the lot associated with 52 Water Street during the 7 Hanover Square Block excavations unearthed the carbonized remains of Gannett's gunny sacks. Finding organic material on a site is rare, but sometimes its details may be preserved as a "design" in charcoal as can be seen in figure 4.1. After the fire, the rebuilding was swift. Within a year, a new building was built by the Classons, who owned the property Gannett rented. Gannett had moved his operation east to 175 Water Street, an address spared by the fire.[4]

THIRST FOR WATER

The early years of the republic saw the transformation of New York from a sprawling town to a dense urban metropolis. By a half-century after the Revolution, one could no longer walk easily from one end of the city to the other. Gone were the garden plots growing vegetables in the midst of the city. The City Commons had become the governmental center, containing City Hall (a New York City landmark), constructed between 1802 and 1811, and other public buildings. Immigrants swelled the population far beyond the imagination of the earlier settlers. Population density, industry, and shipping soared. With this transformation came big-city problems: drinkable water had to be provided, public health became an issue, housing was needed for the new urbanites, and their children needed educating.

In 1799, the state legislature passed a bill allowing the Common Council to authorize the provision of "pure and wholesome water." To this end, they granted an exclusive charter to the Manhattan Company.[5] Under the charter, the Manhattan Company, run by Aaron Burr and some other Republicans, was allowed to use the surplus funds generated by water sales in any legal way. This was a new wrinkle; other chartered companies were constrained by law to use funds only for their chartered purpose, such as building bridges, canals, or roads.

After digging a well near the Collect Pond and constructing a reservoir on Chambers Street, the company eventually laid about twenty-five miles of wooden pipe serving about two thousand customers. These pipes have been excavated in several archaeological digs in Lower Manhattan, including those from Coenties Slip (figure 4.2).[6] Sites on Beekman Street in Lower Manhattan revealed a junction of two pipe lengths connected and fused by an iron band.[7] From the outset, customers complained constantly about the service and water quality. No wonder, for the real purpose of the Manhattan Company was to use the excess funds generated by water sales to open a bank to rival the Bank of New York.[8] Alexander Hamilton and his fellow Federalists were highly displeased. They were the directors of the Bank of New York, which had had a charter and a monopoly on banking in New York since 1784. While the Manhattan Company's water delivery sputtered out over the next three decades, finally motivating the Common Council to take over water distribution, the banking arm of the Manhattan Company thrived. It has undergone many mergers over the centuries and is known today as

FIGURE 4.2
Wooden water mains found within the street bed of Coenties Slip in Lower Manhattan, after they were removed from the ground. Now in the collections of the New-York Historical Society. Photograph by Joan Geismar.

JPMorgan Chase & Co. More than two hundred years later, the modern bank still maintains records from its history as the Manhattan Company.

New York was subject to periodic epidemics of cholera, typhoid, and yellow fever, all of which, without a general theory of germs, were blamed in part on unhealthy water. The polluted neighborhood wells were thought to be sources of contagion, as were the open privies, animal carcasses, and graveyards. The Common Council periodically passed laws regulating these ostensible health hazards, but to no avail. Various plans to bring water from cleaner sources in the Bronx or from farther north in the state were proposed in the first quarter of the nineteenth century but never acted upon by the city. It was not until the cholera epidemic of 1832 and the Great Fire of 1835 that the Common Council acted on plans to import water, this time from the Croton River some thirty-five miles north of the city, near Ossining. This required constructing several reservoirs, including the four-acre Murray Hill Reservoir at the corner of Forty-Second Street and Fifth Avenue (figure 4.3), now the site of the New York Public Library (a New York City landmark), that held twenty million gallons of drinking water, as well as aqueducts, tunnels, and iron piping, while overcoming political and technical difficulties.[9] On July 4, 1842, the infrastructure was complete, and Croton water poured into Manhattan for the first time, to the great rejoicing of the populace.[10] The wooden water mains of the Manhattan Water Company

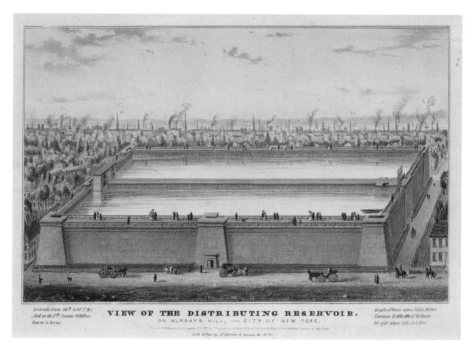

VIEW OF THE DISTRIBUTING RESERVOIR.
ON MURRAYS HILL, — CITY OF NEW YORK.

FIGURE 4.3
The Egyptian-style Distributing Reservoir at Forty-Second Street and Fifth Avenue in 1882 1882. The main branch of the New York Public Library and Bryant Park (a New York City landmark) now occupy this location. Image: Currier & Ives, 1842 Library of Congress Prints and Photographs Division.

were now a thing of the past. This bounty was not distributed equally to all parts of the city. Poorer neighborhoods did not get connected to Croton water for years. Ironically, in the vote approving construction of the Croton project, opposition came from the less affluent parts of the city, where residents feared the cost of Croton water would be too high for them. Reflecting the racism (and class structure) of the society at the time, these same neighborhoods, occupied by newer immigrants and Black people, were also the last to be connected to the city sewers and to get trash removal.[11] The city, in this case, was Manhattan; there were different timelines for different boroughs.

BIG PLANS

By 1810, the city was bursting at its seams. Reacting to this, the city government took two actions that would relieve the pressure and lay the foundation for New York to become the financial and cultural center of the new republic. For both of these, we have the forethought of DeWitt Clinton to thank. DeWitt Clinton (1769–1828) was the nephew of New York governor George Clinton. Educated at Yale and Columbia, he served as mayor of New York City from 1803 to 1815 and governor of New York State from 1817 to 1822 and again from 1825 to 1828.[12] As mayor, he initiated the work that produced the Commissioners' Plan in 1811. This plan overlaid the grid of future streets—so much a part of today's city—on the relatively lightly populated landscape north of the jumbled streets of Lower Manhattan. The work began with John Randel, Jr., the surveyor who carefully mapped the island and precisely recorded the elevations of its hills and valleys. He surveyed everything down to potential locations for fire hydrants and the sizes of future house lots (figure 4.4).

Some of Randel's marking posts still exist in Central Park, and one is on display at the New-York Historical Society (the park and the society are New York City landmarks). This visionary early nineteenth-century projection of a future city made massive population growth possible. It also made fortunes for John Jacob Astor and other land speculators. The grid laid out by Randel is essentially the map of modern Manhattan, with one notable difference: Central Park would not be envisioned until the 1850s.

De Witt Clinton's second dream was a canal to link the Great Lakes trade network with New York City. This was accomplished in a surprisingly short time, between 1817 and 1825 (figure 4.5).[13] The United States was rapidly expanding its territory west of the Mississippi River, starting with the 1803 Louisiana Purchase from France. Now the Erie Canal, running from Albany to Buffalo, opened the new riches of the West to the industrially developing East Coast. It also cemented New York as the preeminent port along that coast, eclipsing Baltimore, Philadelphia, and Boston. Goods from Europe could be off-loaded in New York and transshipped via canal boat and barge up the Hudson, through the canal, into the Great Lakes, and directly to Chicago. Before the canal, a journey like this would have taken months and cost $100 per ton of cargo. After the canal, it took about a week and cost about $10.

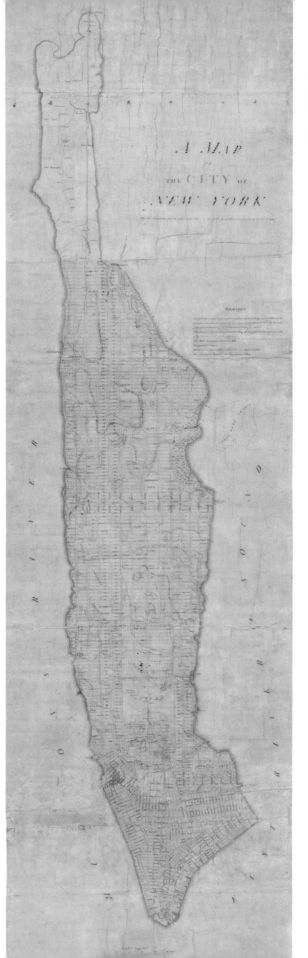

FIGURE 4.4
"Plan of Manhattan Island," John
Randel, 1811. Usually referred to as
the Commissioner's Plan of 1811.
From the manuscripts and archives
collections of the New York Public
Library Digital Collections.

FIGURE 4.5
"Dewitt Clinton Mingling the Waters of Lake Erie with the Atlantic," 1825.
From the New York Public Library Digital Collections.

The economic boost to the City and the State of New York was enormous. The canal's construction was also a magnet for European immigrants.[14] Most of the work on the Erie Canal and the Croton water project was done by Irish immigrants. Before 1840, most of these were "Scotch-Irish" Protestants from Northern Ireland.[15] Irish immigration to the colonies had begun well before the Revolutionary War. Between 1815 and 1840, approximately half a million Irish immigrants arrived in the United States. While many of them settled in the rural South, some were drawn to the Northeast and its constant demand for infrastructure labor.[16]

GROWING CITY

New York City's population growth accelerated in the early days of the new American republic. Census figures from 1790 indicate that the city had 33,131 residents. Even before the larger wave of immigration later in the nineteenth century, about five thousand of these were Irish. By the census of 1840, the city's population has expanded nearly tenfold to more than three hundred thousand. Much of the growth was from immigration and, perhaps surprisingly, migration; the largest groups came into New York from neighboring New England, especially in the 1820s.[17] This is before the large Irish immigration during and after the Potato Famine of 1845 to 1849, which is discussed in the next chapter.[18] Most of New York City's population remained concentrated south of Fourteenth Street well into the nineteenth century.

The growing city needed new housing, churches, and public buildings. In Lower Manhattan, that usually required demolishing an older building, a process of change that happened repeatedly, so that few early buildings remain. A surviving building and New York City landmark from this period is City Hall, which was built between 1811 and 1813. As discussed in chapter 3, the park around it, the old Commons of the colonial city, was extensively archaeologically excavated during multiple campaigns from 1988 to 2011 (figure 4.6).[19] City Hall Park is within the African Burial Grounds and the Commons Historic District, which was designated in 1993 to protect the archaeological resources within the entire district.

Archaeological excavations exposed early nineteenth-century features related to City Hall and nineteenth-century water-management features (figure 4.6) as well as earlier civic structures, primarily from the mid- to late eighteenth century, including two jails and an almshouse, as well as two burial grounds—one associated with the Almshouse and the other with the Bridewell Prison. Although in the seventeenth and early eighteenth centuries this area was outside the city, and therefore a good place to situate "undesirables," by the mid-eighteenth century the city had grown around it.

New York has a plethora of records documenting the occupancy of buildings in the city. However, they do not always provide all the information one would like. Archaeological excavations can often fill in the gaps in the documentary record or provide

FIGURE 4.6
City Hall archaeological excavations, 2010. Shown is the north side of City Hall with an eighteenth-century stone-lined well that was repurposed in the nineteenth century as a dry well to contain excess rainwater. Photograph by Chester Higgins, Jr., 2010.

FIGURE 4.7
A nineteenth-century short-stemmed "Turkish" pipe from the Stadt Huys Block excavation. The bowl of the pipe stands vertically while a hollow reed, now missing, would have been inserted in the opening at a forty-five-degree angle to serve as the pipe stem. The pipe is marked K'Azar, for Kiss-Azar, the Hungarian name of Male Ozorovice in southeastern Slovakia, where it was likely made before 1850.
Qi#207037SHB

unexpected evidence for the presence of a known, but uncommon, ethnic group. For instance, consider this unique find from the early nineteenth century in the foundation of a water trough at the Stadt Huys Block excavation: a tobacco pipe bowl of Turkish shape marked with an insect and stamped "KA" between its antennae and with the words "Kis.Azar" (figure 4.7).[20] This is apparently Kiss-Azar, the Hungarian name of the town of Male Ozorovice in southeastern Slovakia, where it likely was produced. It has been dated to before the mid-nineteenth-century mark. It may have belonged to a Slovakian laborer working on the construction of the water trough. Exactly whose it was and how it arrived in New York remains a mystery.[21]

Coal: A Fundamental Change in Domestic Fuel

Coal is found everywhere in nineteenth- and twentieth-century sites in the city. Its impact on New York vastly outweighs its innocuous appearance (figure 4.8). Coal fundamentally transformed the city in the early nineteenth century. By the close of the eighteenth century, populations were expanding and wood as a domestic and industrial fuel source had become increasingly scarce and costly for New York and the other eastern urban centers. The War of 1812 compounded the problem by restricting coal imports from Great Britain.[22] The discovery of bituminous and anthracite coal seams in northeastern Pennsylvania beginning in the late eighteenth century produced a homegrown solution. Coal is decayed plant material deeply buried and transformed by heat

Cm

Stone Street (1998)

FIGURE 4.8
Anthracite coal excavated from Stone Street in lower Manhattan. The discovery of bituminous coal in 1768 and anthracite coal in 1775 in eastern Pennsylvania replaced wood as the primary domestic fuel in New York City.
Qi#4692 SSHD

and pressure over millions of years into a combustible fossil fuel composed predominately of carbon.[23] It has been used by humans for at least five thousand years. The discovery of Pennsylvania coal galvanized merchants and investors to create the infrastructure necessary to deliver coal directly to the city. The Delaware and Hudson Canal was completed in 1828, enabling coal to be carried from Pennsylvanian mines to Kingston, New York, and then transported down the Hudson River to New York City cheaply and quickly. At its peak, the canal carried seven thousand tons of coal a day en route to New York City, before it was replaced by railroad transport.[24]

Primarily a domestic fuel for home heating and cooking, coal also became a powerful source of energy for urban blacksmiths, bakers, brewers, and manufacturers—and even streetlights. In 1823 the New York Light Company began to illuminate the city streets with coal-powered gas lamps. By 1830, New York was a city powered by coal.

The Impact on Cooking Technology

The increasing scarcity and cost of wood for domestic fuel in the coastal cities of the United States also spurred the development of alternative cooking technologies.[25] Open hearths and brick ovens used too much wood and were inefficient. They were soon replaced with cast-iron closed stoves. Between 1835 and 1839 for example, the U.S. Patent Office granted more than one hundred patents for different cookstoves.[26] Some were designed to accommodate either anthracite or bituminous coal, which had differential burn rates. Bituminous burns more quickly than anthracite, but emits more pollutants.[27] The move from wood to coal as a cooking fuel is a transition visible in the city's archaeological record not only in the increasing presence of coal at sites but also in the decline of red earthenware cooking vessels found on sites as the nineteenth century progressed.

Redware pans and dishes (figure 4.9) were well suited to stewing and baking in the coals of the open-hearth fireplace or the fire-fed bake ovens of the seventeenth and eighteenth century. Once at temperature, they retained heat exceptionally well, cooked evenly, and could be taken directly from the kitchen to the table.[28] These qualities did not transfer well to cast-iron stovetop cooking. Quick changes in temperature can cause the clay to crack. Metal cookware made of iron, copper, and tin—and sometimes even glass cookware—although less common, was better suited for stovetop cooking. This cookware could absorb rapid changes in temperature and concentrated heat without damage. As hearths were enclosed and building styles adapted to accommodate cast-iron cookstoves, the demand for redware cooking vessels declined, a disappearance marked in the archaeological record.

FIGURE 4.9
Top: This Slip-trailed redware baking dish with a coggled (or crimped) rim, likely made in Philadelphia, was excavated from a privy unearthed in the 7 Hanover Square excavation. The dish measured thirteen inches in diameter when whole and shows evidence of heavy use. The underside (*right*) is unglazed and exhibits charring from use in the coals of a fireplace or bake oven. *Bottom*: Slip-trailed redware baking pan with green and yellow bands, also likely made in Philadelphia, excavated from City Hall Park. The base of the pan is also charred. These two redware vessels were both used to cook within an open hearth or brick bake oven and could then be served directly at the table. Qi#20748 7HS, Qi# 97540 CHP

TRADE

International commerce was a major industry in New York's busy harbor. The harbor was the shipping center for barrels of salt beef and other provisions for the sugarcane plantations of the Caribbean and ports along the Atlantic coast. Longshoremen, at this time usually enslaved or free Black men, unloaded the wares that came from across the Atlantic, the Caribbean, or down the Hudson and the Erie Canal.[29] Cotton from the south and textiles from New England, household goods (ceramics and glassware) from England and Europe, Pennsylvania coal, and southern tobacco products were coming into New York, as well as being redistributed from the city.

In 2010, archaeologists at the World Trade Center site made one of the most dramatic archaeological discoveries in New York City history: the hull of a buried ship, sunk here as a part of the landfill (figure 4.10). While research is still underway, it appears to be a modified sloop, a small, maneuverable, single-masted sailing vessel dating to the late eighteenth century, likely used for coastal trading.[30] Sloops featured fore-and-aft rigging that made them well suited for navigating shifting winds along coastlines.[31] Its date was determined by dendrochronology, a type of analysis that involves counting the unique pattern of tree rings in timber that accrue for each year of a tree's life and matching it to another known dated ring sequence. Analysis also revealed that shipworms had once made their home in the timber of the hull, which means that the ship had spent some time in the Caribbean, where these boring worms were endemic.

In 1981, archaeologists discovered more evidence of the extent of transatlantic trade at 7 Hanover Square: an unusual deposit of broken ceramic fragments, or sherds, in the backyard of one of the lots on the eastern half of the block. As they dug deeper, more and more sherds cropped up, until they had recovered what was later tabulated as more than

FIGURE 4.10
Discovery of the "World Trade Center Ship" in 2010, photographed looking west toward the Hudson River. The ship was determined to be a late-eighteenth-century modified coastal sloop. It was scuttled to add to the landfill and expand the west side of Manhattan farther into the Hudson. The archaeologists in the foreground are standing in the ship's exposed hull.
Photograph by Fred Conrad, *New York Times*. Redux.

35,000 pieces of British pottery—mostly hand-painted pearlware and creamware (figures 4.11 to 4.13). The pottery was found in the backyard of what had been two late-eighteenth- and early-nineteenth-century shops that sold ceramic wares. These were owned successively by John Elting (from 1794 to 1795) and John Manley (from 1798 to 1820).[32]

The deposit seems to have been created all at once, or at least very rapidly, so it was hypothesized that these broken pieces were part of a shipload carrying wares from England to America that encountered very rough seas or perhaps were poorly packed, so that all the dishes were broken. None of the dishes had any signs of use or wear, which supports this theory.

Lab analysis made it clear that most of the wares were either undecorated creamware (more than 15,000 pieces) or polychrome hand-painted pearlware, which were primarily decorated before the pottery was glazed (more than 11,000 sherds). There were also almost two thousand pieces of Chinese porcelain, some other pearlware, some decorated creamware fragments, and some other eighteenth-century types. The average date (called the "mean ceramic date") for all the sherds was 1800. The creamware included serving pieces, pitchers and jugs, and dinner plates. Many of the beautiful hand-painted pearlware pieces were from tea sets: teapots, bowls, teacups, and saucers. Analysts counted about ninety different painted patterns among these pieces (figure 4.13).

FIGURE 4.11

Overview of some of the 35,000 ceramic sherds that were recovered from a single archaeological deposit at 7 Hanover Square—a "ceramic dump" of broken ceramics discarded from a ceramic, glass, and earthenware shop. These painted pearlware sherds represent broken bowls and saucers all with the same pattern. Context 624.7.783 7HS, Ceramic Shop Deposit.

FIGURE 4.12

This overglaze printed creamware pitcher from 7 Hanover Square dating to circa 1760 to 1780 was found among many thousands of ceramic sherds. Two distinct transfer prints adorn the two sides of the pitcher. One side depicts the allegorical figure of Hope kneeling beside an anchor in the foreground with a ship in harbor in the background (*left*), the other a three-masted ship under full sail flying the Union Jack (*right*). Qi#206611 7HS

FIGURE 4.13

A sampling of the ninety different polychrome painted patterns that analysts found in the dump of late-eighteenth- and early-nineteenth-century ceramics from 7 Hanover Square. These pearlware saucers illustrate the two different saucer sizes found in the ceramic dump assemblage, some with matching teacups and some without.

Saucers, top row Qi#206687 7HS, Qi#206668 7HS; *middle row* Qi#206667 7HS, Qi#206615 7HS, Qi#206614 7HS; *bottom row* Qi#206672 7HS, Qi#206824 7HS; *figure 4.13b saucer* Qi# 206652 7HS and *teacup* Qi#209582 7HS.

STONEWARE: IMPORTED AND LOCAL

Polychrome painted wares, such as those pictured in figure 4.13, were popular in New York City between around 1795 and 1815 and would have been purchased from merchants who imported ceramics and glass from England. North American potteries were manufacturing redwares and stonewares by the late seventeenth and early eighteenth century, but earthenware potteries were not established until 1850. The majority of New York's ceramics at this time were imported from England; hard-paste porcelain was imported from China as well as some from Europe. These painted pearlware vessels were manufactured in Staffordshire and shipped by canal boat to Liverpool, where they were loaded onto ships bound for New York City. The minimal use of cobalt in these patterns is because of the break in the supply of cobalt to Staffordshire potters during the Napoleonic wars. The colors used instead consist of oxides of copper green, antimony yellow, iron brown, and manganese brown.[33]

The style of dry-bodied stoneware pictured in figure 4.14 was perfected by English potter Josiah Wedgewood in 1768 and copied by many manufacturers into the early nineteenth century. Dry-bodied stonewares were nonporous and thus did not require glaze to hold liquids. The ceramic was intended to replicate basalt, a hard, volcanic rock introduced to Europe through the antiquities collected during European colonial

Stadt Huys Block (1987)
Cm

FIGURE 4.14
Fragments of four English "Black Basalt" or "Egyptian Black" stoneware inkwells excavated from the Stadt Huys Project, Lower Manhattan, that became popular in the United States after the Revolutionary War. Unfortunately, the archaeological site was looted and many artifacts were stolen. While these inkwells were left by the thieves, they were not found in situ, so the archaeologists cannot reconstruct how they were deposited and with what other items, which would have let them draw deeper insights. Qi#203027 SHB

expansion into Egypt and the classical world. Neoclassical styles inspired by archaeo-logical excavations in Greece and Rome and Egyptian themes worked their way into the artwork, clothing, ceramics, furniture, and architecture of nineteenth-century Europe and its colonies.

These particular inkwells are copies of a design by Josiah Wedgewood and his partner, Thomas Bentley, that was touted as "the best and most convenient" ink-stand available. The design was illustrated and described in Wedgwood's 1787 catalog (figure 4.15 *left*): the center cone (D) filled with ink to a set level (E) when a small iron cork was removed from a hole at the top (C). Another chamber (B) held the quill and was closed at the bottom to prevent the ink from drying, as pictured below in the right foreground. The caps that would have sealed the central cone when not in use are miss-ing.[34] The neoclassical design on the exterior of these inkwells was made by turning the leather-hard clay on a lathe while the potter cut the design into the vessel, a form of dec-oration known as engine-turned. Every office or shop in the days before typewriters and word processors needed at least one inkwell. They were also a necessity at home. To purchase an inkstand, New Yorkers would have visited a stationer's store, such as Thomas A. Ronalds at 188 Pearl Street, which was very near where these objects were found. In this 1817 notice from *New York Commercial Advertiser* (figure 4.15 *right*), Ronalds advertised his latest shipment of inkstands and book stands.[35]

Aside from the commercial importance of the port of New York for the import-export trade, the city was itself a center of industry. We have seen the large-scale production of refined sugar beginning in the eighteenth century and the early craft production of cheap (buttons) and expensive (silver) items. The early nineteenth century also brought larger industrial operations like beer brewing, leather tanning, and the continuation of pot-tery manufacture. Distinctive New York stoneware, often large heavy storage vessels, is found in many sites in the city. These were widely used in kitchens and pantries for storing

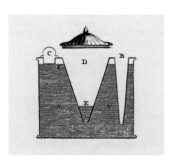 

FIGURE 4.15

Left: An illustration of the inner workings of a Wedgwood Jr. & Bentley inkwell printed in a 1774 French ceramic catalog. *Right:* An advertisement of Thomas A. Ronalds, Stationer, in the *New York Commercial Advertiser* in December 17, 1816, announcing the sale of "black Wedgewood inkstands" at his shop at 188 Pearl Street in Lower Manhattan. *Left:* Smithsonian Library and Archive; *Right: New York Commercial Advertiser*, January 3, 1887, page 1 courtesy of the American Antiquarian Society.

everything from flour to pickles. Archaeologists at the City Hall Park excavations found stoneware plates, shaving bowls, and dishes for eating porridge. Many were "seconds," ruined in firing, possibly donated or sold to the almshouses in the Commons. Based on German originals, the stoneware products were created and produced by a small number of family businesses (associated with the Crolius and Remmey lineages) who had long established kilns on Pot Bakers Hill to the north and west of today's City Hall. Their stoneware was common from the mid-eighteenth to the mid-nineteenth century (figure 4.16).

FIGURE 4.16

John Remmey III stoneware jar stamped with "Manhattan-Wells New-York" made between 1791 and circa 1831 found during the Van Cortlandt House excavations. In the collections of the National Museum of American History, there is a similar and complete jar decorated with a cobalt fish (National Museum of American History, Remmey III stoneware jar, identification number CE.300894.007). The Repository's jar has traces of cobalt by the remaining lug-type handle, suggesting that it too was decorated, but that side of the vessel is missing. Manhattan-Wells was located in Lower Manhattan near today's Foley Square. Qi#5531 VCP

THOMAS COMMERAW, A FREE BLACK POTTER

Among the stoneware potters working at Pot Bakers Hill was a man named Thomas Commeraw, a free Black man. From around 1793 to 1819, he lived and worked in Corlear's Hook at the north end of today's Water Street and Cherry Street on the Lower East Side. His stoneware can be identified by his stamp, seen on many stoneware vessels, or by a distinctive pattern—an impressed cobalt swag and tassel—that is a calling card of his work (figure 4.17).[36]

We know Commeraw was a free Black man from the 1800 census, in which he is recorded as "Thomas Commeraw, Black" (figure 4.18). He was the head of a seven-person household, all of whom were also free Black people. By 1810, seventeen years before New York's official date of emancipation, Commeraw was one of nearly eight thousand free Black people living and working in New York City. We do not yet know where he was born or where he learned his craft, but historians surmise he may have worked with the stoneware potter families of Crolius and Remmey.[37] By 1820, Commeraw had shuttered his pottery and left the Seventh Ward for Sierra Leone, the founding leader of a settlement sponsored by the American Colonization Society.

At least one of his neighbors in the Seventh Ward, Daniel Johnson, was a free Black oysterman who had a fresh oyster stand at 273 Water Street, near Commeraw's

FIGURE 4.17
Thomas Commeraw salt-glazed stoneware jar made between 1793 and 1819. The tri-lobed "tassel" of his trademark swag and tassel is incised on each side of the handle, with the swags draping to either side. Both are infilled with cobalt. This jar was found in the cellar of a boarding house at 263 Pearl Street in Lower Manhattan (the Fulton Street Project) in the same context as the oyster jars mentioned in figure 4.19. Qi#209115 FPS

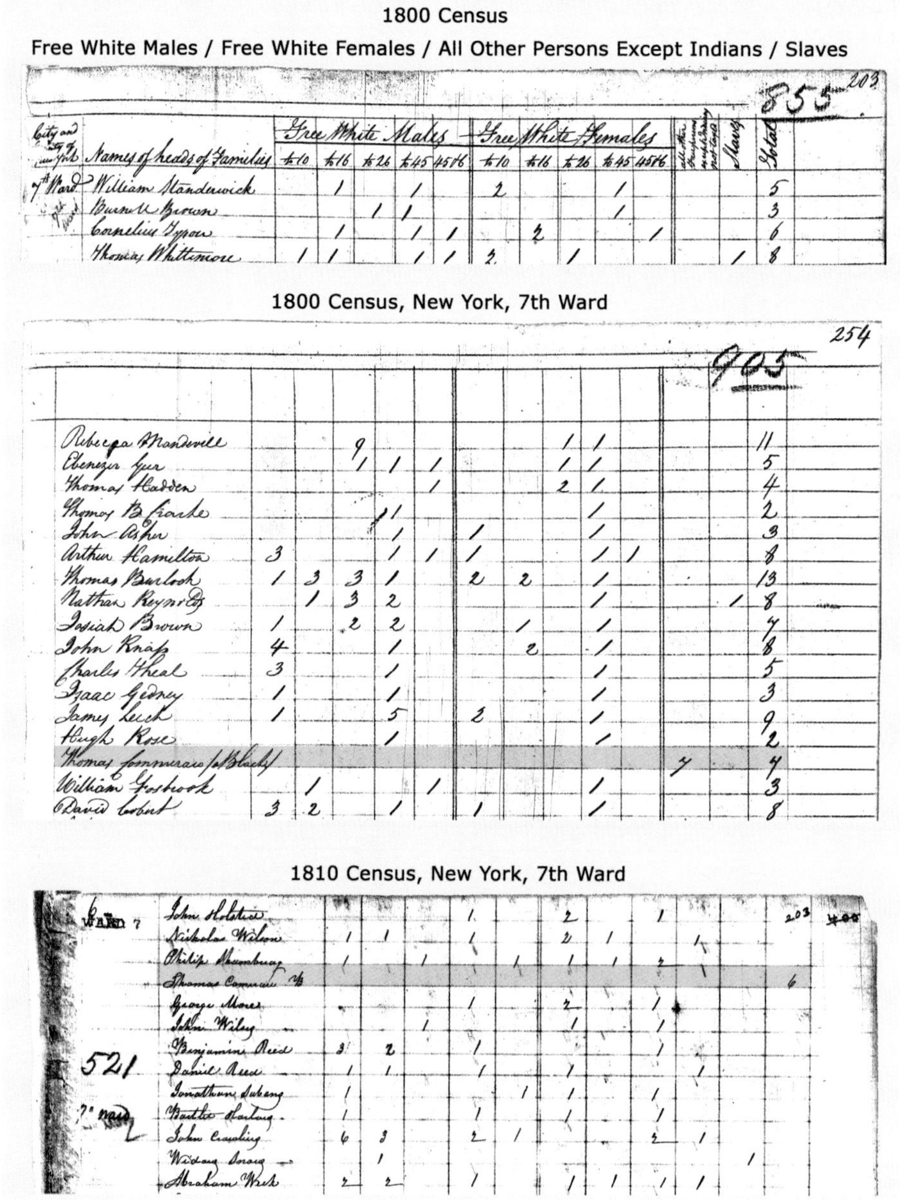

1800 Census

Free White Males / Free White Females / All Other Persons Except Indians / Slaves

1800 Census, New York, 7th Ward

1810 Census, New York, 7th Ward

FIGURE 4.18

The 1800 and 1810 New York State Census records for New York City's Seventh Ward showing that stoneware potter Thomas Commeraw was a free Black resident, as were the six others residing with him. There was no category for "free Black" in either the 1800 or 1810 census, hence Commeraw's racial identity "Black" and "B" is marked by the census taker after his name. The 1820 census was the first to include a distinct column or category for free Black people.

Images courtesy of Ancestry.com.

location.[38] A stoneware oyster pot stamped with Johnson's name and address was found during the creation of Corlear's Hook Park and is in the collection of the New York State Museum in Albany. Commeraw is thought to have manufactured these distinctive-looking oyster pots, and he also made the jars for his neighbor, Johnson. Pickled and brined oysters were popular for much of the eighteenth and nineteenth centuries. Recipes allowed home cooks to prepare their own (Figure 4.19), while the stoneware jars allowed the perishable meat to travel far and wide. New York oysters were shipped throughout the Atlantic and to the Caribbean as well as South America.[39] Some, however, stayed at home, like the pair of oyster jars excavated from the basement of a boarding house in 263 Pearl Street in Lower Manhattan (figure 4.20).[40]

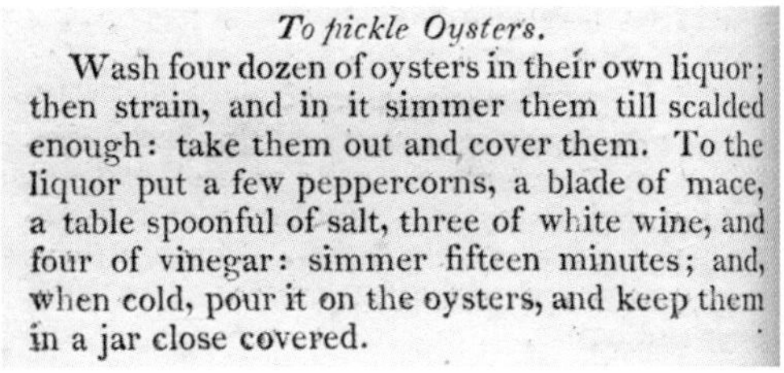

FIGURE 4.19
Pickled oyster recipe from *A New System of Domestic Cookery, formed upon principles of Economy and adapted to the use of private families*, by A Lady (Philadelphia, 1807). Pickled oysters were a highly valued and desirable food that typically sold for six times more than raw oysters (Mark Kurlansky, *The Big Oyster: History on the Half Shell*. [New York, Random House, 2007]).

To pickle Oysters.
Wash four dozen of oysters in their own liquor; then strain, and in it simmer them till scalded enough: take them out and cover them. To the liquor put a few peppercorns, a blade of mace, a table spoonful of salt, three of white wine, and four of vinegar: simmer fifteen minutes; and, when cold, pour it on the oysters, and keep them in a jar close covered.

FIGURE 4.20
Stoneware jars used to store pickled and preserved New York oysters that were shipped to Philadelphia, Charleston, and the Caribbean, as well as to Guyana and Surinam. The jars were sealed with a cork and then the well surrounding the cork was filled with wax. These jars are unmarked but were likely made in the city. To date, these are the only such jars that have been found in an archaeological context. They were excavated from what had been the cellar of 263 Pearl Street (today 40 Fulton Street) in Lower Manhattan (the Fulton Street Project). Qi#209662 FPS and Qi#209663 FPS

MANUMISSION AND EMANCIPATION IN NEW YORK STATE

The census of 1790 recorded that 19 percent of white families living in New York City held Black people in bondage.[41] Most of these families enslaved one person who was classed as a "household servant." Five of the roughly six thousand white families enslaved more than nine people. The legal fight to abolish slavery in New York was complicated by the city's deep economic ties to the slave-owning states of the American South. However, antislavery sentiment was growing, as evidenced by the formation of the Manumission Society in 1785. *Manumission* means release from slavery, or the act of enslavers setting their enslaved people free. *Emancipation* implies government action, making the practice of slavery illegal.

Quakers, who had freed their enslaved people in 1779, figured heavily in the Manumission Society, as did the Federalists. In 1785, the New York state legislature passed an act forbidding the importation of enslaved people for sale in the state, followed by the prohibition of selling any person brought into the state. An act of 1799 required that children born of enslaved people after July 4, 1799, must be emancipated by 1827.[42]

Between the 1790 census and the 1820 census, the number of enslaved people in what is now Manhattan declined from nearly 2,400 to about five hundred.[43] During the same period, the number of free Black people in the city rose from a little more than a thousand to more than ten thousand. Freedom did not bring rights, however. For example, a New York State law passed in 1820 (before the deadline for manumission) required that Black men must own property worth at least $250 to become eligible to vote; this property requirement did not apply to white men after 1826. The purchase and ownership of property was one of the incentives for the founding of Black communities such as Weeksville in Brooklyn, Sandy Ground in Staten Island, and Seneca Village in Manhattan. These communities have all been subjects of archaeological study.[44]

Sandy Ground was settled in 1833 by Black families fleeing the restrictive laws affecting oyster fishing and selling, predominantly the occupations of Black people, in Maryland. They were joined by other Black families from New Jersey, Delaware, and Virginia. Possibly, some families from Commeraw and Johnson's Seventh Ward joined them as well. They specialized in providing shellfish, including oysters, to the growing city and for export (see figure 4.20).[45] Archaeology was completed within Sandy Ground in the 1970s. Unfortunately, the discoveries were never fully analyzed or reported upon, but the preliminary analysis indicated that there were intact archaeological resources related to the nineteenth-century settlement.[46] The site was investigated again from 2009 to 2012, confirming those earlier results, but the recovered materials have not yet been sufficiently analyzed to reveal the full significance of what has been uncovered, or what may yet be revealed about this community.[47]Several New York City landmarks also both preserve and commemorate Sandy Ground, including the Rossville A.M.E. Church, the A.M.E. Zion Church Cemetery, and the Reverend Isaac Coleman and Rebecca Gray Coleman House.[48]

In addition to Sandy Ground, there were other communities of Black oysterman, including in New York's Seventh Ward, where according to the 1810 census, more than two-thirds of the oystermen were Black men. Oystering was an especially important industry for southwestern Staten Island in the nineteenth century.[49] While oyster beds could be found throughout the Hudson River estuary, those found along the southern and eastern shores of Staten Island were ideal for commercial use. Exploding population growth coincided with the decline of New York's oyster beds and, by 1830, resulted in the first effort to reseed the Staten Island beds with seed oysters from the Chesapeake.[50] Oysters remained a popular food throughout the nineteenth century.[51] As the century came to a close, however, the beds were slowly smothered by the continual dumping of waste and sediment into New York's waters and by pollution from industrial uses in the harbor, such as sugar refineries.[52] Efforts are now underway to restore the city's oyster beds.[53]

EDUCATION

In 1805, at the urging of Dewitt Clinton when he was mayor of New York City, a group of New Yorkers founded the Free School Society, with the goal of educating those children who did not belong to any religious organization and therefore were not eligible for the charity schools that the various churches maintained.[54] Clinton served as its first president. Housed in a workshop adjacent to the Almshouse, the school soon outgrew its quarters and relocated to a larger building, the Old Arsenal on the corner of Chambers Street and Tryon Row (between today's Park Row and Centre Street). The city provided funds—supplemented by private donations—for the renovation and functioning of the school, known as Number 1.

More than five hundred students, many from the Almshouse, filled the school, which soon was joined by schools numbered 2, 3, and 4. By 1820, more than three thousand students attended the Free Schools. The schools were riven by controversies. Should they be free or collect one or two cents per week from each student who could afford it? Were the poorer students from the Almshouse morally unfit to learn with the more affluent scholars? Should funds also given to the schools run by religious organizations (there were four hundred "private" schools in the city at the time)? To escape these questions, the Free School Society merged with the schools of the Manumission Society and the Female Association, emerging in 1826 as the Public School Society.[55]

But problems around collecting tuition from the "paying scholars" and paying teachers, as well as perceived class differences among the students, bedeviled this attempt at free public education. Education for the manumitted children is difficult to determine. In a school census of 1829, only six out of more than four hundred private schools were for "colored children," but three of these were said to be "excellent." Of the nearly twenty-five thousand pupils in the private schools, only about eight hundred were Black. The six or seven "African schools" administered by the Manumission Society enrolled about 1,400 students before merging into the Public School Society in 1834.[56]

FIGURE 4.21
Multiple styles of pencil leads, graphite, and chalk found during the archaeological excavations of the Flatbush District Number 1 School, which is located on the same block in Flatbush as Erasmus Hall High School. In the nineteenth century, most students would use lead pencils to mark their reusable slates, which was much more economical than using paper. In this era, lead was more common than chalk. The various styles reflect that the site was used as a school from the mid-nineteenth century until 2000.
Qi# 212376 FABG; Qi#212377 FABG, QI#212378 FABG

Excavations on the campus of Erasmus Hall High School in Flatbush, Brooklyn (New York City landmark), around the foundations of the old (1787) Erasmus Academy (also a New York City landmark), gave archaeologists some clues to activities on the site.[57] The Academy building in the center of the high school quadrangle was moved to its present location in 1940 when the south structure of the campus was built. It was therefore not on its historic foundation, and the excavation turned up mostly artifacts and building features from the expansions of 1826 and 1897. However, enough earlier artifacts were preserved to show something about early nineteenth-century student life. Pipe stems and bowls indicated leisure activities on the campus. Slates and slate pencils, seen in figure 4.21, were used for schoolwork instead of more expensive pens and paper.[58]

CEMETERIES

As the city grew, everyday aspects of life changed. In the Dutch city, graveyards had been situated in its center. In the nineteenth century, with the city expanding and growing wariness of the dangers of "bad air" and contagion from dead bodies, the cemeteries not connected with churches were moved uptown.

In the seventeenth century, paupers were buried in the same graveyards as everyone else. In the eighteenth century, this changed, and they were interred in "Potter's Fields," which were moved farther and farther outside of the city.[59] One of these graveyards was in what is now Washington Square Park, which is located within the Greenwich Village Historic District. When the park was reconstructed from 2008 to 2013, the associated archaeological work discovered and documented intact burials, which were then protected in place, as well as fragmentary remains that were reinterred in the park in 2021. One of the discoveries was a headstone of James Jackson (figure 4.22), an Irishborn man who died of yellow fever in 1799 in the midst of a summer outbreak. At this time, the city issued a directive that anyone who died from the disease, whether impoverished or not, must be interred in the city's potter's field as a public-health measure.[60] In the nineteenth century, the dead were put somewhere out of sight, eventually moved from the city center to outside the city entirely. The changing attitude toward death and burial culminated in the parklike settings of graves of elite New Yorkers in Green-Wood in Brooklyn and Woodlawn in the Bronx in the later nineteenth century. This only widened the gap between elite "Old New Yorkers" and the new immigrants. To a lesser extent, African Americans, at the bottom of the social scale, felt the same pressure.

The second African burial ground was begun in 1795 in what is today the Lower East Side about a mile north of the first African Burial Ground at 290 Broadway. It was still in use until 1853, when burials were disinterred and moved to Cypress Hills Cemetery in Brooklyn. Not all the graves were moved, as was discovered in 2006 during the construction of the New Museum. Archaeological testing uncovered human remains, which were subsequently also reinterred in Cypress Hills after consultation with St. Philip's Church, which is the descendent church for the cemetery now located in Harlem (and is a New York City landmark).[61] This uptown movement of the cemetery is the result of not only a growing free Black population, enforced by legislation related to permitted burial ground locations throughout the first half of the nineteenth century, but also a change in attitude about death and burial not exclusive to the city's elite. Again, while earlier burials were close to the living, by the mid-nineteenth century, the dead were shunted farther away from the neighborhoods occupied by live New Yorkers.

After the Revolutionary War and into the nineteenth century, New York grew tremendously quickly. With this growth came problems of urban density, problems that the small eighteenth-century town at the foot of Manhattan could ignore but that the burgeoning nineteenth-century urban center had to solve. Immediate issues such as policing, education, and access to clean water reflected the underlying challenges of planning and a vision of what the city landscape might become. The Commissioners' Plan of 1811 foresaw the necessity of a larger planned city, the Croton water project relieved the need for clean water, and the building of canals to and from the north and west brought major changes in the shipment of goods and commerce. In the second half of the nineteenth century, New York built its reputation as a center of population, culture, and commerce.

FIGURE 4.22

Sandstone grave marker for James Jackson from County Kildare, Ireland, who died of yellow fever in New York City on September 22, 1799, at age twenty-eight. His gravestone was found during archaeological excavations at Washington Square Park, the location of an eighteenth-century potter's field.

Image: Joan Geismar, 2009.

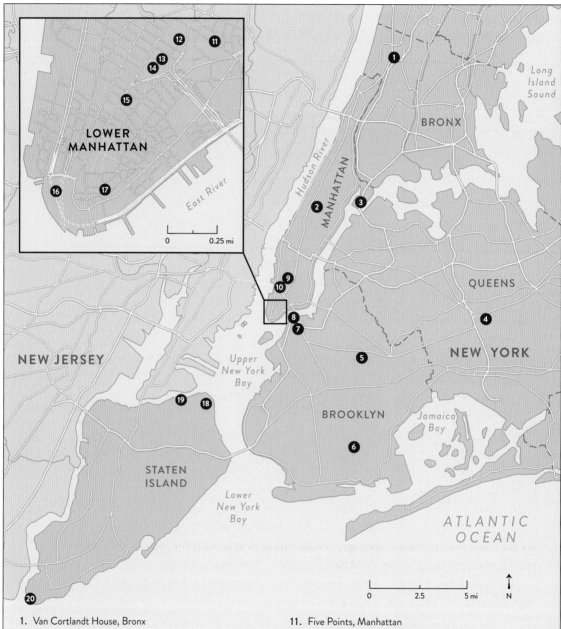

Long
Island
Sound

BRONX

Hudson River

MANHATTAN

QUEENS

NEW YORK

Upper
New York
Bay

NEW JERSEY

BROOKLYN

Jamaica
Bay

STATEN
ISLAND

Lower
New York
Bay

ATLANTIC
OCEAN

0   2.5   5 mi   ↑ N

LOWER MANHATTAN

East River

0   0.25 mi

1. Van Cortlandt House, Bronx
2. Seneca Village, Manhattan
3. Ward's Island, Emigrant Refuge, Manhattan
4. King Manor, Queens
5. Weeksville, Brooklyn
6. Lott House, Brooklyn
7. 84 Tillary St, Brooklyn
8. Empire Stores, Brooklyn
9. Washington Square Park, Manhattan
10. Spring Street Presbyterian Church
    Burial Ground, Manhattan

11. Five Points, Manhattan
12. African Burial Ground, Manhattan
13. Tweed Courthouse, Manhattan
14. City Hall Park, Manhattan
15. Corbin Building Well, Manhattan
16. South Ferry Terminal Project, Manhattan
17. Stadt Huys, Manhattan
18. Quarantine Grounds, Staten Island
19. Sailor's Snug Harbor, Staten Island
20. Aakawaxung Munahanung (Island Protected from the Wind)
    Archaeological Site, Staten Island

5

DEVELOPMENT OF THE MODERN CITY,
1840–1898

Between 1840 and 1898, New York City rapidly became the metropolis that we can recognize today. This was the time when fresh water became readily available at the turn of a tap, sewers and sanitation became municipal priorities, new bridges allowed greater movement of residents, the first skyscrapers were built, new immigrants moved into the southern parts of Manhattan, and consolidation in 1898 joined the boroughs together to become today's New York.

Massive immigration from Ireland, Germany, and Eastern Europe, along with migration of both white and Black people from the southern states after the Civil War,[1] brought more diversity to the city, tied it firmly into historical events at home and abroad, and reinforced the city's long-standing cosmopolitan outlook. Commerce thrived. Newcomers joined a labor pool, stoking the growing interregional and international trade, and sometimes became inventors, artisans, restaurateurs, and self-made millionaires. New York City's port continued to be essential both to the city's growth and to that of the nation. Railroads carried foreign and domestic goods to the interior of the country and returned with agricultural products to support the growing city. The new transcontinental railways tied New York to the West, and the West to New York.

But rapid growth was not without its problems. A growing population meant growing demands on sanitation, housing, health facilities, education, and the food supply. Periodic economic fluctuations undercut poor New Yorkers in particular, from how they earned a living to what they ate to where and how they lived. The gap between rich and poor yawned wider. Tensions emerged between earlier residents and anyone who belonged to a newly arrived group. Sometimes tensions erupted into riots and gang warfare. Political corruption was rife. Horse (and often human) waste polluted the streets faster than it could be cleaned. With all of this, by the dawn of the twentieth century, New York was the largest city in the United States. A decade later, it eclipsed London to become the largest city in the world.

New York City in 1840

In 1840, New York City had a population of 313,000.[2] As can be seen in figure 5.1, most people lived south of Fourteenth Street in what is now Lower Manhattan and in downtown Brooklyn. While the area that is now New York City once contained many outer-borough towns, such as Jamaica, West Farms, Flatbush, and New Brighton, most areas

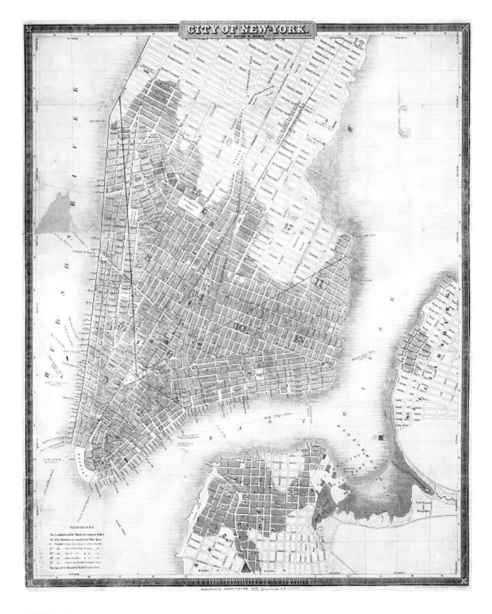

FIGURE 5.1
David Burr's Map of the City of New York in 1842, including the downtown Brooklyn waterfront and Williamsburg. From the New York Public Library Digital Collections.

north of Fourteenth Street in Manhattan and outside of such settlements were largely agrarian. Public transportation was in its infancy, so getting from place to place would have been challenging.[3] In 1890, the city's population was 1.5 million, an almost fivefold increase in just fifty years.[4] By then, development had expanded throughout the city. While some people moved to New York City from other parts of the United States— part of the urbanization of the era—most of the population increase came from immi- gration, especially from Ireland.

Between 1845 and 1852, successive potato crop failures in Ireland brought widespread famine. More than a million people died of starvation and disease, and almost twice that many left the country for better prospects. Some Irish immigrants went to other parts of the United Kingdom, others to Australia, but many came to the United States, and most of those entered through the Port of New York. In 1854 alone, more than three hundred thousand Irish immigrants entered New York.[5] By the next year, about 87 per- cent of the unskilled workforce in the city was Irish.[6] New York had seen waves of immi- grants before, but this was unprecedented, and it posed new challenges to the city. Not only was the volume of immigrants tremendously high, but many of them arrived mal- nourished, making them particularly vulnerable to diseases like cholera and smallpox. Sometimes they were even infected while traveling to New York.

QUARANTINE GROUNDS AND THE EMIGRANT REFUGE AND HOSPITAL

Archaeological excavations of the Quarantine Grounds and the Emigrant Refuge and Hospital Institution helped illuminate the real risks that immigrants took. From 1799 to 1860, the U.S. Marine Hospital Quarantine Grounds operated in St. George, Staten Island (figure 5.2). A walled institution, it included a hospital, several outbuildings, and a cemetery. This was before the advent of germ theory, and the cause and prevention of contagious diseases were poorly understood. But it was believed that quarantining the sick would help maintain public health.

A doctor from the city boarded all ships that entered the Port of New York to check the passengers' and crew's health before they disembarked. Anyone determined to be ill was taken to the Marine Hospital for treatment. Records indicate that sick people from the city were also sent to this hospital, most likely people of limited means who could not pay for their own medical care. Unsurprisingly, among the thousands of people who were treated in this hospital, many died. The residents of St. George had long petitioned the government to move the Quarantine Grounds, in part because they blamed it for the yellow fever outbreaks in their own community.[7] In 1858, after moving the sick and infirm from the hospital, the residents burned it down. The property was subsequently sold and used for other purposes.[8]

From 2006 to 2012, archaeologists examined the site of the old Marine Hospital Quarantine Grounds ahead of the construction of the Staten Island Criminal Court and

FIGURE 5.2
An 1833 depiction of the view of the New York Quarantine Hospital Grounds in St. George, Staten Island, in operation from 1799 to 1866. Note the cluster of ships near the Quarantine Grounds awaiting their turn for sick passengers to be admitted into the complex. Also note the rural nature of this part of Staten Island. From the New York Public Library Digital Collections.

Family Court complex. The testing revealed that burials from the cemetery remained at the site; ultimately, thirty-eight in situ burials and more than sixty isolated human remains were recovered. The archaeology revealed that unclothed burials in plain wooden coffins were placed either in individual graves or side by side in trench burials. Analysis indicated that the burials were primarily men of European ancestry, most of whom exhibited signs of nutritional deficiencies, repetitive work stressors, and trauma.[9] The remains were reinterred at the site in 2014.

In 1847, a Board of Commissioners of Emigration was created by the New York State legislature and charged with reforming the immigration process. This included overseeing the Quarantine Grounds. They created the Emigrant Refuge and Hospital on Ward's Island (now Randalls and Wards Islands in the East River). In the mid-1850s, it was the largest hospital complex in the world (figure 5.3).[10] Archaeologists examined this site in 1993 and uncovered the remains of at least twenty people, likely those who had died in this hospital. It was a small sample of what had been a much larger cemetery. The excavated burial population included men, women, and children. Most of the adults had died in midlife. Subsequent analysis indicated that at least one was of African ancestry and several others of European ancestry. The bones of several people displayed signs of heavy repetitive physical labor, and some had suffered degenerative joint disease and episodes of trauma by the time they died.[11]

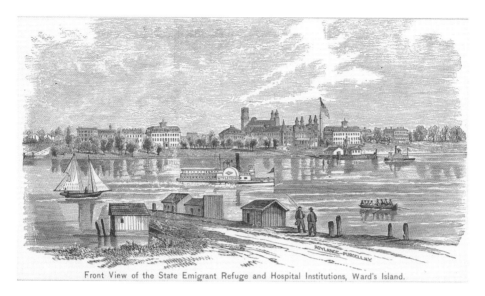

Front View of the State Emigrant Refuge and Hospital Institutions, Ward's Island.

FIGURE 5.3
Emigrant Refuge and Hospital Institutions, Ward's Island. Created in 1847, it was in use until the end of
the nineteenth century. Archaeology completed at the site in 1993 uncovered burials associated with the
institution.
From the New York Public Library Digital Collections.

In 1855, the Board created a new immigration center in Castle Garden in Battery
Park in Lower Manhattan (later known as Castle Clinton and today a New York City
landmark). This center was responsible for receiving and processing all immigrants
until it closed in 1890. More than eight million people passed through Castle Garden.[12]
Castle Garden was initially built in 1808–1811 as part of New York's fortification system,
in preparation for the War of 1812. Ultimately, it was not needed for that purpose.[13] Back
then it was called the Southwest Battery. Later it was transformed into the immigration
center and then an aquarium; today it is a place where tourists buy tickets to visit the
Statue of Liberty and Ellis Island (both New York City landmarks).

Nineteenth-century maps show that Castle Clinton was originally located on an
island accessed by a long bridge from the shoreline (figure 5.4). The area around it has
been filled in over time, and today the Hudson River shoreline is 125 feet west of Castle
Clinton. Around 2004, a new subway tunnel and station were planned within Battery
Park, so an archaeological examination of the area occurred.[14] Archaeologists uncovered portions of the eighteenth-century Battery defenses discussed in chapter 3 and
also exposed the many episodes of landfilling that connected the park to the mainland.
Modern visitors to Castle Clinton can see a permanent archaeological exhibit called
"Walls Within Walls," which displays a portion of the Battery walls.

In the seventeenth to nineteenth centuries, made land, which archaeologists call
landfill, almost always included garbage, such as the ink bottle shown in figure 5.5. (City
regulations today require landfill to be clean earth, concrete, rock, gravel, stone, and
sand.[15]) Archaeologists use artifacts found in the landfill to date when the landfill was

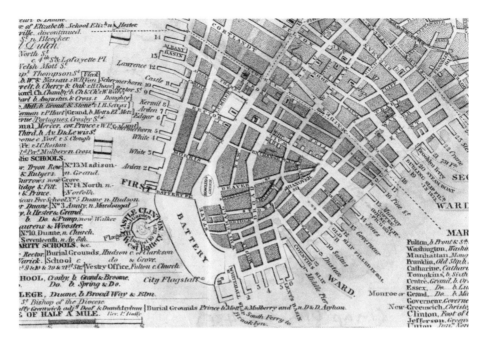

FIGURE 5.4

Detail of Castle Clinton, middle left, then on an island in the Hudson River.

From *Hooker's New Pocket Plan of the City of New York, 1838.* Lionel Pincus and Princess Firyal Map Division,
From the New York Public Library. New York Public Library Digital Collections.

created, by using the manufacturing dates of the items. They provide a *terminus post quem* (TPQ), or the earliest date the deposit could have been created. For example, if a deposit of artifacts includes a coin from 1860, then 1860 is the earliest year in which the landfill could have been created.

Immigration continued throughout the late nineteenth century, but in the 1880s the immigration patterns changed. Up until then, the majority of immigrants were from northern Europe. But in this period, immigrants' origins changed so that most came from southern and eastern Europe. In addition, whereas the initial waves of immigrants were predominantly Protestant and Catholic, in this period they shifted to being predominantly Catholic, Jewish, and Orthodox Christian. While each group had its own reasons for coming, all sought to improve their economic circumstances as conditions in southern and eastern Europe were difficult, with high levels of poverty and few opportunities for those living there to better their lives if they remained.

Unfortunately, immigrants were not universally welcomed to New York. A group called the Know Nothing Party viewed the "Famine Irish" with special antipathy. It began as a secret society that initially focused on antislavery and temperance efforts, but emerged—and flourished—in the 1850s as a nativist political party that was vehemently anti-immigration and anti-Catholic.[16]

FIGURE 5.5
A mid-nineteenth-century brown salt-glazed master ink bottle, stamped "Bournes' Improved Vitreous Stone Bottle, Guaranteed Not to Absorb." The bottle was manufactured by the Bourne Pottery in Denby, England. When stoneware clays are fired at a high temperature, they become dense and nonabsorbent—in other words, a perfect container for ink. Bulk volumes of ink were sold in "master" ink bottles and decanted into inkwells as needed. This bottle was excavated from landfill in Battery Park near Castle Garden.
Qi#113430 SFT

The Know Nothing Party was also a small part of the temperance movement that emerged in the 1820s. This was before there was widespread access to potable water, and tea, coffee, and hot chocolate were relatively expensive. So alcoholic beverages like cider and beer were the most common drinks, and many even thought of them as excellent energy sources. In time, more and more people began to see alcohol as a societal ill. Religious leaders spoke against it as an impediment to a righteous life. Key among these was Father Mathew, an Irish Catholic priest. After he gained fame for his work in Ireland, he was asked by leaders of the temperance movement to come to the United States to provide moral guidance to Irish Americans. He was in the United States from 1849 to 1851, preaching that crime and poverty were a direct result of drunkenness. Many ceramic vessels expressing the sentiments and ideals of the movement such as "temperance" and "industry," like the teacup and plate rim in figure 5.6, were sold to his supporters and to those who supported the temperance movement.[17] These particular vessels were found at two different sites—hinting at the popularity of Father Mathew and his message with New Yorkers. Other Father Mathew vessels have been excavated elsewhere in the city but are not in the Repository's collection.[18] Artifacts that indicate political alignment are rare, so the archaeological discovery of Father Mathew vessels at different sites is noteworthy.

Nativist Americans viewed the Irish as carriers of disease and a drain on the medical resources of the city. The Irish did have a higher rate of hospitalization and death than other groups of New Yorkers—not surprising as many Irish immigrants arrived in the United States malnourished, only to live in squalid housing and find dangerous and low-paying work such as construction (see the pipe in figure 5.7, found at a nineteenth-century construction site).[19] The Know Nothing Party had only limited success in its persecution of the Irish. By the end of the nineteenth century, many Irish people had risen to prominent positions in New York City.

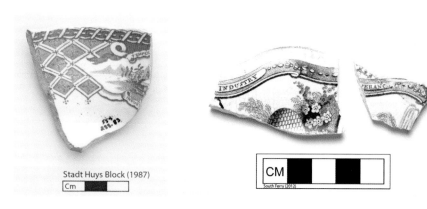

Stadt Huys Block (1987)

FIGURE 5.6

Teacup and plate rim fragments associated with the Father Mathew temperance movement, found at the Stadt Huys (*left*), and South Ferry (*right*) sites in Lower Manhattan. The sherds include several clues about their association, including portions of the words "temperance," and "industry" and the stylized beehive, which symbolized industry. These vessels were likely made by William Adams IV & Son[e]s in Staffordshire, England.

Qi#201514 SHB and Qi#102483 SFT

City Hall Park (2013)

FIGURE 5.7

Smoking pipe stamped with a harp and shamrocks found in City Hall Park in a context associated with the construction of Tweed Courthouse from 1861 to 1881. Personal items such as pipes were a way for people to display individual allegiances to home countries or belief systems. This pipe was likely smoked by a proud Irishman who helped to build Tweed Courthouse.

Qi#123434 CHP

MINERAL WATER

In the second half of the nineteenth century, many households had access to potable water, but certainly not everyone did. Mineral and soda water grew in popularity. The temperance movement promoted them as an alternative to alcohol. They may also have been an important link for many immigrants to their homeland, where they were regarded as being curatives. At Five Points (located in what is now part of the Civic Center in Lower Manhattan), archaeologists found, through associated contexts, that Irish families had more soda-water bottles than other families; these may have been used to treat illness, as was the case with the mineral-water bottles shown in figure 5.8.[20]

FIGURE 5.8

Top: Hunyadi János mineral-water bottles from the Rufus King Manor Excavations in Jamaica, Queens. A Hungarian water-bottling company featured Hunyadi Janos, a fifteenth-century Hungarian hero, stating that this mineral water fought "the evil consequences of indiscretion in diet" and was a primary elixir for relieving hemorrhoids (Gonzalez 2017). This product was widely advertised, even on the New York City subway, as shown in the lower photograph from 1905.

Bottom: Canal Street, West Side, Manhattan, [interior of Canal Street Station], Contract One, May 4, 1905. Subway Construction Photograph Collection, New-York Historical Society, PR 069-10-5797. New York Transit Museum and New-York Historical Society.

Qi#212368 RKP to Qi#212375 RKP

FIGURE 5.9
German salt-glazed stoneware mineral-water bottles that contained naturally carbonated water imported to New York in the mid- to late nineteenth century. Both bottles were excavated from the Stadt Huys site in Lower Manhattan.
Qi#201376 SHB and Qi#201832 SHB

The use of mineral and soda water was widespread throughout the city. The mineral-water bottles in figure 5.9 were found during the Stadt Huys excavations.[21] The standing bottle on the left would have contained approximately three English pints of mineral water. It is impressed with "Roisdorfer Mineralquelle," and it dates to circa 1876. The brand is still in production today, although the water is no longer sold in these bottles. The bottle on the right is stamped with "selters" encircling a lion rampant and dates from circa 1846 to 1866.[22] Missing are the words "Hersogthum Nassau" stamped below the seal, indicating that the bottle contained mineral water from the Niederselters Spring in the Dutchy of Nassau in Northern Germany—the genesis of the generic word *seltzer* for carbonated water in English.

While New Yorkers drank many imported brands of mineral water, these beverages were also manufactured in the city. Archaeologists found D. L. Ormsby bottles, which

FIGURE 5.10

Left: D (Dornan). L. Ormsby stoneware mineral-water, beer, or root-beer bottle excavated from the Seneca Village Site in Central Park. We can determine from city directory entries, like the 1846 excerpt shown here, that the stoneware bottle was manufactured, brought to Seneca Village, and disposed of sometime between 1844 and 1856. We know it was discarded before 1857 because that is when Seneca Village was cleared through the law of eminent domain. *Right:* a D. L. Ormsby & Son glass bottle from the Stadt Huys site, made sometime between 1860 and 1864, when Dornan was in business with his son.

Doggett's New-York City Directory for 1846 and 1847. New York: John Doggett, Jr., page 300. New York Public Library Digital Collections.

Qi#210483 SVP and Qi#203273 SHB

held either mineral water, root beer, or beer, in both the Stadt Huys and the Seneca Village excavations (figure 5.10). According to New York City business directories, D. L. (Dorman Leonard) Ormsby operated as a root-beer manufacturer at 255 West Sixteenth Street in 1844. By 1860, he had moved to 423 West Sixteenth Street, where he was in business with his son as a soda- and mineral-water producer. By 1874, he moved his operations uptown to 168th Street, east of Amsterdam. While archaeological sites can provide insights into the lives of individuals who lived and worked at the excavated sites, in this case it was the discovery of bottles brewed by the same company at two archaeological sites that led archaeologists to pursue more research on the Ormsby business and family.[23]

Spring Street Presbyterian Church

In 2006, during the construction of the Trump SoHo Hotel on Spring Street in Manhattan, subsequently renamed the Dominick, workers uncovered human remains. As was required by law, work stopped and the New York City Office of the Medical Examiner, which includes a Forensic Anthropology Department, visited the site. They determined that the remains were historical—meaning not recently interred burials—and asked the Landmarks Preservation Commission Archaeology Department to advise, although the site was not under the jurisdiction of the Commission. Subsequently, archaeologists from URS Corporation and AKRF investigated and discovered that the site had once been home to the Spring Street Presbyterian Church and associated burial ground.[24]

The Spring Street Presbyterian Church was established in the early nineteenth century. By 1820, it provided full membership to people of African ancestry, at a time when slavery was still legal in New York State. The church included a burial ground that was in use from 1820 to 1850. The church became especially known when, on July 11, 1834, it was attacked by an anti-abolitionist and anti-Black mob.[25] Their anger was likely sparked by the church's reverend, Samuel Cox, who stated that Jesus Christ may have been of a "dark Syrian hue."[26] The church population included people of both European and African ancestry, both working class and members of the emerging middle class.

While the documentary research indicated that there may have been as many as six hundred people interred in the site's burial vaults, the skeletal analysis confirmed only about two hundred individuals. Being able to analyze such a large historic burial population is unusual in urban archaeology. At this site, more than seventy burials were analyzed by bioarchaeologists, who determined that most of the skeletal material represented individuals who had died of diseases that did not affect bone. There were a few noted exceptions, including one individual whose remains exhibited signs of cancer and two others who had tuberculosis.[27] The archaeologists were also able to analyze dental material and noted that about 50 percent of the adult teeth examined had caries (cavities). The analysis indicates that men lost more teeth than women. The project analysts also noted the presence of dental care: they documented three gold fillings, a gold dental bridge, and a false tooth made of stone. In the nineteenth century, self-care, including care of the teeth, was an emerging part of "Americanness," stretching across ethnic and class boundaries as part of democracy and national character. Self-care was linked—or so early Americans thought—to self-governance.[28] But in comparison to other contemporaneous populations, this congregation had poor dental health, likely stemming from a reliance on sugar for calories, which is commonly associated with poorer people. Ultimately, the remains were reinterred with a memorial service at the First Presbyterian Church in October 2014.[29]

Hygiene

The city in this period was far dirtier than it is today. Soot from wood and coal fires filled the air, and the streets were usually covered with filth, including large quantities of horse manure. Many jobs, such as keeping livery stables and working in early industrial-age factories, made people very dirty. While some households could simply turn a tap to wash, most of the population could not. This meant that it took real effort for most people to keep themselves clean. Cleanliness, therefore, emerged as a significant class marker, as did hygienic practices designed to promote good health. At this time, they were associated with refinement and good breeding, which were seen as upper- and middle-class attributes. Dirt was considered "vulgar" and was associated with the working classes.[30]

Archaeological excavations often uncover evidence about personal hygiene, as in the nailbrush, toothbrush, and cold-cream jars seen in figures 5.11 and 5.12. The nailbrush and toothbrush are both made of animal bone. Although toothbrushes are ubiquitous

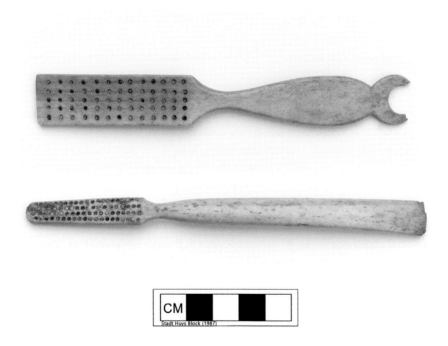

FIGURE 5.11

Mid nineteenth-century nailbrush (*top*) and toothbrush (*bottom*). Both are made of animal bone and would have had bristles, likely made from boar's hair. These artifacts were found in a privy deposit associated with the Jacques and Marsh Druggists at the Stadt Huys Block excavations. Found among the druggists' trash, they were likely never used.

Qi#203110 SHB and Qi#202880 SHB

FIGURE 5.12

Ironstone cold-cream jar with lid. As this lid did not have a manufacturing label, it may have been made to contain homemade cold cream (Sharrow 2001, 238–239), or perhaps it was sold by a pharmacy that made small batches of cold cream and used paper labels that did not survive being buried for 150 years. This jar was found during the Van Cortlandt excavations. Archaeologists believe it was discarded when the mansion was converted from private to public ownership in 1889 (Bankoff, Winter, and Ricciardi 1992, 7).

Qi#197815 VCP

today, their use in the mid-nineteenth century was unusual. Even seventy years later in 1920, only 20 percent of the American population routinely used them.[31] These artifacts came from contexts associated with the Jacques and Marsh Druggists at the Stadt Huys Block excavations. They had not yet been sold and were likely never used. Worked-bone objects were a cottage industry; people made them at home for a set price per object. The bones were purchased from slaughterhouses and then boiled down. This bone boiling would have produced very noxious odors. Once clean, the bone would be carved and polished and then be ready for sale.[32] The cold-cream jar (figure 5.12) was found during the Van Cortlandt House excavations and likely dated from the mid-nineteenth century. Cold creams have been used for centuries and were thought to cleanse, heal, and beautify. In the early- and mid-nineteenth century, they were often made of vegetable oils and would quickly spoil, so they were generally either made at home or purchased in small quantities from local pharmacies. In the later nineteenth century, petroleum jelly replaced vegetable oils, which ensured a long shelf life for these products, still widely sold today.[33]

MEDICINE AND PERSONAL CARE

Medical care in the mid- to late-nineteenth century was as stratified as cleanliness. Elite families were attended by doctors, but most people would have depended upon what are today considered folk remedies, as well as products that could be purchased from druggists' shops. There were hospitals for the truly ill, but the cure rates did not inspire confidence, and there was only one hospital that served everyone regardless of their means. That was Bellevue Hospital, a successor to the Almshouse discussed in chapter 3. Bellevue is still an important New York City institution. There were also city dispensaries that were largely used by New York's poor.[34]

Druggists' shops sold their own formulas alongside patent medicines. Before the Pure Food and Drug Act of 1906, purchasing medicine was a "buyer beware" situation. Medicines often contained opiates, alcohol, and even mercury and lead. Examples of patent-medicine bottles can be seen in figure 5.13, all of which were found in the Van Cortlandt House excavations and were used by the same household. The bottle on the left dates from 1840 to 1860 and is embossed with "Osgood's India Cholagogue, New York." It was marketed to purify the blood and promote the discharge of bile and was sold both as a cure and as a preventive measure for those traveling in "bilious climates." It should be noted that biliousness was a common symptom of cholera. The bottle in the middle, Dr. O'Toole's Cough Remedy, is also from the mid-nineteenth century. It was marketed in the mid-nineteenth to early-twentieth centuries as curing a wide array of illnesses that caused coughing fits, including tuberculosis, although there was no effective cure for tuberculosis at that time. The bottle on the right is an Ayer's Cherry Pectoral cough-medicine bottle. Marketed for coughs, croup, asthma, and sore throats

FIGURE 5.13

Examples of patent-medicine bottles commonly used in the late-nineteenth century from the Van Cortlandt House excavations. The bottle on the left is embossed with "Osgood's India Cholagogue, New York"; the bottle in the middle contained Dr. O'Toole's Cough Remedy; the bottle on the right was for Ayer's Cherry Pectoral cough medicine.

Qi#199595 VCP, Qi#199733 VCP, and Qi#199721 VCP

Stadt Huys Block (1987)

FIGURE 5.14
Top: Jacques and Marsh stoneware bottle with their address from 1832 to 1835 at 56 Pearl Street. *Bottom:* Jacques and Marsh Hive Syrup glass medicine bottle. Hive syrup was used to treat croup, a bronchial infection commonly seen in children. Given how small the Hive syrup bottle is, many bottles would likely need to be purchased to treat one illness (Czerkowicz 2016). This bottle was found at the Stadt Huys Block excavations adjacent to where the Jacques and Marsh Druggists were located from 1832 to 1851.
Qi#201474 SHB and Qi#202882 SHB

Stadt Huys Block (1987)

in children and adults, it was sold in the nineteenth and early-twentieth century. It initially included heroin, morphine, and alcohol.[35]

One druggists' establishment from which, we have surviving artifacts is the Jacques and Marsh Druggists, originally located on Pearl Street in Lower Manhattan, though the shop moved locations and changed proprietors a few times. The bottles in figure 5.14 are from their 56 Pearl Street days, between 1832 and 1835, and were found within the Stadt Huys excavations in Lower Manhattan. The bottles were likely disposed of shortly after Jacques and Marsh moved from 56 Pearl Street.[36] Another pharmacist identified through archaeological excavation was George L. Peck and his Hall of Pharmacy on 356 Fulton Street (today Jamaica Avenue) in Jamaica, Queens (figure 5.15).

The Peck Pharmacy bottles were found near the Rufus King Manor, in Jamaica, Queens, which suggests that someone in that household sought relief from that pharmacy.[37] George Peck was in business from 1857 to 1906.[38] Bottles from druggists are helpful for dating sites, as the bottle styles frequently changed and one can use historical records to match the bottle to when and where the businesses existed.[39] Archaeologists have used pharmacy bottles to understand the ailments that residents suffered. They also use city directories to learn where these businesses were located and can then

FIGURE 5.15
A collection of identical pharmacy bottles from the George L. Peck Hall of Pharmacy, Jamaica, Long Island, found during the Rufus King Manor archaeological excavations in Queens, indicates that someone in the household was struggling with a significant or reoccurring ailment and was determined to find relief. Qi#212346 RKP to Qi#212349 RKP

trace people's paths through the city by seeing how the shops they visited relate to the archaeological site.[40]

THE MCEWEN FAMILY

Significant information about the health and habits of the McEwen family were revealed by archaeology. In 2014, excavations at 84 Tillary Street in downtown Brooklyn uncovered a dry-laid stone rectangular privy.[41] It was likely built in the 1840s and filled with domestic rubbish in the 1850s and early 1860s by the McEwen family when their house was connected to the public water and sewer system. The 1860 census, which recorded the names of the people in the household, where they were from, their ages, and professions, records that Robert McEwen, his wife Janette, and their three children were all born in Scotland and that Robert was a grocer. Besides the usual mid-nineteenth-century domestic artifacts that are almost always found at New York City sites—like the white Gothic granite teapot shown in figure 5.16—the archaeological assemblage included artifacts that revealed significant details about this family. Remnants of expensive cuts of meat were found, suggesting that the family was well off, although they may have received the meat in payment from one of their tenants, who was a butcher. There

FIGURE 5.16
Gothic-style white granite teapot. It was manufactured by T & R Boote between 1845 and 1851. This ceramic type is a hallmark of mid-nineteenth-century New York sites because of its ubiquity. Found during the NYC College of Technology Archaeological Excavations in Brooklyn.
Qi# 212197 NYCCT

were also a number of medicine bottles that were primarily marketed to cure indigestion, suggesting that someone in the household was unwell.

Documentary research revealed that Mrs. Janette McEwen had testified to the efficacy of Dr. Francis Tumblety's "Indian cure" for digestive issues in an 1863 newspaper advertisement. This doctor, an infamous fraud, was also suspected by some to have been Jack the Ripper.[42] In this period, "Indian cures" and "Indian doctors" were presented as being steeped in special esoteric healing knowledge gained from Indigenous Peoples. But most of these practitioners, like Dr. Tumblety, had no such training and were simply quacks.[43] Mrs. McEwen died a few months after this advertisement appeared. The examiner reported the cause of death as a disease of the heart.[44]

Macrobotanical analysis examined plant materials preserved within the McEwen privy. The oldest level included maple seeds, the middle levels had many weeds—carpetweed, jimsonweed, and grass—and the most recent levels (likely deposited just before the privy was closed) had seeds from fruits like raspberries, blackberries, and grapes (figure 5.17). This indicates that in its earliest use, the backyard was likely not cultivated, but the seeds that were present toward the end of use likely passed through

FIGURE 5.17
Blackberry seeds under a microscope, found in the
privy at 84 Tillary Street, Brooklyn. The blackberries
were likely consumed by the residents of the house.
Image: Justine McKnight, Archeobotanical
Consultant.

human digestive tracts rather than having grown naturally in the backyard as the plant
remains found in the earliest levels likely had. This analysis also documented ash in the
earlier deposits, which perhaps indicates that the owners were dumping their fire waste
into the privy.[45] We do not know whether that was done simply out of convenience or for
potential reasons of hygiene.

FEEDING LATE-NINETEENTH-CENTURY NEW YORK

As in earlier periods, late-nineteenth-century New York City was diverse. Many people who lived there were born in other parts of the world, and they often held onto
their food traditions and introduced them to the city. For example, Eastern European
Jews are said to have introduced bagels—now a key staple of the modern New Yorker's
diet—in the late nineteenth century.[46] Archaeology can shed light on the different food
choices residents made and what those differences mean.

In 1985, the Landmarks Preservation Commission conducted archaeological excavations of features associated with Sailors' Snug Harbor in Staten Island (a complex that
includes multiple New York City landmarks). This institution was established in 1801
near Washington Square to provide institutional care for "aged, decrepit and worn-out
sailors." In 1831, it was moved from Manhattan to the northern shore of Staten Island.
Today it is a cultural center. Snug Harbor was a planned community with different activity areas and residential areas for the managers of the complex, including a steward and
a matron, its employees, and its residents. Because of the well-documented and discrete
areas of the site, archaeologists were able to compare artifacts (and, in this case, faunal
remains) from the various groups. One aspect of the analysis suggests that, not surprisingly, there was a direct correlation between affluence and the meat cuts selected. This
relationship held for the two periods they uncovered, 1845–1872 and 1872–1900. Specifically, they found that the steward, who managed the institution, had both a greater
variety of expensive tableware and more good meat cuts in his rubbish than did the residents and the female employees.[47]

The Uses of Faunal Analysis

The examination of animal bones from Sailors' Snug Harbor makes use of a set of techniques called faunal analysis. This powerful form of analysis requires the expertise of archaeologists who can identify the kind of animal to which a bone or sometimes only a part of a bone belongs. A series of steps are required.

First the analyst looks at the entire collection and sorts the bones into rough categories: mammal, bird, rodent, and so on. Bones within these categories are then further categorized where possible: what kind of animal or bird or reptile is it, and what part of the body is represented (hind or foreleg, skull, ribs, etc.)? With many animals it is possible to distinguish, for example, a left humerus (arm bone) from a right. If the remains are too fragmentary or worn to establish the species, these remains are often classified (if mammals) into large, medium or small. And there is always a residual category in any collection for "unidentified." The better the analysis, the smaller the "unidentified" category will be.

The second step involves quantification of each type of bone. There are several ways to count bones. One is the number of identifiable specimens (NISP), which can give a rough sense of the proportions of each type of creature. However, if the archaeologist wants to know what proportion of the *diet* is contributed by each species, a cow bone is clearly more important in this regard than a songbird bone (if both were part of the diet). Another way to tabulate bone is by minimum number of individuals (MNI). The use of this technique necessitates identifying which specific bone, from which side of the body, was found. It is also important to distinguish the age and gender of the animal from which the bone came, if possible. Thus, three left femurs (thigh bones) classified as adult male pig implies there were portions of three pigs consumed in this particular context. The ability to refine these identifications is essential to the definition of MNI.

Some analysts investigate what cuts of meat are represented by specific bones. Were residents of the site eating steaks like sirloin or round, for example, or stews made from other smaller or tougher cuts of meat? Were they eating young animals (figure 5.18), usually more tender, or older ones, often less costly? This kind of detail allows the archaeologist (as in the Sailors' Snug Harbor report) to link faunal material with another type of classification, such as social status or race.

The faunal analysis undertaken by the archaeologists examining the material from the Five Points site (another excavation that will be discussed later in the chapter), which included the review of historical records and cookbooks, was undertaken in part to see what relationships could be discerned between what was eaten and the ethnicity and class of the consumers. Historical records indicated that in working-class households, meat was eaten multiple times a day, especially pork, because it was one of the most affordable meats then available. Archaeologists noted that the faunal assemblages at Five Points were consistent

CM

City Hall Park (2013)

FIGURE 5.18
The butchered end of a cow (*Bos taurus*) femur with a sawn edge at left. The epiphysis, or rounded head of the femur, is unfused with the bone shaft, indicating that the animal was young when it was butchered. Found in the City Hall Park 2010–2011 excavations.
Qi# 207106 CHP

with this expectation; they had a high mammal component, with pork particularly prevalent. The assemblages also included a good deal of fish and a lower quantity of poultry. Archaeological analysis at other sites indicated that middle-class households tended to have higher proportions of poultry, likely reflecting preferences as well as the relative cost of each in the period.

The archaeologists also analyzed the faunal remains in terms of the ethnicities of specific households. It was determined that while pork was widely used in Irish households, it did not appear to be used in the one Jewish household examined. Since pork is not kosher, observant Jews would not eat it, but it was impossible to conclude if culture or economic concerns affected the one household that did not consume pork.[48]

Other attributes that faunal analysts may also look for are signs of food processing: was a bone chopped or sawed to create a portion? These differences have temporal implications, as the saw was introduced in the nineteenth century, whereas an axe was used to cut up carcasses in the eighteenth. Gnawing on bones by dogs or rats may suggest that the bones were left on a ground surface for a while.

Weathering also implies exposure. Burning may suggest cooking style or that the bones were being disposed of as refuse.

Not all these qualities are examined for every project. It depends on the condition of the bones involved and the research questions that the analyst asks of the assemblage. However, faunal analysis of a relatively intact collection, in conjunction with other forms of material recovered (such as ceramics, for example) can be incredibly productive of information.

Faunal analysis can also be an important way to understand how dramatically the environment has changed over time. For example, passenger pigeons were once the most abundant bird in North America; there are many historical accounts of the sky darkening when flocks would fly by (Figure 5.19). In 1914, the passenger pigeon was declared extinct, likely as a result of overhunting and the destruction of their nesting and feeding habitats. Therefore, one should be able to find passenger pigeon bones in early deposits and far fewer in those dated to the late nineteenth century. New York City faunal assemblages to date cannot reinforce this idea, as current samples are too small.

FIGURE 5.19
Passenger Pigeon femur (*left*) and clavicle (*right*) excavated from Battery Park during the South Ferry archaeological project between 2004 and 2006. Passenger pigeons, now extinct, were once the most abundant bird in the country.
Qi#198349 SFT and Qi#199078 SFT

SLAVERY AND EMANCIPATION FROM 1840 TO 1898

While emancipation occurred in New York State on July 4, 1827, and theoretically ended slavery there, in fact Black people were not permitted the same rights or legal protections provided to white people. Until 1841—a full fourteen years after emancipation—New York allowed nonresident enslavers to keep enslaved people within the state for up to nine months. And the Fugitive Slave Act of 1850, passed by the U.S. Congress, stipulated that "escaped" enslaved people could be taken from New York (and other free states) and returned to bondage in the South. This law was in effect until the Civil War. In 1822, the New York State constitution was amended to require that men of African ancestry hold property worth at least $250 (approximately $8,000 today) in order to be eligible to vote. The same amendment removed the suffrage property requirements for white men, and in 1826, New York State abolished the remaining tax and residency requirements so that all white men could vote. In 1846, 1860, and 1869, referendums were put forward to remove the voting restrictions for men of African ancestry; each one was defeated. It was only the passage of the Fifteenth Amendment in 1870 that granted the vote to all men of African ancestry;[49] it would be another forty-seven years before women could vote in New York State.

The city's economy remained tied to the institution of slavery even after emancipation. The city's banks were a critical support to the southern economy, and some went so far as to accept enslaved people as collateral for loans.[50] New York City shipowners transported goods such as cotton, rice, tobacco, and sugar that were produced through enslaved labor, meaning that not only owners but also dockworkers and related industries were linked to slavery. Brokers in New York City traded goods including cotton and sugar as commodities, and many factories in the city used those goods to make their products. And some people, such as shipbuilders, were directly tied to the trade of enslaved people.[51] Finally, many southern enslavers spent time and considerable money in the city and its establishments, both to conduct business and for pleasure.[52]

SENECA VILLAGE

Seneca Village was a community in what was then Upper Manhattan but today is part of Central Park. It lies between today's West Eighty-First and West Eighty-Ninth streets, from Eighth Avenue east to what would have been the extension of Seventh Avenue (figure 5.20).[53] It was first settled in 1825 by a few free Black individuals, including Andrew Williams, who purchased the land from a white family called the Whiteheads. Another early landowner was Epiphany Davis, who acquired land for the African Methodist Episcopal (AME) Mother Zion Church for use as a cemetery. Downtown cemeteries, which were primarily church properties, were filling up, and most of the land downtown had been developed. Space to bury anyone—and especially Black people—was hard to come by.[54]

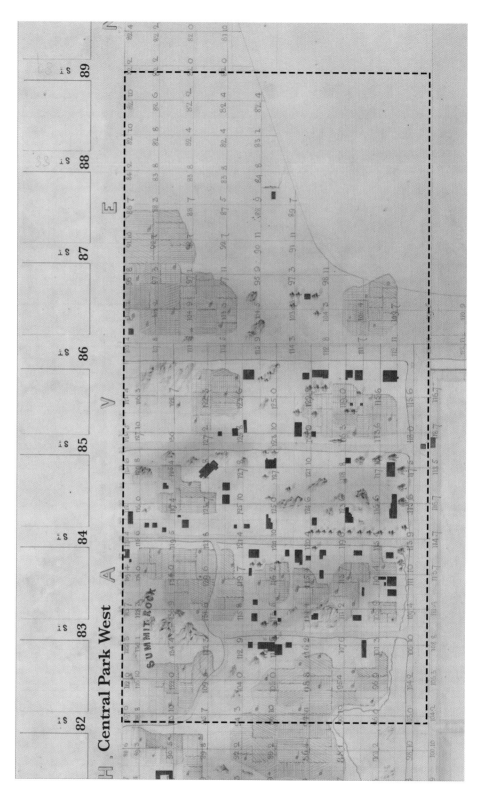

FIGURE 5.20

Egbert Viele's 1855 Topographic Survey of Central Park with the added outline of Seneca Village located between Eighty-Second and Eighty-Ninth streets within today's Central Park.

Municipal Archives, City of New York.

In the 1820s and 1830s, most of the land in Seneca Village was acquired by Black buyers. Likely these land purchases were motivated by the 1822 New York State law that linked property ownership to voting. Later, in the 1840s and 1850s, other people settled in the village, principally Irish and German immigrants. In 1856, the approximately three hundred Seneca Villagers were removed through the use of eminent domain and required to leave their homes so that Central Park could be built. They were compensated, but many felt inadequately.[55] While there is some information as to where the Villagers went, the community itself shattered, as people dispersed around New York City. In order to create the Park, a total of 1,600 people were removed from all the land needed for it, including those from Seneca Village.

Seneca Village appears to have been a meaningful community to its nearly three hundred residents. It was a refuge for many from the incessant and overt racism of the downtown city. By 1855, there were more than fifty houses, three churches, and at least one school. The houses were laid out on the city grid, close to a local spring. Church records of baptisms and marriages show that residents participated in each other's lives, even across racial lines, suggesting a close and supportive community.

Scholars became interested in this community and what archaeological resources might still be present because very little was known about Black domestic life in the city. In 2011, after many years of preparation, including documentary research, soil borings, and ground-penetrating radar studies, archaeologists and students from New York City conducted an eight-week excavation. They discovered, not far beneath the surface, the foundation walls of a house belonging to William Godfrey Wilson. Wilson was the sexton of the All Angels' Church, and he had lived in this house with his wife, Charlotte, and many children. This wood-frame building, approximately four hundred square feet, was originally three stories tall and had a tin roof and a brick fireplace. Inside, the archaeologists found many artifacts, including earthenwares, stoneware, porcelain, glass, cooking pots, a toothbrush, a comb, a three-cent coin, a child's shoe, and a slate pencil (figure 5.21). Slate pencils were used on slate writing boards by adults and schoolchildren alike. Colored School No. 3, established in 1840 in Seneca Village in the African Union Methodist Church, was one of only a handful of Black schools in New York City at the time. The 1850 census indicates that all five of the Wilsons' school-age children attended school, as did three-quarters of other Seneca Village children. The archaeologists compared the school attendance of Seneca Villagers to that of another Black community in downtown New York from the same period and found that a third more Seneca Village children attended school. They concluded that the parents of Seneca Village were more likely middle class, who both valued education and were able to ensure that their children attend school rather than work at a young age.[56]

To the southeast of the Wilson house, archaeologists came upon the shallowly buried original ground surface of the village, which they identified by its soil color and texture, which differed from the layer below. This area was in the backyard space of two other houses. Comparison of artifacts with those of the Wilson house was interesting because of their differences. Artifacts here included a handsome, well-made, large blue-on-white transfer-printed pitcher (figure 5.22), a number of beer bottles, quite a few

FIGURE 5.21
Slate pencil from Seneca Village excavations. This slate pencil was found beneath the floorboards of the Wilson house. Slate pencils were used on slate writing boards by adults and schoolchildren alike.
Qi#210691 SVP

smoking pipes, and a good proportion of the faunal remains recovered from the site as a whole. Many of these objects seemed related to backyard use rather than the ceramics, kitchen equipment, and glass from the Wilson house.

The analysis of materials from the site, including relevant historical records, yielded a number of conclusions. First, and most significant, this was a community of middle-class Black people, based on landowning, the importance of education in the community (seen in census records), and the significance of the moral community to its residents.[57] A few other middle-class Black communities have been identified according to these same criteria in Boston; the Washington area; New Philadelphia, Illinois; Sacramento and West Oakland, California; and Weeksville in Brooklyn. In all these communities, the church was the center of community life, and education was highly valued. However, they varied in important ways, such as men's occupations.[58]

Archaeologists compared the ceramics from the Wilson house to samples of ceramics from two white middle-class New York households from the same time period: the Robsons and the Hirsts, who both lived in Greenwich Village. While the samples were rather small, and all three assemblages contained mainly similar ceramics, there are some interesting differences. First, the Wilsons used more transfer-printed plates, while the two white families used more molded ironstone dishes. Second, while all families had porcelain dishes, only the wealthiest white family had painted porcelain tea wares, perhaps reflecting their cost. Third, the dishes in the Wilson assemblage, although all blue-and-white prints, did not match, which is a pattern that has been described in other assemblages associated with Black people. It has been suggested that this might be a legacy of enslavement, where there were few forms of

FIGURE 5.22
Gothic-shaped ceramic teapot with a printed "Florentine" pattern, made at the Thomas, John, and Joseph Mayer pottery in Burslem, Staffordshire, England, between 1842 and 1855. It was found in a house yard shared by the Webster and Philips families, who also resided in Seneca Village. In the nineteenth century, sharing tea was for many women an important way to form friendships and build a community.
Qi#210415 SVP

self-expression available—the choice of one's own plate might be one.[59] Fourth, the Wilsons had relatively more small bowls than either of the white middle-class families; again, a possible inheritance from African cuisine, which favored soups and stews over steaks and chops. The archaeological analysis of the soil differences among the layered strata also showed that some Seneca Villagers swept their yards, another trait thought to derive from Africa, where the swept yard was an extension of the home.

News about the existence of Seneca Village has been making its way through the contemporary New York City community. Several books, including two for children, a play, two books of poetry, a website suggesting clothing design for Village women, and various other forms of art (paintings, textile, film, exhibits) have begun to tell the story of this community. It is also being incorporated into some New York City school curricula. The Metropolitan Museum of Art created a period room that imagines what a Seneca Village house might look like, had the Village not been destroyed. The existence of middle-class nineteenth-century Black communities is an emerging and important area of investigation. It is hoped that more archaeological research will further enhance the understanding of these communities.

New York City and the Civil War

The American Civil War lasted from 1861 to 1865 and was fought between northern states committed to retaining the Union and southern states that had seceded to form the Confederate States of America so they could preserve the institution of slavery. While many New Yorkers today would assume that New York City would always have been supportive of the Union side and its soldiers (figure 5.23), in fact, in the early stages of the Civil War, many New Yorkers did not want New York City to fight for the Union. Mayor Fernando Wood, for instance, was primarily concerned with the potential economic impact of the war if slavery were abolished. Wood advocated for New York City to become an independent city-state that would remain neutral and could maintain trade with both the Union and the Confederacy.[60] But in 1861, after the Confederacy threatened to disrupt trade and invalidate the millions of dollars in debt Southerners owed New York banks, the New York elite finally became supporters of the Union, if only to ensure their own economic interests. The loss of Confederate markets—and especially those related to the cotton trade—crashed the city's economy, but New York quickly rebounded. During the war, trade from western and midwestern states that had once flowed through the Mississippi and New Orleans to Europe was rerouted through New York. Wartime industries such as shipbuilding and uniform manufacture boomed within the city. This boosted the economy, but it also encouraged some profiteering. Companies such as Brooks Brothers, founded in 1818, won large contracts for manufacturing soldiers' uniforms (figure 5.24). The company was accused of profiteering by charging high fees yet providing uniforms of such poor quality they were said to have dissolved in the rain. This uniform scandal is said to have introduced the modern meaning of the word *shoddy* into the English lexicon.[61]

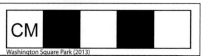

FIGURE 5.23
Smoking pipe made of ball clay found in Washington Square Park during archaeological excavations. The interior is blackened from use. Based upon the hats and uniforms the figures are wearing, the image is likely of three Civil War soldiers, two of whom are shaking hands (Geismar 2013, 14).
Qi#207036 WSP

FIGURE 5.24
This copper-alloy Brooks Brothers button dating
to the second part of the nineteenth century was
found during the 2010 City Hall Park archaeological
excavations. Brooks Brothers was founded in 1818
as Brooks Clothing Store at the corner of Catherine
and Cherry streets in Manhattan.
Qi#122743 CHP

The wealth that poured into New York City during the Civil War was not evenly distributed. Some companies, primarily those involved in manufacturing war supplies, made
vast fortunes. But for most people, these years were very difficult. The working class was
particularly hurt by housing shortages and rising inflation. Many workers fought back,
striking for higher wages and better working conditions. Rather than meeting these
demands, companies brought in other workers to cross the picket lines. The new workers
were often Black people, as in general they had few employment options and were willing
to accept the poor working conditions. Rather than targeting company owners for their
actions, some white workers instead resented Black people for accepting the work.[62]

They were not alone in having negative views about Black people. When Abraham
Lincoln issued the Emancipation Proclamation, which freed more than 3.5 million
Black people, it was met with consternation by many New Yorkers of all classes. Significant individuals from New York governor Horatio Seymour to Samuel F. B. Morse,
the inventor of the telegraph system, opposed abolition. According to them, freeing
enslaved peoples would ensure that the United States could never compete with economies like Brazil that remained dependent on enslaved labor.[63]

In March 1863, Congress passed a national conscription lottery; up until then, the
Union army had been made up of volunteers, including those from New York. The draft
was not well received, especially as wealthy men could pay $300 to buy their way out of
it. On July 11, 1863, the draft came to New York City. The first names were selected without incident. But tension quickly mounted, and just two days later, on July 13, 1863, what
became known as the Draft Riots began.

Groups of European Americans poured out of depressed neighborhoods such as Five
Points. The rioters seemed strategic and coordinated at first, as they worked together to
destroy telegraph poles and railroad tracks. Soon this devolved into mob violence, and they
took to assaulting and often murdering any Black person they came upon. The mob burned
the Colored Orphan Asylum on Fifth Avenue at Forty-Second Street, which was home to
more than two hundred children. Fortunately, most of the children were not there at the time.

The riot lasted for four days and was not quelled until six thousand Union troops came into the city to restore order. At least 119 people died—though the number may have been much higher—and thousands were injured, almost all of them were Black people. There was also extensive property damage: one hundred buildings were burned down, including some owned by abolitionists (figure 5.25), and twice as many damaged. Ultimately, sixty-three people were tried, but very few received any significant sentence.[64] The riots spurred an exodus from the city, including about 20 percent of

FIGURE 5.25
Lamartine Place Historic District, designated in 2009, is on the north side of West Twenty-Ninth Street between Eight and Ninth avenues. Abby and James Sloan Gibbons, prominent abolitionists, lived at 339 West Twenty-Ninth Street. Draft rioters attacked and partially burned down their house because of their known association with the abolitionist movement.
Image: Christopher D. Brazee, LPC.

the Black population. The Draft Riots had many causes. Obviously, racism was primary among them, but blame must also be assigned to poor governmental oversight, insufficient enforcement, and economic inequality.[65]

HOUSING AND SANITATION

After the Civil War ended, veterans and immigrants moved to New York City. Housing was already in high demand, and the influx of new residents caused massive housing shortages. Some areas were particularly densely populated, such as the Fourth Ward (today known as Two Bridges in Lower Manhattan). At the peak of the housing shortage, the Fourth Ward held 290,000 people per square mile.[66] By comparison, today the city's average population density per square mile is 27,000 people; Manila, considered the world's most densely populated city in 2021, has about 119,600 people per square mile.[67]

Not surprisingly, living conditions were squalid. In 1866, New York State established the nation's first comprehensive building code to address the most significant issues. A year later, the Tenement House Law required that all buildings have fire escapes and that all rooms have ventilation, and it instituted a tenant occupancy maximum of how many people could be housed in each unit. It also outlawed all animals except dogs and cats and established that there must be one "water closet" (toilet) per twenty residents; this presupposed that all buildings had access to public water and sewer, which was not always the case.[68]

This last change had a significant impact on historical archaeology. Builders stopped building privies and cisterns, and many property owners closed the ones that existed to meet the new requirements. Usually this meant filling them with household rubbish. Historical archaeologists rely on the material disposed of in privies and cisterns as a time capsule of what life was like for the building's inhabitants. In addition, use of one common household item—the chamber pot—was sharply curtailed. These were used both as an alternative to privies and as a way to avoid a nighttime trip to the privy (figure 5.26). They ranged in form and design from the ultra-simple to nicely decorated. While not frequently used today, some exist, ranging from plastic containers used in hospitals to "potties" commonly used for toilet training.

The 1991–1992 Five Points excavations uncovered many such archaeological features and almost one million artifacts, including those from the cesspool reconfigured into a water closet shown in figure 5.27. In 1864, a tenement was built at 472 Pearl Street in what had been in the rear of the property, and a water closet was placed over this existing eleven-foot-diameter cesspool originally built to drain the sewage of the adjacent tenements. This plumbing fixture may have been periodically flushed using collected rainwater.[69]Unfortunately, practically the entire archaeological assemblage was stored at the World Trade Center and destroyed in the September 11, 2001, terrorist attacks. Some artifacts from the African Burial Ground collection (although not the burials and associated artifacts) were also stored there but amazingly survived. All that now remains of the Five Points collection are the excavation reports and eighteen artifacts that had been on exhibit at the time.[70]

FIGURE 5.26
Brown transfer-printed chamber pot decorated with the "Antiquarian" pattern; these were commonly used before the introduction of indoor plumbing. This chamber pot dates to the mid-nineteenth century. The romantic Antiquarian pattern depicts a grand estate in the background with a Gothic-spired gatehouse in the foreground.
Qi#199545 VCP

In addition to eliminating privies and cisterns, the building code reforms also required that garbage be removed from individual sites and taken to garbage dumps, where it would comingle with thousands of other people's trash. Some archaeological projects have focused on these multifamily sites. For example, the Riverside Project on West End Avenue between Sixtieth and Sixty-First streets on the Upper West Side uncovered fill deposits (figure 5.28) that indicated that the local residents owned Gothic-style ceramics (typical of middle-class homes), used gas lighting, gave their children toys, and displayed other harbingers of "respectability."[71]

In 1865, the Citizens' Association of New York Council of Hygiene and Public Health published the Sanitary Report. It found that 50 to 70 percent of tenement dwellers were sick at any one time, and preventable diseases like smallpox were still prevalent. The report spurred the creation of the Metropolitan Board of Health in 1866, with the

FIGURE 5.27
Cesspool reconfigured with water closet found during the Five Points excavation project.
Photograph by John Milner Associates Inc, "Tales of Five Points: Working Class Life in Nineteenth-Century New York," Vol. I prepared for Edwards and Kelcey Engineers, Inc. and the General Services Administration.

FIGURE 5.28
Excavation photograph showing layers of fill, sand, and older sand from the Riverside Project.
Photograph by Geoarchaeology Research Associates.

power to order people to hospitals and order landowners to improve conditions, such as cleaning filth from backyards. They were also empowered to rid streets of filth and to improve the water supply.[72]

POSTWAR DEVELOPMENT BOOM AND CORRUPTION

After the Civil War, the city embarked on an intense period of development intended to address the continually expanding city. William M. "Boss" Tweed—formerly elected to the U.S. House of Representatives and later to the New York State Senate—was a notorious politician and at one point the third largest landowner in the city, before he was convicted for embezzling immense amounts of money from the city. He promoted the expansion of the urban core of New York from Lower Manhattan and appointed engineers to oversee the installation of public sewers, water lines, and roads throughout the Upper East Side, Harlem, and the Upper West Side, to ensure that the developing city was well planned. But Tweed was also known for major corruption. Arguably the best-known example was the construction of the New York County Courthouse at 52 Chambers Street, now known as the Tweed Courthouse (figure 5.29). This project

FIGURE 5.29
The Tweed Courthouse. New York County Courthouse, built from 1861 to 1881 and designed by, architects Thomas Little, John Kellum, and Leopold Eidlitz. A New York City landmark, it is located at 52 Chambers Street in Manhattan.
Photograph by Amanda Sutphin, LPC.

included fraudulent bills from almost all the contractors involved. It was estimated that $9,000,000 (equivalent to about $173,000,000 today) was lost to corruption. Construction began in 1861, and the building was completed in 1881, during which time Tweed was convicted for forgery and larceny.

TWEED COURTHOUSE ARCHAEOLOGY

In 1999, the City of New York began to renovate the Tweed Courthouse. Because it is a New York City landmark and also within the African Burial Ground and the Commons Historic District, archaeology was required. Archaeologists uncovered intact burials likely associated with the First Almshouse, which stood there from 1736 to 1797, and Bridewell prison, which was there from 1775 to 1838. They also found archaeological features likely associated with the Second Almshouse (1797–1857) and British barracks (1757–1790).[73]

The archaeologists found no features associated with the construction of the Tweed Courthouse, such as distinctive builder's trenches that might contain artifacts from the period of construction. But the archaeologists did uncover many interesting artifacts

FIGURE 5.30
Jacob J. Teufel & Bro clinical thermometer.
This medical-equipment company was based in
Philadelphia in the second half of the nineteenth
century. The thermometer was found during the
Tweed Courthouse reconstruction excavations and
may be related to the Second Almshouse.
Qi#4122 CHP

such as the Jacob J. Teufel & Bro clinical thermometer (figure 5.30) likely used by someone in the Second Almshouse. More significantly—as in the City Hall Park reconstruction archaeological project (discussed in chapter 3)—they found ossuary-like deposits in which they uncovered concentrations of human remains. These remains were mainly partial segments of skeletons; in general, the groupings did not include the typically smaller and more fragile bones of the body. This indicates that the bones were moved from where they had been originally interred after the bodies had decayed to skeletal remains, and that the movers had taken only the recognizably human bones.[74] Given that this relocation took place sometime after the original interments, the archaeologists surmise this occurred while the Tweed Courthouse was being constructed. No records have been found about the discovery and movement of the remains, so perhaps the workers took this removal upon themselves. The archaeological projects protected intact burials in place and disinterred fragmentary remains for subsequent study.[75] Those remains were later reinterred in the northeast corner of City Hall Park in 2010 and 2013.

PUBLIC ENGINEERING PROJECTS

After the Civil War, the city engineers laid out development plots, expanding the grid in accordance with the Commissioner's Plan of 1811 to the Upper East Side, Harlem, and the Upper West Side, and defined places for schools, parks, and hospitals. They also considered public transportation and ensured that public water and sewers would be available. Workers uncovered traces of New York's earlier history that would be highly valued by archaeologists today, including a graveyard for British soldiers that was uncovered at 104th Street and Lexington Avenue, and tore down structures such as the Beekman Mansion on East Fifty-First Street, built in 1763.[76]

Arguably the greatest engineering project of this period was the construction of the Brooklyn Bridge (a New York City landmark). Prior to its construction, about fifty million people a year traveled between Manhattan and Brooklyn by ferry.[77] The bridge design challenged the technology of the era: it had to be tall enough for tall ships to sail under it and strong enough to withstand the East River currents. It also had to withstand political opposition. Powerful uptown Manhattan landowners did not want the bridge to be built, because they thought Brooklyn neighborhoods would then compete with their development sites in Manhattan. This is exactly what happened: Brooklyn neighborhoods near the bridge experienced a development boom after the bridge was finished.

One such neighborhood includes part of what is now Brooklyn Bridge Park. It was dominated by the Empire Stores, 53–83 Water Street, within the Fulton Ferry Historic District (figure 5.31), built in 1870 and 1885 for the general storage of coffee, sugar, molasses, animal hides, and grain imported by cargo ship from Cuba, South America, and Africa. In 1870, this part of Brooklyn was so densely developed by tall warehouses that it was known as the walled city.[78] Archaeological excavations completed at this site in 1978 and 1979 revealed that the area had been developed through multiple stages of landfilling, beginning in the eighteenth century.[79]

FIGURE 5.31
The Brooklyn Bridge in the background, behind the Empire Stores in Brooklyn Bridge Park.
Photograph by Amanda Sutphin, LPC.

SKYSCRAPERS

Another important advancement in the 1870s and 1880s was the skyscraper, which permitted much denser development than other types of architecture. Skyscrapers relied upon several inventions, including reliable passenger elevators, iron floor beams, "fireproof" construction, and metal framing. The first skyscrapers were commercial and usually no more than twenty stories tall, which is considerably shorter than today's skyscrapers. They were largely clustered on Park Row near City Hall Park, where the eighteen-story Manhattan Life Insurance Company Building (64–66 Broadway, now demolished) is credited with being the first skyscraper.[80] The Corbin Building, located at 11 John Street and a New York City landmark, was constructed around 1888 and is eight-and-a-half stories tall. Although it has the hallmarks of a traditional skyscraper, because it has masonry bearing walls it is classified as a transitional building.[81] In 2009, during work to create a new subway entrance at Fulton Street Station, workers uncovered a brick shaft feature underneath a portion of the Corbin Building (figure 5.32).

FIGURE 5.32
1857 Perris Map with overlay of well location and Corbin Building lot (*yellow highlight*). This insurance map includes the outlines of all standing structures and what they were made of as well as their addresses. Archaeologists use atlases like this one to document site changes through time in order to assess archaeological potential.
Image by AKRF, Inc., 2010 created for NYCT.

Because of the challenging location and condition of the discovery, only limited archaeological analysis was possible; it indicated that it had been a late-eighteenth- to early-nineteenth-century public well, crucial to local residents in a city before running water was available for most households.[82]

BURIAL GROUNDS IN THE NINETEENTH CENTURY

From the colonial era on into the early nineteenth century, burial grounds were located in the center of the settlement, essential reminders that death is always present. But by the mid-nineteenth century, several beliefs merged to ensure that burial grounds were relocated to the city's hinterlands. One was that burial grounds were injurious to public health because people thought, in a time before there was a widespread understanding of germ theory, that burial grounds released miasmas of poisonous gas that caused disease.[83] Another was that it was more respectful to the dead to have them at a remove from the dirty, crowded city. And the third consideration was simply that land values increased exponentially in this period.

One of the United States' first rural cemeteries was Green-Wood Cemetery (figure 5.33), which was founded in 1838 in what is today Greenwood Heights, Brooklyn, and contains several designated resources. Like other cemeteries that were part of the rural cemetery movement, it was deliberately designed to be a beautiful, serene oasis. More than half a million people per year visited Green-Wood in the early 1860s, making it second only to Niagara Falls as the most visited site in the United States.[84] Then there is Woodlawn Cemetery in the Bronx, founded in 1863, which contains mausoleums that interred some of the wealthiest New Yorkers of that era and were designed by some of the greatest architects of the day, including McKim, Meade, and White, and Carrere and Hastings. Many scholars have argued that the popularity of these sites led to the development of large urban parks such as Prospect Park in Brooklyn.

As burial ground locations shifted from inside the city to its hinterland, the city passed multiple laws banning burials in densely developed areas. People from all classes were interred in new burial grounds outside the settled areas, ranging from places like Green-Wood to the city's potter's field, which is still in use on Hart Island. Many of the city's burial sites were subsequently redeveloped, and some still contain human remains. Today when Landmarks' archaeologists review proposed development projects, the agency considers whether the area was ever a burial ground. If it was, that triggers in-depth research to learn what may have happened to the burial ground and whether there is a descendant group connected to those burials.

FIGURE 5.33
Green-Wood Cemetery Gate, a New York City Landmark. Designed by Richard Upjohn and Sons and completed in 1865.
Photograph by LPC.

DEVELOPMENT OF ARCHAEOLOGY IN NEW YORK CITY

Arguably the first archaeological work in the United States was completed by Thomas Jefferson when he oversaw the excavation of an Indigenous Peoples' burial mound on his estate in Virginia. However, it was not until the late nineteenth century that archaeology became a profession, largely because of people like Englishman William Flinders Petrie, often called the "father of archaeology." Those early professionals tended to focus their attention on the Near East, Egypt, and Ancient Greece and Rome. In the early twentieth century, many archaeologists lived in New York and worked for city institutions such as the Metropolitan Museum of Art or the Brooklyn Museum of Art but directed their professional efforts to other parts of the world.

One of the earliest archaeological projects within New York City was conducted by George Hubbard Pepper in 1893 for the American Museum of Natural History. He excavated within what is now the Aakawaxung Munahanung (Island Protected from the Wind) Archaeological Site, a New York City landmark located in Conference House Park in Tottenville, Staten Island (see chapter 1).[85]

Archaeological Field Schools

Dr. H. Arthur Bankoff

Today there are many archaeologists who live and work in New York City. While some of them work for the city's universities and museums and study other parts of the world, others, such as the authors of this book, focus on New York City. To become an archaeologist, one must participate in archaeological field schools that give practical experience to those who wish to have more than a theoretical grasp of archaeology (figure 5.34). Usually run by universities during the summers, they provide the budding archaeologist and interested student with a chance to actually "do archaeology" or "get one's hands dirty." Field schools may be given in many places, from urban parks or empty lots to Classical ruins or prehistoric monuments. Often students take the field school for college credit, opting to spend some time outdoors rather than in a summer-school classroom. Field schools may be part of a faculty research project, lowering labor costs by using unpaid labor, or partially funded by student fees. A good field school gives solid training in many phases of a project, from research design through artifact conservation and exhibit preparation.

Archaeology is a team endeavor. Students usually dig in small groups of four to six, supervised by a more experienced person, often a graduate student or a faculty member. They quickly find out that field archaeology demands the skills of a construction worker (moving heavy rocks, digging with a pick or shovel) and

FIGURE 5.34
2010 Archaeological Field School, H. Arthur Bankoff with Total Station.
Photograph by Wayne Powell.

a gardener (cleaning delicate contexts with a brush and trowel). It also requires
the attention to detail of an artist or an engineer (surveying, mapping a trench,
or drawing artifacts). And of course, it helps to have the patience of a saint and a
sense of humor. I have directed field schools both in New York and abroad for the
past forty-five years. We have dug in locations as far apart as New York and Israel.

We have dug in every borough except Queens. In all these projects, I was fortunate to have students to instruct and to learn from. For almost a decade, Erasmus Hall High School students took the Brooklyn College Archaeological Field School for college credit. The field schools in New York were conceived as opportunities for a true archaeological experience that cost no more than a subway fare. We are not training them to be professional archaeologists as much as giving them some appreciation of what an archaeologist knows and does (and what gets reported in the news).

Field schools arise for different reasons. Work at the Lott House in Brooklyn (a New York City landmark) was the result of the city's acquisition of the Lott property, while work at the Van Cortlandt House in the Bronx occurred because its basement flooded and they had to excavate to install new drains.

Not every excavation was equally productive of artifacts. A summer digging at Fort Greene Park in Brooklyn produced only a bare handful of objects, while excavations at Van Cortlandt turned up thousands of artifacts. Imagine the surprise when, while looking for the location of a former barn at Van Cortlandt, we found instead two stone-lined root cellars each filled with nineteenth-century ceramics and other artifacts, probably thrown there when the Van Cortlandts moved to their estate up the Hudson at Phillipsburg. It was like diving in the dumpster of an elite New York family: dinnerware, wine bottles, even a set of false teeth. Several summers of Brooklyn College field schools at the Lott House in Marine Park exposed the lifestyle of Brooklyn Dutch farmers. We found German nineteenth-century doll heads, which attested to the local family's contacts with the wider world. Another surprise was the discovery of several unexpected rooms within the Lott House itself. Behind a closet on the second floor was a small hidden space. The wallpaper that concealed this small room was backed by newspaper dating to the 1850s, which lent credence to the Lotts' oral history that they were a stop on the Underground Railroad. Beneath the floorboards of a room above the kitchen, in the oldest part of the house, we found corncobs in a cross-shaped pattern known (from other sites and inscribed artifacts) to be ritually significant to West African peoples. Most likely they were hidden in this attic room by enslaved Africans at the Lott farm. Different generations of the Lott family clearly had very different views about slavery.

But whether one found things or not, the practical aspects of the field schools were the same. The problems and joys of intensely investigating a small piece of the past transcended the dearth or abundance of finds. One of the first things that a field school stresses is that archaeologists dig for information, not for artifacts. Archaeology is basically destructive. In most cases, at its end it leaves an empty hole in the ground (which then has to be backfilled). It is rewarding and fun to find things, especially lovely and sometimes valuable things, but these are but means to an end: information about the lives of people in the past. This information is as fragile as the artifacts, easily lost through a careless move or poor record keeping, and more precious than any object. Field school participants usually find that the joy of archaeology is not just holding the past in one's hand but solving the riddles of its meaning. Archaeology is as much an intellectual exercise as a physical one.

CONSOLIDATION

On January 1, 1898, the City of New York was incorporated to include its current boundaries, famously uniting the City of New York with the City of Brooklyn and the smaller communities of western Queens, Staten Island, and the east Bronx. At the time, New York City was the largest city in the United States, and Brooklyn the second largest (figure 5.35).

There were three motivations behind consolidation. One was a long-standing effort by merchants to centralize control of New York's harbor and the development of associated railroads, shipping, and utilities. The second was that enlarging New York City meant more city services and lower taxes for residents, because it would increase the tax base to include corporations and businesses in Manhattan. The third, and most essential argument for Brooklynites, was that the City of Brooklyn—which pumped ninety-four million gallons of water a day from Long Island—was running out of water and had neither the finances nor the political capital to gain access to more. New York City, however, through the Croton Aqueduct (initially completed in 1842, with the New Croton Aqueduct completed in 1890) had enough water to supply itself, the City of Brooklyn, and all the other communities in consolidation.[86]

On that day of unification in 1898, New York City suddenly had a population of 3.4 million people, making it the largest North American city. It was twice the size of the next largest city at the time, Chicago, which had a population of 1.7 million.[87]

Greater New York has grown and expanded through massive building projects, the world's largest subway system (as measured by number of stations), and the construction of super-tall buildings. In each era, New York City's population has grown in size and become more diverse; structures and infrastructure have emerged and been replaced; visitors from all over the world have come to see the sights. Yet through it all, New Yorkers continue to hold essential truths about the city: wonderful things from one's youth have disappeared, everything is too expensive and too crowded—and yet, there is no better place to be.

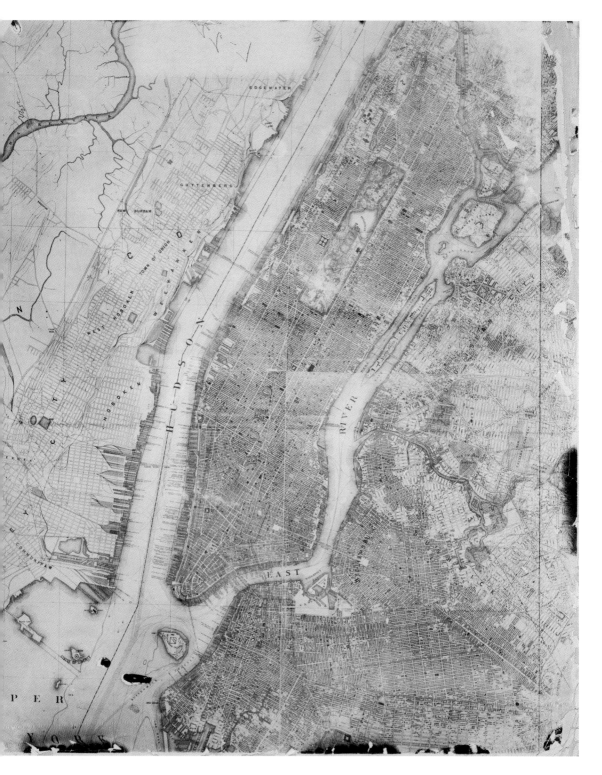

FIGURE 5.35

Portion of the Risse Map, "General Map of the City of New York, Boroughs of Manhattan, Brooklyn, Bronx, Queens, and Richmond, New York, Board of Public Improvements," created in 1900 to map the newly consolidated City of New York.

Lionel Pincus and Princess Firyal Map Division, The New York Public Library. New York Public Library Digital Collections.

Riverdale Park (1989)

Stadt Huys Block (1987)

South Ferry Terminal Project (2012) – Battery Wall

Stadt Huys Block (1987)

CONCLUSION

When we consider the enormity and complexity of New York City today, it is hard to imagine that just four hundred years ago it was a small European colonial port community of about 250 people. Its residents, clustered together, depended on each other to survive. They also counted on help from the Indigenous Peoples who had lived in the area long before any Europeans arrived. Back then, the land was somewhat hilly, spotted with rich marshes and swamps, an environment that supported many kinds of birds, animals, plants, and humans. When European settlers arrived, they first adapted to local conditions and then began to change them, reworking the environment many times. The same terrain that supported a few hundred settlers would come to support thousands of residents after the colonial period, tens of thousands as America flourished, and millions today.

The story of the people who have made this area home has been told here through artifacts from the New York City Archaeological Repository: The Nan A. Rothschild Research Center (figure C.1). Archaeology reveals these changes in the land, the

FIGURE C.1

Figure C.1. Examples of Artifacts from the NYC Archaeological Repository: The Nan A. Rothschild Research Center. *Clockwise from top left*:
Chert Lamoka Side-Notched Projectile Point, Riverdale Park Archaeological Project, Qi#213111
New York Redware Mug, Stadt Huys Project, Qi#202412
Triangular-Mouthed Stoneware Crucible, 7 Hanover Square, Qi#209646
Bone Syringe, Beekman Street, Qi#210413
Marshall & Co. Green Glass Soda Water Bottle, Stadt Huys Project, Qi#203992
Gothic Patterned Ironstone Plate, Seneca Village, Qi#210540
Painted Pearlware Punch Bowl, South Ferry Project, Qi#206613
Tin-Glazed Earthenware Wall Tile, South Ferry Project, Qi#108135

people, and their culture. It is the "ground truth" of history. The collections in this volume cover at least fourteen thousand years of New York City prehistory and a few hundred years of European settlement. They are the result of more than a hundred years of archaeology, and they tell the city's story as a site and as part of a broader landscape, one connected to its own hinterland and to countries across the ocean. Archaeological collections can show us things that are not available in documentary sources, especially glimpses of mundane, workaday life. Artifacts reveal how people of the past solved common problems, from the most basic ones, like getting, storing, and preparing food and constructing homes, to the advanced ones, like creating communal spaces, protecting themselves against enemies, and regulating life according to laws and shared principles.

Beginning with the long period before European colonization, this book considered certain consistent themes that each successive population—Indigenous Peoples, Dutch, British, and American—have addressed. How will we use the land? What is the best way to make a living? In what kinds of communities will we live? How shall we govern ourselves? How shall we treat the people we live among as well as foreigners? With whom shall we trade and wage war?

Archaeology does not provide every answer, but it can reveal at least something about all of these. It is especially useful in illuminating cultural diversity, which is perhaps more distinctive of New York's character than of any other American city. Indigenous groups descended from thousands of years of Indigenous people were the land's first occupants, but after them came a variety of European peoples, beginning with different groups from the United Provinces (now known as the Netherlands) and subsequent waves of British and Irish. These settlers brought, increasingly over the seventeenth and eighteenth centuries, enslaved Africans, who were forced to come. All of these groups have left the signatures of their presence in material culture and land use. For instance, the lower Manhattan street grid is a relic of the Dutch period. The pottery archaeologists have found are remnants of cultures from the Indigenous Peoples to the Chinese. We see the presence of some groups even etched on the landscape. The Bronx and northern Manhattan, for instance, were once covered by forests. Today those lands, as well as the rest of the city, are the site of houses, skyscrapers, malls, hospitals, and offices.

Economic forces shaped the landscape. Maps made first by Europeans and then by Americans bear witness to these changes. And even though maps are documents produced to demonstrate control of the land, to repress minority representation, or to express a particular point of view, we can use them alongside other documents such as censuses and tax lists. They show how the town expanded under the Dutch and the English, up to and beyond the northern fortification that we now mark as Wall Street. The grid plan of 1811 and the Erie Canal of 1825 each changed the city; the latter made New York City the dominant port of the United States. With the exploding population, feeding the city also became more complex. Backyard gardens were eliminated, markets sprang up, and by the mid-eighteenth century, urban residents changed their diets to include bigger fish, such as cod, and more poultry. Food imports appeared, and sugar took its place as the dominant local and exportable product.

New York, with its bounteous lands and thriving economy, attracted many kinds of immigrants. Skilled craftsmen and laborers alike arrived through the seventeenth to nineteenth centuries. The mid-nineteenth century especially brought waves of Irish immigrants. Here, archaeologically recovered materials can sometimes offer evidence of ethnicity. Evidence of social class is more often visible in people's uses of ceramics. Do affluent residents simply have more of the same objects as poorer folk, such as more dishes? Or do they have distinctive wares in their homes? Archaeology can answer this: the assemblage from the Van Cortlandt family of the nineteenth-century Bronx contained a range of serving vessels not found in poorer homes. Evidence from the many thousands of enslaved Africans who once lived in the city may best be seen in the labor they were required to do, constructing New York's streets, wharves, and defenses such as the Battery. Human remains from the African Burial Ground National Monument evidence this labor in skeletal alterations from muscle attachments.[1] This and the other African burial grounds that remain in the city are important memorials.

This book has touched upon the lives of many people. Archaeology requires teams and the hard work of collaborators, from excavators to researchers to lab analysts. It is not just digging in the ground; it also requires analysis and interpretation to create meaning from what we have recovered. And the work does not end even there. As new research questions and new analytic techniques emerge, we return again and again to old artifacts to look at them anew. Archaeological deposits still remain throughout the city, buried under the streets, and archaeological research will one day find them, shedding new light upon the past and bringing us close to the lives of past New Yorkers.

We cannot know now what future archaeological research will reveal. But we do know it will likely build on what is happening right now. We can imagine a time when community-informed archaeology will become more common, with more intense collaboration among archaeologists, communities, and historians. Archaeology is particularly useful in opening up the history of groups poorly represented in documents, giving voice to those whose past is absent or barely present in the archives. This commitment to underrepresented narratives—to protect, support, and engage with stories of the city's diversity, past and present—is important; in fact, it may be one of contemporary archaeology's most significant contributions. This work includes Indigenous Peoples, who may appear to some to have been long gone from New York City but in fact are still here and are still connected. This same commitment is readily seen in work that began when the African Burial Ground was excavated in 1991. That rediscovery energized many to understand the lives and importance of enslaved peoples, and why their contributions to the emerging city have been ignored, forgotten, and dismissed. Since 1991, several other African burial grounds have been identified throughout the city.

FIGURE C.2
NYC Archaeological Repository: The Nan A. Rothschild Research Center interior. Dr. Arthur Bankoff and Dr. Jessica Striebel MacLean sharing some of the Repository highlights with visitors.
Photograph by Kait Ebinger.

But not all the work of archaeology is excavation and identification. There is also research into existing artifacts and sites (see figure C.2), and the Repository offers two important possibilities to that end. First, it allows the public to digitally access the city's collections and to understand this past for themselves. And, second, it provides data to foster and answer new questions that arise about the past. Many of the stories in this book were realized at the time of discovery, but some were not revealed until much later, when archaeological techniques and methodology had evolved to meet them.

The Repository and other collections like it are essential to this endeavor. The artifacts in the Repository are not "museum pieces" frozen in time. Rather they can respond to each new question asked of them, revealing something we did not know before, often again and again. Since the Repository opened its doors in 2014, many research projects have been undertaken. One study examined a collection of early-nineteenth-century ceramics to assess the formation of an American identity in the aftermath of the American Revolution.[2] Another used oxygen isotope analysis on pig bones to reveal that upper-class New Yorkers imported pork whereas poorer New Yorkers ate pork from pigs that roamed the city and ate its garbage.[3] Another study, underway at the time of this writing, is analyzing oyster shells to understand the tremendous environmental changes in the city's waterways. There are others, and many more lie ahead of us.

New York City is not alone in its wealth of urban archaeological sites and collections, although there are few repositories as comprehensive as New York's. A number of research projects have examined urban formations using cross-city comparisons. New techniques and research questions are constantly emerging. Even today, New York's vitality and commerce are creating the archaeological sites of the future. The artifacts tie us to the unbroken history of occupation in the city for the past fourteen thousand years. They allow us to understand the ways New York differs from other cities. They are a testimony to its unique character. Each artifact in the Repository contains part of the New York story. Archaeology lets us hear that story.

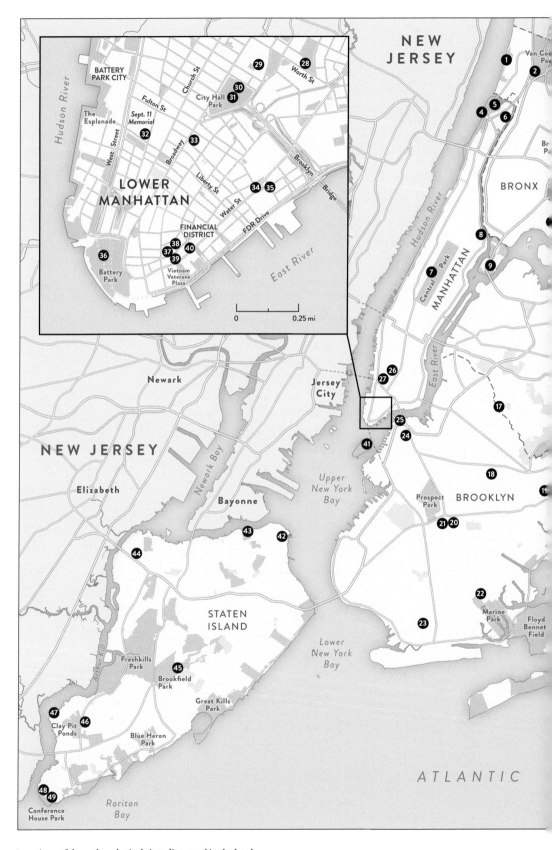

Locations of the archaeological sites discussed in the book

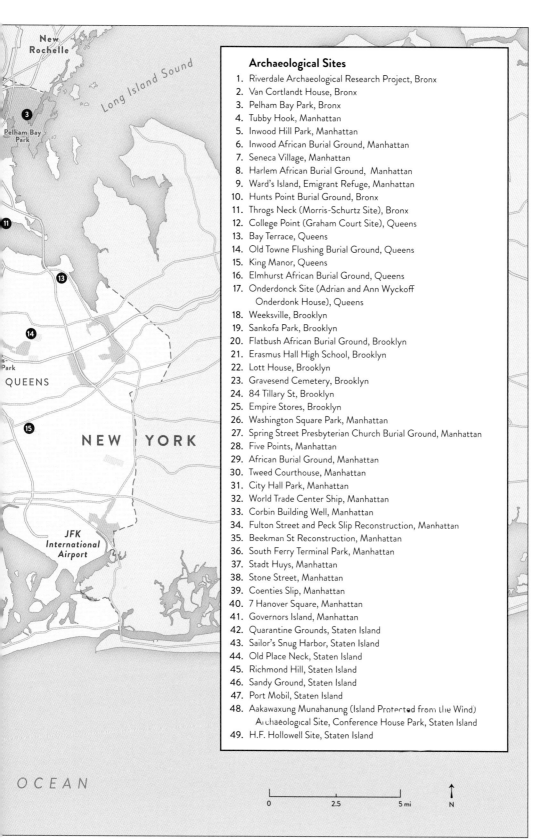

Archaeological Sites

1. Riverdale Archaeological Research Project, Bronx
2. Van Cortlandt House, Bronx
3. Pelham Bay Park, Bronx
4. Tubby Hook, Manhattan
5. Inwood Hill Park, Manhattan
6. Inwood African Burial Ground, Manhattan
7. Seneca Village, Manhattan
8. Harlem African Burial Ground, Manhattan
9. Ward's Island, Emigrant Refuge, Manhattan
10. Hunts Point Burial Ground, Bronx
11. Throgs Neck (Morris-Schurtz Site), Bronx
12. College Point (Graham Court Site), Queens
13. Bay Terrace, Queens
14. Old Towne Flushing Burial Ground, Queens
15. King Manor, Queens
16. Elmhurst African Burial Ground, Queens
17. Onderdonck Site (Adrian and Ann Wyckoff
    Onderdonk House), Queens
18. Weeksville, Brooklyn
19. Sankofa Park, Brooklyn
20. Flatbush African Burial Ground, Brooklyn
21. Erasmus Hall High School, Brooklyn
22. Lott House, Brooklyn
23. Gravesend Cemetery, Brooklyn
24. 84 Tillary St, Brooklyn
25. Empire Stores, Brooklyn
26. Washington Square Park, Manhattan
27. Spring Street Presbyterian Church Burial Ground, Manhattan
28. Five Points, Manhattan
29. African Burial Ground, Manhattan
30. Tweed Courthouse, Manhattan
31. City Hall Park, Manhattan
32. World Trade Center Ship, Manhattan
33. Corbin Building Well, Manhattan
34. Fulton Street and Peck Slip Reconstruction, Manhattan
35. Beekman St Reconstruction, Manhattan
36. South Ferry Terminal Park, Manhattan
37. Stadt Huys, Manhattan
38. Stone Street, Manhattan
39. Coenties Slip, Manhattan
40. 7 Hanover Square, Manhattan
41. Governors Island, Manhattan
42. Quarantine Grounds, Staten Island
43. Sailor's Snug Harbor, Staten Island
44. Old Place Neck, Staten Island
45. Richmond Hill, Staten Island
46. Sandy Ground, Staten Island
47. Port Mobil, Staten Island
48. Aakawaxung Munahanung (Island Protected from the Wind)
    Archaeological Site, Conference House Park, Staten Island
49. H.F. Hollowell Site, Staten Island

APPENDIX A

The New York City Landmarks and Historic Districts Discussed in the Book

Designated New York City landmarks and historic districts discussed in the book are presented here in alphabetical order. All designation reports are available through the Landmarks Preservation Commission's website.

Landmark name	Landmark address	Date of construction	Architect(s) or builder(s)	Borough	Date designated
Aakawaxung Munahanung (Island Protected from the Wind) Archaeological Site, LP-2648	298 Satterlee Street	Associated with over 8,000 years of occupation by Indigenous Peoples.	N/A	Staten Island	June 22, 2021
African Burial Ground and the Commons Historic District, LP-1901	Multiple blocks in the Civic Center	Burial Ground in use by 1713	N/A	Manhattan	February 25, 1993
American Museum of Natural History, LP-0282	Central Park West at West 77 Street	1874–1877; 1889–1900; 1906–1908; 1922–1924; 1931–1935; 1931–1933; 1935	Vaux & Mould (1874–1877); Cady, Berg & See (1906–1908); Trowbridge & Livingston (1922–1924; 1935); John Russell Pope (1931–1935)	Manhattan	August 24, 1967

(*continued*)

Landmark name	Landmark address	Date of construction	Architect(s) or builder(s)	Borough	Date designated
Billiou-Stillwell-Perine House, LP-0380	1476 Richmond Road	c. 1679; additions 1700, 1750, 1790, 1830	Unknown	Staten Island	February 28, 1967
565 and 569 Bloomingdale Road Cottages, LP-2415 (within Sandy Ground)	565 and 569 Bloomingdale Road	c. 1887 and 1898	Unknown	Staten Island	February 1, 2011
Brooklyn Bridge, LP-0098	Spanning the East River	1867–1883	John A. Roebling, Emily Roebling and Washington A. Roebling	Manhattan and Brooklyn	August 24, 1967
Brooklyn Institute of Arts and Sciences (Brooklyn Museum), LP-0155	Eastern Parkway at Washington Avenue	1894; altered 1936	McKim, Meade & White	Brooklyn	March 15, 1966
Bowne House, LP-0143	37-01 Bowne Street	1661; additions 1680, 1691; altered 1830	Unknown	Queens	February 15, 1966
Castle Clinton, LP-0029	Battery Park	1807	John McComb, Jr.	Manhattan	November 23, 1965
Central Park Scenic Landmark, LP-0851	5th Avenue to Central Park West and West 55th to West 110th Street	1858	Frederick Law Olmsted and Calvert Vaux	Manhattan	April 16, 1974
City Hall, LP-0080	City Hall Park	1802–1811	Joseph-Francois Mangin and John McComb, Jr.	Manhattan	February 1, 1966
Reverend Isaac Coleman and Rebecca Gray Coleman House, LP-2414 (within Sandy Ground)	1482 Woodrow Road	Before 1859	Unknown	Staten Island	February 1, 2011

Landmark name	Landmark address	Date of construction	Architect(s) or builder(s)	Borough	Date designated
Conference House, LP-0393	7455 Hylan Boulevard	c. 1675	Unknown	Staten Island	February 28, 1967
Corbin Building, LP-2569	11 John Street	1888–1889	Francis H. Kimball	Manhattan	June 23, 2015
Cubberly-Britton Cottage, LP-0942	3737 Richmond Avenue	c. 1670; additions c. 1700 and c. 1750	Unknown	Staten Island	November 9, 1976
Dyckman House, LP-0309	Broadway between 204th and 207th streets	c. 1783	Unknown	Manhattan	July 12, 1967
Ellis Island Historic District, LP-1902	Ellis Island	1880s–1930s	Boring & Tilton, under supervision of James Knox Taylor	Manhattan	November 16, 1993
Empire State Building, LP-2000	350 5th Avenue	1930–1931	Shreve, Lamb & Harmon	Manhattan	May 19, 1981
Erasmus Hall High School, LP-2130	899-925 Flatbush Avenue	1905–1906, 1909–1911, 1924–1925, 1939–1940	C. B. J. Synder, William Gompert, Eric Kebbon, Superintendents of School Buildings for the New York City Board of Education	Brooklyn	June 24, 2003
United States Custom House (Federal Hall National Memorial), LP-0047	28 Wall Street	1834–1842	Town & Davis; Samuel Thompson; William Ross and John Frazee	Manhattan	December 21, 1965
Flatbush District No. 1 School, LP-2285	2274 Church Avenue	1878; addition c. 1890–1894	John Y. Culyer	Brooklyn	November 20, 2007

(continued)

Landmark name	Landmark address	Date of construction	Architect(s) or builder(s)	Borough	Date designated
Flatbush Dutch Reformed Church, Expanded Site, LP-0170E	866 and 890 Flatbush Avenue	1793–1798 (no. 866); 1922–1924 (no. 890)	Thomas Fardon (no. 866); Meyer & Mathieu (no. 890)	Brooklyn	January 9, 1979; amendment to the designation of March 15, 1966
Fort Greene Historic District, LP-0973	Many blocks in Fort Greene	Primarily nineteenth century	Multiple	Brooklyn	September 26, 1978
Friends Meeting House, LP-0141	137-16 Northern Boulevard	Built in 1694; altered 1716–1719.	Unknown	Queens	August 18, 1970
Fulton Ferry Historic District, LP-0956	On the East River below the Brooklyn Bridge	Primarily late nineteenth century	Multiple	Brooklyn	June 28, 1977
Governors Island Historic District, LP-1946	North side of Governors Island	Eighteenth century–1930s	Multiple	Manhattan	June 18, 1996
Greenwich Village Historic District, LP-0489 (includes Washington Square Park)	Many blocks within Greenwich Village	Primarily nineteenth century	Multiple	Manhattan	April 29, 1969
Green-Wood Cemetery Gate, LP-0149	5th Avenue at 25th Street	1861–1865	Richard M. Upjohn & Son	Brooklyn	April 19, 1966
Fort Hamilton Parkway Entrance and Green-Wood Cemetery Chapel, Green-Wood Cemetery, LP-1233	500 25th Street	1876–1877 (parkway entrance); 1911–1913 (chapel)	Richard Mitchell Upjohn (parkway entrance); Warren & Wetmore (chapel)	Brooklyn	April 12, 2016

Landmark name	Landmark address	Date of construction	Architect(s) or builder(s)	Borough	Date designated
Havemeyers & Elder Filter, Pan and Finishing House (later known as the American Sugar Refining Company and the Domino Sugar Refinery), LP-2268	292-314 Kent Avenue	1881–1884	Theodore A. Havemeyer with Thomas Winslow and J. E. James	Brooklyn	September 25, 2007
Houses on Hunterfly Road, LP-0769; LP-0729; LP-0730; LP-0731; LP-0732; LP-0733	1698–1708 Bergen Street	c. 1830	Unknown	Brooklyn	August 18, 1970
Lamartine Place Historic District, LP-2324	West 29th Street between 8th and 9th avenues	Mid-nineteenth century	Unknown	Manhattan	October 13, 2009
Lent Homestead, LP-0135	78–03 19th Road	c. 1729	Unknown	Queens	March 15, 1966
Hendrick I. Lott House, LP-1705	1940 East 36th Street	1720; addition 1800	Unknown	Brooklyn	October 3, 1989

(continued)

Landmark name	Landmark address	Date of construction	Architect(s) or builder(s)	Borough	Date designated
Metropolitan Museum of Art, LP-0410	1000 5th Avenue	1880–1894; additions 1902, 1911, 1913, 1916, 1926, 1956, 1965	Calvert Vaux and Jacob Wrey Mould; early wings by Thomas Weston and Arthur Tuckerman; Central Pavilion by Richard Morris Hunt and R. H. Hunt; additions on Fifth Avenue by McKim, Mead & White	Manhattan	June 9, 1967
New York Courthouse (also known as Tweed Courthouse), LP-1437	52 Chambers Street	1861–1881	Thomas Little, John Kellum and Leopold Eidlitz	Manhattan	October 16, 1984
New-York Historical Society, LP-0281	170 Central Park West	1903–1908; addition 1937–1938	York & Sawyer (1903–1908); Walker & Gillette (1937–1938)	Manhattan	July 19, 1966
New York Public Library, Astor, Lenox and Tilden Foundations LP-0246	476 5th Avenue	1898–1911	Carrere & Hastings	Manhattan	January 11, 1967
New York Stock Exchange, LP-1529	8–18 Broad Street	1901–1903	George B. Post	Manhattan	July 9, 1985
New Utrecht Reformed Dutch Church Cemetery, LP-1978	8401–8427 16th Avenue; 1602–1622 84th Street; 1601–1621 85th Street	Established c. 1653–1654	N/A	Brooklyn	January 13, 1998

Landmark name	Landmark address	Date of construction	Architect(s) or builder(s)	Borough	Date designated
Old Gravesend Cemetery, LP-0921	Gravesend Neck Road at McDonald Avenue	First burial in the mid-seventeenth century	N/A	Brooklyn	March 23, 1976
Prospect Park Scenic Landmark, LP-0901	Bounded by Prospect Park West, Flatbush Avenue, Ocean Avenue, Parkside Avenue, and Prospect Park SW	1866–1873	Frederick Law Olmsted and Calvert Vaux	Brooklyn	November 25, 1975
Reformed Church on Staten Island, Sunday School Building, and Cemetery, LP-2384	54 Port Richmond Avenue	Cemetery in use by 1704; 1844 (church); 1898 (Sunday school)	James G. Burger (1844); Oscar S. Teale (1898)	Staten Island	March 23, 2010
Rossville A.M.E. Zion Church, LP-2416 (within Sandy Ground)	584 Bloomingdale Road	1897	Andrew Abrams (builder)	Staten Island	February 1, 2011
Rossville A.M.E. Zion Church Cemetery, LP-1399 (within Sandy Ground)	Crabtree Avenue	Established 1852	N/A	Staten Island	April 9, 1985
Rufus King House, LP-0145	Jamaica Avenue and 150th Street, King Park	1730; additions 1755 and c. 1806	Unknown	Queens	April 19, 1966
Kingsland Homestead, LP-0005	40-25 155th Street	c. 1801	Unknown	Queens	October 14, 1965

(continued)

Landmark name	Landmark address	Date of construction	Architect(s) or builder(s)	Borough	Date designated
Saint Mark's-in-the-Bowery Church, LP-0229	East 10th Street at 2nd Avenue	1799; 1828 (steeple); 1854 (portico)	Tower by Ithiel Towne	Manhattan	April 19, 1966
Saint Paul's Chapel and Graveyard, LP-0075	Broadway at Fulton Street	1764–1766; 1794	Thomas McBean	Manhattan	August 16, 1966
Saint Philip's Protestant Episcopal Church, LP-1846	210–216 West 134th Street	1910–1911	Vertner W. Tandy and George W. Foster, Jr.	Manhattan	July 13, 1993
Sailors' Snug Harbor, Building A, LP-0022	914–1000 Richmond Terrace	1879	Richard P. Smyth	Staten Island	October 14, 1965
Sailors' Sung Harbor, Building B, LP-0023	914–1000 Richmond Terrace	1839–1840	Minard Lafever	Staten Island	October 14, 1965
Sailors' Snug Harbor, Building C, LP-0024	914–1000 Richmond Terrace	1831–1833	Minard Lafever	Staten Island	October 14, 1965
Sailors' Snug Harbor, Building D, LP-0025	914–1000 Richmond Terrace	1831–1841	Minard Lafever	Staten Island	October 14, 1965
Sailors' Snug Harbor, Building E, LP-0026	914–1000 Richmond Terrace	1880	Richard P. Smyth	Staten Island	October 14, 1965
Sailors' Snug Harbor, Chapel, LP-0027	912 Richmond Terrace	1854	James Solomon	Staten Island	October 14, 1965

Landmark name	Landmark address	Date of construction	Architect(s) or builder(s)	Borough	Date designated
Sailors' Snug Harbor, North Gatehouse, LP-0742	982 Richmond Terrace	1873	Richard P. Smyth	Staten Island	May 15, 1973
Sailors' Snug Harbor, Iron Fence, LP-0743	Extending along Richmond Terrace and Snug Harbor Road between Tysen Street and Kissel Avenue	1842	Frederick Diaper (architect); William Alexander (fabricator)	Staten Island	May 15, 1973
Shearith Israel Graveyard, LP-0091	55-57 Saint James Place	Burial ground founded in the Seventeenth century	N/A	Manhattan	February 1, 1966
Statue of Liberty National Monument LP-0931	1 Liberty Island	Erected in 1886	Frederic Auguste Bartholdi, Richard Morris Hunt	Manhattan	September 14, 1976
Street Plan of New Amsterdam and Colonial New York, LP-1235	Multiple streets within Lower Manhattan	Seventeenth century	Unknown	Manhattan	June 14, 1983
Trinity Church and Graveyard, LP-0048	Broadway at Wall Street	1846	Richard Upjohn	Manhattan	August 16, 1966
United States Custom House, LP-0020	Bowling Green	1901–1907	Cass Gilbert	Manhattan	October 14, 1965
Frederick and Frances Jay Van Cortlandt House, LP-0127	Van Cortlandt Park, Broadway and West 242nd Street	1748	Unknown	Bronx	March 15, 1966

(continued)

Landmark name	Landmark address	Date of construction	Architect(s) or builder(s)	Borough	Date designated
The Pieter Claesen Wyckoff House, LP-0001	5816 Clarendon Road and Ralph Avenue	c. 1652	Unknown	Brooklyn	October 14, 1965
The Adrian and Ann Wyckoff Onderdonck House, LP-1923	1820 Flushing Avenue	1750–1775; reconstructed 1980–1982	Giorgio Cavaglieri (1980–1982)	Queens	March 21, 1995

APPENDIX B

Archaeological Sites Within New York City

Discussed in the Book

Site	Principal archaeologists	Fieldwork years	Overview and key discoveries	Location of archaeological collection and final report
Aakawaxung Munahanung (Island Protected from the Wind) Archaeological Site (also known as Ward's Point), Conference House Park, Tottenville, Staten Island)	More than nineteen projects, including American Museum of Natural History and Jerome Jacobson	Nineteenth century–2019	Indigenous Peoples' cultural complex spanning over 8,000 years. The area also contains historic resources from the Colonial to nineteenth centuries.	The collections are in multiple locations including the American Museum of Natural History and the Staten Island Museum as are the reports but some can be found on the LPC website.
African Burial Ground, Manhattan	Analysis and report— Dr. Michael Blakey, Dr. Warren Perry, Dr. Jean Howson, et al., Howard University; fieldwork—Historic Conservation and Interpretation and John Milner and Associates	1991–1992	Colonial burial ground for the interment of people of African ancestry. In use by 1712 until 1795. In the heart of Lower Manhattan today, but on the outskirts of the settlement at the time. Archaeology was completed in one section of the burial ground, and 419 individuals were identified. Most burials were supine and placed in the same body position. They were generally shrouded and interred in wooden coffins. A few of the graves had distinctive African adornments such as waist beads and teeth filing. The skeletal analysis revealed indicators of hard work, illness, and nutritional stressors for almost all of the individuals studied. In situ burials remain at the monument site.	The burials and associated artifacts were reinterred at the African Burial Ground National Monument, which is open to the public and includes an interpretive center at 290 Broadway. The National Parks Service curates the remaining archaeological collection. The final reports are in multiple volumes and can be found on the LPC website.

Site	Investigator	Date	Description	Curation/Report
Bay Terrace, Queens	Stanley Wisniewski & Ralph S. Solecki	1940s	Mid- to late Archaic through late Woodland periods	Collection curated at the NYC Archaeological Repository; no final report.
Beekman Street Reconstruction, Manhattan	Chrysalis Archaeological Consultants, Inc.	2006	Discoveries included remnants of an eighteenth-century wharf/pier that was still controlling water flow in the area, segments of the city's early-nineteenth-century wooden water main system, eighteenth- and early-nineteenth-century landfill, and portions of what was likely an early-nineteenth-century cellar that contained many artifacts.	Collection curated at the NYC Archaeological Repository; final archaeological report can be found on the LPC website.
City Hall Park, Manhattan	LPC with Brooklyn College Archaeological Project	1989	Multiple archaeological features uncovered, attributed to the first Almshouse (1736–1797)	Collection curated at the NYC Archaeological Repository; final archaeological report can be found on the LPC website.
City Hall Park, Manhattan	Hunter Research, Inc.	1995	A segment of a stone foundation discovered that may have been part of the eighteenth-century British barracks	Collection curated at the NYC Archaeological Repository; final archaeological report can be found on the LPC website.
City Hall Park, Manhattan	Analysis and report—Brooklyn College Archaeological Research; fieldwork—Parsons Engineering Science	1998–1999	More than fifty archaeological features documented, including in situ eighteenth-century burials and multiple episodes of trash dumping in the eighteenth and early nineteenth centuries. Project resulted in a very large archaeological collection. In situ burials were protected in place, and fragmentary remains were reinterred in the northeast corner of the park.	NYC Archaeological Repository; multivolume final archaeological report can be found on the LPC website.

(continued)

Site	Principal archaeologists	Fieldwork years	Overview and key discoveries	Location of archaeological collection and final report
City Hall Park, Manhattan	Chrysalis Archaeological Consultants and URS Corporation	2010–2011	More than forty archaeological features, including features associated with the Bridewell prison and City Hall as well as multiple episodes of trash dumping in the eighteenth and early nineteenth centuries. Project resulted in a large archaeological collection. Fragmentary human remains were reinterred in the northeast corner of the park.	NYC Archaeological Repository; multivolume final archaeological report may be found on the LPC website.
Coenties Slip, Manhattan	Joan Geismar	2005	Early-nineteenth-century wooden water mains recovered associated with the Manhattan Water Company (now JP Morgan Chase).	Wooden mains now in the collections of the New York Historical Society; report can be found on the LPC website.
College Point, Queens (Graham Court Site)	Stanley Wisniewski & Ralph Solecki	1934	A headless dog burial was excavated from this site, likely from the Late Woodland period.	Collection at the NYC Archaeological Repository; no report.
Corbin Building Well, Manhattan	AKRF, Inc., and URS	2009–2010	Early-nineteenth-century public well uncovered during construction monitoring	No associated collection. Report on the LPC website.
Dogan Point (not in NYC)	Louis Brennan and later Cheryl Classen	1974–1995	Middle Archaic shell midden, radiocarbon dated to between 6900 and 4400 BP, located thirty miles north of NYC on the Hudson River	Classen report available online.
Elmhurst African Burial Ground, Queens	Initial fieldwork—Celia Bergoffen; later work—Chrysalis Archaeological Consultants	2007 to present	Nineteenth-century burial ground for the interment of people of African ancestry associated with St. Mark A.M.E. Church. Multiple burials recovered including a well-preserved woman of African ancestry who was interred in an iron coffin.	Human remains to be reinterred. Reports on the LPC website.

Site	Investigator	Date	Description	Disposition
Empire Stores, Brooklyn	Ralph Solecki et al.	1980	At least four fill deposits, from the late eighteenth century to the twentieth century, were found adjacent to the foundations of the 1870 and 1885 warehouse	Artifacts on display at the Brooklyn Historical Society Waterfront exhibit; larger collection curated by the New York State Parks, Recreation, and Historic Preservation. Report on the LPC website.
Erasmus Hall High School, Brooklyn	H. Arthur Bankoff, Director, Brooklyn College Archaeological Research Center	1987, 1988, 2004, 2010	Archaeological field school-documented archaeological resources associated with the original 1787 Academy building, its 1826 addition, and later construction episodes	Artifacts at Erasmus Hall High School; partial collection in NYC Archaeological Repository. Report on the LPC website.
Five Points, Manhattan	Analysis and report—John Milner Associates; fieldwork—Historic Conservation and Interpretation	1991–1992	More than twenty-four archaeological features and almost one million artifacts, including mid-nineteenth-century sanitation features and resources associated with specific households and a brothel	Collection destroyed on 9/11. The Museum of the City of New York has the remaining eighteen artifacts that were on loan at the time. Final Report on the LPC website.
Flatbush African Burial Ground, Brooklyn	Historical Perspectives, Inc.	2001; pending	Colonial to nineteenth-century burial ground for the interment of people of African ancestry. Archaeological testing uncovered human remains, which were reinterred. Future site plans to be determined.	Archaeological collection at the NYC Archaeological Repository; human remains have been reinterred. Archaeological reports on the LPC website.
Fulton Street and Peck Slip Reconstruction, Manhattan	Chrysalis Archaeological Consultants, Inc.	2009–2014	More than one hundred features, including early eighteenth-century well and wharf structure, a power station utility box from the late nineteenth century that was part of Thomas Edison's Electric Illuminating Company, and more than 45,000 artifacts primarily dating from the eighteenth and nineteenth centuries	NYC Archaeological Repository.

(continued)

Site	Principal archaeologists	Fieldwork years	Overview and key discoveries	Location of archaeological collection and final report
				Final report can be found on the LPC website.
Governors Island, sawmill excavation, Manhattan	University of Massachusetts at Amherst	1998	Excavation uncovered postholes and nails likely associated with the 1625 Dutch sawmill.	Collection and final report with the National Parks Service.
Gravesend Cemetery, Brooklyn	H. Arthur Bankoff, Frederick A. Winter, Brooklyn College Summer Archaeological Field School	1977–1978	Survey of tombstone dates and styles; artifacts revealing nineteenth-century use of the cemetery for recreational outings; twentieth-century refuse attesting to the cemetery's disuse.	Material in Brooklyn College Archaeological Research Center.
7 Hanover Square, Manhattan	Nan Rothschild, Diana diZerega Wall, Arnold Pickman	1981	Dozens of archaeological features and thousands of artifacts, including seventeenth-century foundations from Dutch (and other) families, remnants of Simeon Soumaine's early-eighteenth-century silver workshop (his silverwork can be seen today at institutions like the Metropolitan Museum of Art), and remnants of the Great Fire of 1835	NYC Archaeological Repository; the final report can be found on the LPC website.
Harlem African Burial Ground, Manhattan	AKRF, Inc.	2015	Colonial to nineteenth-century burial ground for the interment of people of African ancestry. Human-remains fragments uncovered from previously disturbed burials likely associated with what is now known as the Harlem African Burial Ground.	NYC Archaeological Repository, pending reinterment; the final report can be found on the LPC website.

Site	Investigator	Date	Description	Reference
H. F. Hollowell Site, Staten Island	Donald Hollowell, Albert and Robert Anderson, Joseph Bodner, and Donald Sainz	Early twentieth century	Early Archaic stratified site discovered by avocational archaeologists. Reported on in Ritchie and Funk 1971.	Ritchie, William A., and Robert E. Funk. 1971. "Evidence for Early Archaic Occupations of Staten Island." *Pennsylvania Archaeologist* 41 (3): 45–59.
Hunts Point Burial Ground, Bronx	Jessica Striebel MacLean	2016	Colonial to nineteenth-century burial ground for the interment of people of African ancestry. Documentary research and ground-penetrating radar (GPR) have indicated that associated burials remain within Drake Park in Hunts Point.	Report on the LPC website. There is no associated collection.
Inwood African Burial Ground, Manhattan	Multiple projects including by Reginold Bolton and AKRF, Inc.	Multiple including 1903, 1904 and 2021	Colonial to early-nineteenth-century burial ground for the interment of people of African ancestry. Archaeological testing in 2021 indicated that the site no longer contains human remains.	Reports on LPC website. Location of human remains discovered in the early twentieth century is unknown. 2020 and 2021 AKRF reports can be found on LPC's website.
Inwood Hill Park, Manhattan	Multiple projects including by Alanson Skinner and Alexander Chenowith	1920s	Resources associated with Indigenous Peoples' habitation have been documented, including rock shelters, middens, and a village site. The park also has important historical archaeological resources, including those associated with the Revolutionary War Cock's Hill Fort, a Revolutionary War–era encampment, and the nineteenth-century estates and institutions that once were within the park.	Reports are in early archaeological journals.

(continued)

Site	Principal archaeologists	Fieldwork years	Overview and key discoveries	Location of archaeological collection and final report
Rufus King House, Queens	Multiple projects including Hofstra University, Linda Stone, and Joan Geismar	1984–2020	Archaeological fieldwork has uncovered multiple features associated with the house.	NYC Archaeological Repository. Reports can be found on the LPC's website.
Lott House, Brooklyn	Brooklyn College Summer Archaeological Field School	1998–2001, 2005, 2007, 2009, 2012–2014	Archaeological testing and fieldwork uncovered the stone kitchen, the privy, brick walks, and several trash features around the farmhouse. Recovered artifacts document the purchase of local and imported goods. Possible quarters for enslaved persons were found in the house attic.	Artifacts stored in the Brooklyn College Archaeological Research Center; site reconstruction by the NYC Department of Parks and Recreation is open to the public; no final archaeological report.
Old Place Neck, Staten Island	Public Archaeology Laboratory	2011–2012	Features and artifacts indicating that Indigenous Peoples had visited the site for short periods of time to hunt, fish, and collect foods such as nuts over a ten-thousand-year span	Staten Island Museum; final report on the LPC website.
Old Towne Flushing Burial Ground, Queens	Early work—Linda Stone; later work—Chrysalis Archaeological Consultants	1999 and 2020	Colonial to nineteenth-century potter's field that included the interment of people of African ancestry. Documentary information and ground-penetrating radar (GPR) indicate that the burial ground is still in situ in this park.	No archaeological collections. Reports available on the LPC website.

Site	Investigators	Dates	Description	References/Notes
Onderdonk Site, Queens (also known as Adrian and Ann Wyckoff Onderdonk House)	Multiple projects including Nan Rothschild	1975–1986	Archaeological work focused on the construction episodes of the house and outbuildings at the site from the seventeenth to twentieth centuries.	The house is open to the public; the associated archaeological collections are at the house.
Pelham Bay Park, Bronx	Edward J. Kaeser; Goodwin & Associates; John Milner Associates; Eugene Boesch; HPI, Inc.; Chrysalis Archaeological Consultants	1957, 1958, 2000, 2003, 2012, 2015	Indigenous Peoples' sites from the Late Woodland period through to historical period sites. The Late Woodland Archery Range Site was excavated by Edward J. Kaeser in the 1950s. Subsequent work included survey, monitoring, and Phase 1B testing in advance of park renovations and construction. The Eastchester Marine Pipeline survey included work on Hunter Island, now a peninsula within the park.	Kaeser, Edward J. 1970. "The Archery Range Site Ossuary Pelham Bay Park, Bronx County, New York." *Pennsylvania Archaeologist* 40(1–2): 9–34. Project reports from 2000 onward are available on the LPC website or on file with LPC's Department of Archaeology. The NYC Archaeological Repository contains the artifacts from the 2000 Eastchester Marine Pipeline as well as from the Chrysalis Archaeological Consultants 2015 project.
Port Mobil, Staten Island	Herbert Kraft; Bert Salwen	1967, 1977	Collection of three Paleo-Indian sites located in southwest Staten Island, first identified by avocational archaeologists (Joseph Bodnar, Albert and Robert Anderson, the Mayti brothers, and Donald Sainz). Preliminary excavations were conducted by Dr. Bert Salwen in 1967. His findings, along with an analysis of the artifacts collected by the avocational archaeologists, are documented in Kraft 1977.	Kraft, Herbert. 1977. "The Paleo-Indian Sites at Port Mobil, Staten Island." In *Current Perspectives in Northeastern Archaeology*, ed. R. E. Funk and C. Hayes, New York Society of Anthropology and Archaeology Researches and Transactions, 171–19.

(continued)

Site	Principal archaeologists	Fieldwork years	Overview and key discoveries	Location of archaeological collection and final report
Quarantine Grounds, Staten Island	Historical Perspectives Inc.	2006–2012	Thirty-eight in situ burials and more than sixty isolated human remains were recovered, providing information about the people who died at the Quarantine Grounds, which were in use circa 1799–1860.	The remains were reinterred, and there is a memorial on site. The final report is on the LPC website.
Richmond Hill, Staten Island	Multiple	Early twentieth century	Archaic period Indigenous Peoples' site discovered by avocational archaeologists. Reported on in Ritchie and Funk 1971.	Ritchie, William A., and Robert E. Funk. 1971. "Evidence for Early Archaic Occupations of Staten Island." *Pennsylvania Archaeologist* 41 (3): 45–59.
Riverdale Archaeological Research Project, Bronx	Laurie Boros with contributions by Valerie DeCarlo and Barbara Hildebrand	1980s	Eight sites preliminarily identified, including Indigenous Peoples' shell middens and a historical lime kiln.	Collection at the NYC Archaeological Repository. There is no final report.
Sailor's Snug Harbor, Staten Island	LPC	1985 (two episodes)	Sailor's Snug Harbor served aged and sick seamen from 1833 to 1976; it was one of the first retirement homes for sailors. Testing uncovered remains associated with Matron's Cottage and a sheet midden deposit from the second half of the nineteenth century.	Collection at the NYC Archaeological Repository. The report is on the LPC website.

Site	Investigator	Dates	Description	Reporting / References
Sandy Ground, Staten Island	William Askins and William Schuler; later project by AKRF	1974–1989; later project 2009–2012	Free Black nineteenth-century community that specialized in shellfish and especially oysters.	Collection at the Sandy Ground Historical Society. Reporting: Askins, William. 1980. "The Sandy Ground Survey: Archaeological and Historical Research in Support of a National Register Nomination." On file at the New York State Office of Parks and Recreation and Historic Preservation. Schuyler, Robert. 1974. "Sandy Ground: Archaeological Sampling in a Black Community in Metropolitan New York." In *The Conference on Historic Site Archaeology Papers 1972*, 7:13–51. The Institute of Archaeology and Anthropology, University of South Carolina, Columbia. ——. 1980. "Sandy Ground: Archaeology of a Nineteenth-Century Oystering Village." In *Archaeological Perspectives on Ethnicity in America*, ed. R. L. Schuyler, 48–59. AKRF report on file with the NYS Office of Parks, Recreation and Historic Preservation.
Sankofa Park, Brooklyn	Hartgen Archaeological Associates	2018; pending	Colonial to nineteenth-century African burial ground associated with the New Lots Dutch Reformed Church. Archaeological documentary study and testing completed.	Human remains reinterred. Archaeological reports on the LPC website.

(*continued*)

Site	Principal archaeologists	Fieldwork years	Overview and key discoveries	Location of archaeological collection and final report
Seneca Village, Manhattan	Institute for the Exploration of Seneca Village History, Inc.	2011	Multiple features found, including resources associated with the Wilson household and backyards of multiple dwellings. Seneca Village was once the largest community of free Black property owners in mid-nineteenth-century New York. It was settled in the 1820s and taken through eminent domain in the 1850s to create Central Park.	Collection is at the NYC Archaeological Repository. Report is on the LPC website.
South Ferry Terminal, Battery Park, Manhattan	Fieldwork—Dewberry; analysis and final report—AKRF, Inc., and URS Corporation	2006	Multiple features uncovered, including portions of the mid-eighteenth-century Battery, segments relating to the construction of Whitehall Slip, and artifacts from the historical era landfill.	A portion of the Battery wall can be seen within the South Ferry station; another segment is on display at Castle Clinton. Collection is at the NYC Archaeological Repository. Report is on the LPC website.
Stadt Huys, Manhattan (includes Lovelace Tavern)	Nan Rothschild and Diana Wall	1979–1980	First large-scale archaeological excavation completed within New York's urban center. Multiple features found, including remains of Lovelace Tavern, built in 1670, that served as an interim town hall in the late seventeenth century.	Archaeological features can be seen in the plaza area of 85 Broad Street. Collection is at the NYC Archaeological Repository. Report is on the LPC website.
Stone Street, Manhattan	LPC	1998	Archaeological monitoring completed; no significant archaeological resources recovered.	Collection is at the NYC Archaeological Repository. Report is on the LPC website.
Throgs Neck, Bronx (also known as the Morris-Schurtz Site)	Edward Kaeser	1950s	Avocational project that uncovered evidence of extensive trade during the Middle Woodland, including more than 150 plates of sheet mica.	Reporting in *New York State Archaeological Society Bulletins*.

Site	Principal archaeologists	Fieldwork years	Overview and key discoveries	Location of archaeological collection and final report
84 Tillary Street, Brooklyn	AKRF, Inc.	2013	Truncated privy containing mid-nineteenth-century artifacts likely linked to residents of 84 Tillary Street, including Dr. Francis Tumblety, one of the many men suspected to have been Jack the Ripper.	Collection is at the NYC Archaeological Repository. Report is on the LPC website.
Trump SoHo (Spring Street Presbyterian Church), Manhattan	AKRF, Inc., and URS Corporation	2006–2007	Nineteenth-century burials and burial vaults associated with the integrated Spring Street Presbyterian Church were documented archaeologically. The remains were analyzed.	The remains were reinterred by the Presbytery; the related reports are on the LPC website.
Tubby Hook, Manhattan	Alanson Skinner, Amos Oneroad	1919	Shell midden from the Late Archaic excavated in Washington Heights. The collection includes projectile points, woodworking tools, and knives.	Skinner, Alanson. 1920. "Archaeological Investigations on Manhattan Island, New York City." *Indian Notes and Monographs* 2(6). Museum of the American Indian, Heye Foundation, New York.
Tweed Courthouse, Manhattan	Hartgen Archaeological Associates	2000–2001	Many archaeological features uncovered, including an eighteenth-century burial ground likely associated with the Almshouse and Bridewell, fragmentary human remains, a privy, and a cold-storage unit from the nineteenth century.	The remains were reinterred in the northeast corner of the park. Collection is at the NYC Archaeological Repository. Report is on the LPC website.
Van Cortlandt House, Bronx	Brooklyn College Archaeological Research Center	1990–1992, 2003, 2005	Archaeological field school excavations uncovered several features and a large number of eighteenth- and nineteenth-century artifacts that were likely discarded when the house was no longer used as a home for the Van Cortlandt family.	The Van Cortlandt House is open to the public. The archaeological collection is at the NYC Archaeological Repository. The reports are on the LPC website.

(continued)

Site	Principal archaeologists	Fieldwork years	Overview and key discoveries	Location of archaeological collection and final report
Ward's Island, Emigrant Refuge, Manhattan	Greenhouse Consultants	1993	More than twenty burials were recovered, likely interred between 1847 and 1885, which may represent residents of the Emigrant Refuge and Hospital.	The report is on the LPC website.
Washington Square Park, Manhattan	Joan Geismar	2008–2013	Burials from the Potters' Field (in use 1797–1825) were identified. In situ burials were protected in place.	Remains were reinterred in the park in 2021. Collection is in the NYC Archaeological Repository. Report is on the LPC website.
Weeksville, Brooklyn	Fieldwork—CUNY City College and Joan Geismar; analysis and report—Joan Geismar	Fieldwork 1978–1982, 2000–2003; report 2009	Multiple features and artifacts dating from the early 1860s to the early twentieth century associated with Weeksville, a free Black community.	Archaeological collection is at the Weeksville Heritage Center; report is on the LPC website.
World Trade Center Ship, Manhattan	AKRF, Inc.	2010	Ship uncovered in the landfill used to create the area around the World Trade Center site. Research is still under way, but it appears to be a modified sloop dating to the late eighteenth century that was used for coastal trading.	The ship was deconstructed and will be on display at the New York State Museum. The report is on the LPC website.

ACKNOWLEDGMENTS

Many people were extremely helpful in the creation of this book. The authors are especially indebted to their colleagues at the Landmarks Preservation Commission (LPC), including Sarah Carroll, Chair of LPC, and executive staff members: Lisa Kersavage, Mark Silberman, Kate Lemos McHale, and Timothy Frye, and Research Department staff, Margaret Herman and Mary Nell Nolan-Wheatly who, read, edited, and gave suggestions that improved the book. Staff members Sarah Moses and Melanie Dieg created important graphics used in the book. Gardea Caphart assisted us with all financial matters for the NYC Archaeological Repository. Angela Zhinin, an urban archaeologist who worked in the Repository from 2018 to 2021, assisted in multiple ways, including producing many of the artifact images in this book. Carol Weed, who graciously volunteers at the Repository, was an important adviser for the Indigenous Peoples chapter, as was Daniel Pagano of the LPC Archaeology Department who generously shared information and maps. John Yarmick, who also kindly volunteers at the Repository, was instrumental in corralling and organizing the objects used in the book.

We must also thank the material culture specialists and other New York archaeologists who gave us feedback on specific artifacts (such as clay pipes, ceramics, and faunal materials) and sites, confirming that we were interpreting them correctly and providing valuable ideas. They include Eugene J. Boesch, Anne-Marie Cantwell, Diane Dallal, Peter Francis, David Higgins, Jean Howson, Meta F. Janowitz, Amanda Lang, Meredith Linn, Shannon Novak, Chris Pickerell, Marie-Lorraine Pipes, David Taylor, Diana Wall, The Seneca Village Project, The Columbia Center for Archaeology, and the Brooklyn College Archaeological Research Center. The majority of the incredible artifact photographs throughout the book are the work of Matthew Septimus and the Museum of the City of New York. A sincere thanks also goes to those who gave us permission to use their images and took extra steps to help us obtain the images, a process made especially difficult during the COVID-19 pandemic, Joan Geismar, Emily Isakson, Elizabeth Meade, Matthew Reilly, Eric Sanderson, Joseph Schuldenrein,

Marie Warsh, and Rebecca Yamin. We also thank Rev. Dr. Patricia A. Singletary, Sharon Wilkins, and Melissa Mark-Viverito, former New York City Council Speaker, for allowing us to use their image. We thank our NYC colleagues at the Department of City Planning, Department of Environmental Protection, the Economic Development Corporation, the Department of Parks and Recreation, the Municipal Archives, and the Office of the Speaker of the NYC City Council.

We want to gratefully acknowledge the support of The Durst Organization and the Durst family. By providing a climate-controlled home for the Repository, they were instrumental in enabling the Commission to consolidate the city's archaeology collections and begin making them accessible to scholars and the public. KeepThinking designed the database and the Repository's website. Funds for the Repository were provided in part through the Archaeology Project which is managed by the Fund for the City of New York on behalf of the Landmarks Preservation Commission and the Department of City Planning, and in part by grants from Iron Mountain and an anonymous donor. A Furthermore award from J. M. Kaplan Fund allowed the book to include enhanced graphics.

Columbia University Press, and especially our editor, Stephen Wesley, were invaluable throughout the process. Bridget Flannery-McCoy, former editor at Columbia University Press, was the book's initiator. Chang Jae Lee, who composed and arranged the graphics, made the book not only more attractive, but more understandable as well. We would also like to thank James Gulliver Hancock for the cover art. Copy editors Peggy Tropp and project manager Ben Kolstad at KGL handled the details.

Nan Rothschild

Nan Rothschild would like to dedicate this book to her brother and her cousins-- Douglas, Jody, Kristoffer, Laurel, Leslie, Peter A, Peter D, Robin, Steve, and Wendy. Other family members were also important: Alexander, Helena, and David Neil. Their support of the New York Archaeological Repository allowed for the development of the book; without the Repository the book would not have been possible. This support reflects a deep, longstanding family interest in New York City history.

Amanda Sutphin

I would like to thank my friends, family, and colleagues and to especially thank my mother, Jean, who first instilled a love of New York City in me; my father, Derik, who inspired my love of history; my stepmother, Ann, who helped me to understand the built environment; my husband, Andy, for his support; and my daughter Amelia who is my very favorite New Yorker.

H. Arthur Bankoff

I would like to express my deepest thanks to my wife Elizabeth for her love and support throughout this project. My children, Simeon, Sarah, Naomi, Richard, Yael and their spouses encouraged me from the beginning. I also would like to express my appreciation to my friends and colleagues, and, of course, my co-authors, without whom this book would never have been written.

Jessica Striebel MacLean

To Mary, a champion of things material and particular, thank you for your support of this project; thank you to the women of NYC archaeology for the collaborative community you have engendered; and to Simon and Beatrix, I dedicate this book to you.

NOTES

Introduction

1. Eric W. Sanderson, *Mannahatta: A Natural History of New York City* (New York: Abrams, 2009).

2. Very fine comprehensive histories—such as Edwin G. Burrows and Mike Wallace, *Gotham: A History of New York City to 1898* (Oxford: Oxford University Press, 1999)—have mined these historical sources. The archaeological record is the subject of one important previous book about the city's archaeology, although it has a different focus than this one: Anne-Marie Cantwell and Diana diZerega Wall, *Unearthing Gotham: The Archaeology of New York City* (New Haven, CT: Yale University Press, 2001).

3. "People Enslaved at Monticello," accessed May 20, 2021, https://www.monticello.org/slavery/people-enslaved-at-monticello/.

4. Salwen 1973, 1978.

5. Other municipal governments in the United States with urban archaeologists include Washington, D.C.; Boston; Alexandria, Virginia; Phoenix; San Diego; San Antonio, Texas; and St. Augustine, Florida.

6. NYC LPC 2018, "Guidelines for Archaeological Work in New York City."

1. Indigenous Peoples Before the City

1. Boesch 2016; Cantwell and Wall 2001; PAL 2016.

2. Boesch 2016.

3. BP is an abbreviation for Before Present, which is calculated backward from the year 1950.

4. See the discussion of "early colonial" versus "contact" period in Loren 2008, 1–5. Although Giovanni da Verrazzano made landfall in New York Bay and sailed along the coast of Long Island in 1524, we are defining the beginning of the contact period as Henry Hudson's 1609 voyage, which marks the point of first sustained contact with Europeans in the region.

5.   GRA 2016, 19; PAL 2016.

6.   GRA 2016, 19; PAL 2016, 21.

7.   Boesch 2016, 1; Cantwell and Wall 2001, 43, 47; *New York Times* 1925, 15.

8.   Boesch 2016; GRA 2016.

9.   Cronon 2003, 13. See also Cantwell and Wall 2001, 53–54.

10. Cantwell and Wall 2001, 13.

11. See PAL 2016.

12. GRA 2016, 20.

13. Boesch 2016, 1; Cantwell and Wall 2001, 42; GRA 2016, 20; PAL 2016, 25–26.

14. Boesch 2016; *New York Times* 1925, 15.

15. GRA 2014, 27–29.

16. Cantwell and Wall 2001, 40; PAL 2016, 25.

17. Cantwell and Wall 2001; Ritchie 1980.

18. Cantwell and Wall 2001, 41.

19. A Dalton or Dalton-type projectile point is characterized by a concave fishtailed point dating from the late PaleoIndian to the early Archaic period. It is found in the Eastern and Midwestern United States. PAL 2016, 45.

20. Cantwell and Wall 2001, 47.

21. Boesch 2016; GRA 2016.

22. Cantwell and Wall 2001, 46; GRA 2016, 20; PAL 2016, 26.

23. PAL 2016, 27.

24. Grumet 2009, 26; PAL 2016, 26.

25. Cantwell and Wall 2001, 48; GRA 2016, 20. Ward's Point archaeological site is now a Designated City Landmark known by its LPC designation Aakawaxung Munahanung (Island Protected from the Wind). See the text box, Aakawaxung Munahanung in this chapter.

26. Cantwell and Wall 2001, 51–52; Ritchie and Funk 1971, 50–53.

27. Cantwell and Wall 2001, 54.

28. Boesch 2016, 1–2; PAL 2016, 26–27.

29. Cantwell and Wall 2001; GRA 2016.

30. PAL 2016, 27.

31. Cantwell and Wall 2001; GRA 2016; PAL 2016.

32. Cantwell and Wall 2001, 59; GRA 2016, 21.

33. Sanderson 2009, 289–290; Cantwell and Wall 2001, 57.

34. Mast is the fruit produced by trees and shrubs, like acorns, walnuts, and hickory nuts. These nuts are referred to as hard mast, whereas raspberries. blueberries, and other fruits and buds are known as soft mast. The term *mast* is derived from an old English word meaning "fat" or "food."

35. Cantwell and Wall 2001, 57, 307.

36. Cantwell and Wall, 2001, 58.

37. PAL 2016, 27.

38. Weissner 1983.

39. PAL 2016, 27.

40. GRA 2016, 118.

41. Cantwell and Wall 2001; GRA 2016; PAL 2016.

42. Boudreau 2008 17–18; GRA 2016, 21–22; Ritchie 1971, 29, 32, 55.

43. PAL 2016, 27.

44. Tweedie 2014.

45. PAL 2016, 27.

46. Sassman 1993.

47. Ward and Custer 1988, 36.

48. Dixon 1987.

49. Hart et al. 2008.

50. Dixon 1987; Tweedie 2014.

51. The unprovenienced vessels were collected by Dr. Theodore Kazimiroff in the middle of the twentieth century and are part of the Repository's reference collection.

52. Tweedie 2014.

53. Tweedie 2014.

54. Tweedie 2014, iii.

55. Boesch 2016, 2; GRA 2014, 128; 2016, 22–23.

56. Cantwell and Wall 2001, 73–75, 94, 96; GRA 2016, 128; PAL 2016, 27–29.

57. Cantwell and Wall 2001, 73; PAL 2016, 27–28.

58. Cantwell 2013, 7; Cantwell and Wall 2001, 119; Grumet 2009, 3–4; Office of Federal Register 2008, 39777.

59. Cantwell and Wall 2001, 61; GRA 2014, 120.

60. Cantwell and Wall 2001, 87.

61. GRA 2016, 22–23; PAL 2016, 27–28.

62. Cantwell and Wall 2001; GRA 2016; PAL 2016.

63. Bridges 1994; PAL 2016. The isotope analysis cited by Bridges was completed using skeletal material that has been in the collections of the American Museum of Natural History since 1895.

64. Bolton 1922.

65. Cantwell and Wall 2001; PAL 2016; Ritchie 1980.

66. Cantwell and Wall 2001; GRA 2016; PAL 2016; Ritchie 1980.

67. GRA 2016, 23.

68. Rice 1987.

69. Cantwell and Wall 2001; GRA 2016.

70. Cantwell and Wall 2001, 78. The artifacts from the Morris-Schurtz site are not located in the NYC Archaeological Repository. Their present location is undetermined.

71. Kerber 1997, 81.

72. Cantwell 1980, 480.

73. See Lopez and Wisniewski 1958, 17, and Cantwell and Wall 2001, 104–109, for an expanded discussion of dog burials in New York City. Lopez and Wisiniewski attribute the discovery of only one dog burial in Queens and none in Brooklyn to the rapid development of these boroughs and the concurrent lack of intensive archaeological work at the time.

74. Jacobson 1980; NYC LPC 2021.

75. NYC LPC 1967

76. Grumet 1981, 2.
77. NYC LPC 2021; Grumet 1981, 2–3; 2009, 297, Number 17
78. NYC LPC 2021, 12, and endnote 52.
79. Delaware oral history indicates that the Munsee migrated into the New York City region from the west or northwest. Archaeological and linguistic evidence supports the presence of the Munsee in the region by the Late Woodland period (Office of Federal Register 2008, 39777). To call these peoples Munsee is slightly misleading. Munsee is a dialect of the Algonquin language, not a specific group. There was no singular Munsee group or tribe in what became the five boroughs, but rather a number of loosely organized settlements that often temporarily coalesced around leaders or family groups (Cantwell 2013; Grumet 2009). Cantwell notes that the name Lenapehoking, "land of the people," comes from twentieth century Lenape elders and may not be how Native communities in the Late Woodland Period referred to themselves, a point that Grumet also makes Cantwell 2013, footnote 1; Grumet 2009, 13–14.
80. Cantwell 2013; Grumet 2009, 9.
81. Cantwell 2013, 15.
82. Cantwell and Wall 2001; GRA 2016.
83. PAL 2016, 30.
84. PAL 2016 53; Ritchie 1971, 31, 33.
85. Carol S. Weed, 2020, personal communication, re Weed and Warfel 1990.
86. Loren 2008; Rothschild 2003.
87. White 1991, in Rothschild 2003.
88. Rothschild 2003, 3–4.
89. Loren 2008; Cantwell 2013.
90. Bolton 1920; Cantwell 2013; Cantwell and Wall 2001; Grumet 2009.
91. Cantwell and Wall 2001, 120.
92. Otto 2006, 64S.
93. Cantwell 2013, 9.
94. Ceci 1989.
95. Ceci 1989, 63.
96. The Great League of Peace, also known as the Five Nations or the Iroquois Confederacy, was created as a means of ending warfare among the Onondaga, Oneida, Seneca, Cayuga, and Mohawk nations and creating an alliance across their combined territories. The Great Law of Peace established by the Confederacy was written, or recorded, using wampum belts. Snow 1996.
97. Ceci 1989, 63.
98. Rothschild and Wall 2014.
99. Hamell 1983 25.
100. Cantwell and Wall 2001, 133.
101. Cantwell and Wall 2001, 134.
102. Cantwell and Wall 2001, 135; Ceci 1977, 1989.
103. Cantwell and Wall 2001, 137.

104. Cantwell and Wall 2001, 122.

105. Grossman 2011, 87–89, 113.

106. See Cantwell and Wall 2015, 33–34, for a discussion of enslaved Africans' experience during the initial years of New Amsterdam and their relations with Europeans and Indigenous people. Cantwell and Wall also discuss how the experience of enslaved Africans brought to the colony differed from the experience of those taken in bondage later, in the mid-seventeenth century.

107. Cantwell 2013, 18.

108. Grossman 2011.

109. Rothschild 2003.

110. U.S. Department of the Interior Indian Affairs n.d.

111. Grumet 2009, 3–4, notes that the people who spoke the Munsee dialect became known as the Munsee, meaning "the people from Minisink" (near today's Delaware Water Gap), after 1727.

112. Goddard 1978; Grumet 2009.

2. Dutch Beginnings, 1624–1664

1. Throughout this book we use the term *British*. The name comes from Britannia, which was what the Romans called the region. In 1603, the Union of the Crowns created a Kingdom of Great Britain, and in 1707 the United Kingdom of Great Britain was formed by the Act of Union that created a single kingdom with a single Parliament. For more information, see Ben Johnson, "The UK and Great Britain—What's the Difference?" at https://www.historic-uk.com/HistoryUK/HistoryofBritain/The-UK-Great-Britain-Whats-the-Difference/.

2. See Cantwell and Wall 2001, 119.

3. Jacobs 2009, 1.

4. National Historic Landmark (NHL), Ward's Point Archeological Site, Staten Island, New York (aka Burial Ridge, STD 1–3, Tottenville Site), nomination prepared by Jerome Jacobson and Robert S. Grumet, September 11, 1992; listed April 19, 1993.

5. No New York City archaeological sites have uncovered artifacts related to the Vikings. To date, the nearest documented Viking site has been found in Newfoundland.

6. Schama 1987.

7. Van Laer 1924.

8. Hamell 1983, cited in Rothschild 2003, 18.

9. Wheeden 1899, 39.

10. Rothschild 2003.

11. Klooster 2005, 64.

12. Fabend 2017, 19.

13. Jacobs 2009, 19.

14. University of Massachusetts Amherst 2003.

15. Jacobs 2009, 64.

16.   Stiles 1867, 20.

17.   Cantwell and Wall 2001, 168; 2015, 32.

18.   Moore 2005, 31–35.

19.   Fabend 2017, 12, 25.

20.   Jacobs 2009, 30.

21.   The U.S. Customs House is now home to the National Museum of the American Indian.

22.   NYC LPC 1983.

23.   https://www.newnetherlandinstitute.org/history-and-heritage/digital-exhibitions/a-tour
       -of-new-netherland/manhattan/haarlem/

24.   http://digital-archives.ccny.cuny.edu/exhibits/Harlem350/Harlem_2.pdf

25.   HPI 2013, 13.

26.   HPI 2013.

27.   AKRF 2016.

28.   Jacobs 2009, 31; lensonleeuwenhoek.net.

29.   Cronon 2003.

30.   Greer 2018.

31.   Shorto 2005, 57–58.

32.   Rink 2009, 23.

33.   Moore 2005, 37.

34.   See DeCorse 2001; Thomas 1997.

35.   Cantwell and Wall 2015, 36.

36.   Fabend 2017, 24.

37.   Foote 2004.

38.   Maika 2005, 119.

39.   Foote 1993, 2004.

40.   Fabend 2017, 25.

41.   Jacobs 2009, 36, 45; Van den Hurk 2005.

42.   Cantwell 2013; Jacobs 2009, 71.

43.   Fabend 2017, 34

44.   Jacobs 2005, 135; Trelease 1960, 66.

45.   Cantwell 2013, 11–13; Jameson 1967, 208; Van der Donck 2008, 101; Jacobs 2009, 77.

46.   Rothschild, Wall, and Boesch 1987; Rothschild and Pickman 1990; AKRF and URS 2011; AKRF,
       URS, and Stone 2012.

47.   Huey 1985.

48.   New York City landmarks dating from the Dutch period include the Pieter Claessen Wyckoff
       House, the Bowne House, and the Adrian and Ann Wyckoff Onderdonck House. Landmarks
       dating from the late seventeenth and eighteenth centuries built in a similar style include
       the Dyckman Farmhouse, the Billiou-Stillwell-Perine House, the Lent Homestead, and the
       Kingsland Homestead.

49.   See Van den Hurk 2006, 322.

50.   Van den Hurk 2006.

51.   Lucas 1998.

52. Van den Hurk 2005, 140; 2006, 194.
53. Van den Hurk 2006, 173, 201, appendices B and C.
54. Andrews 1956, 65; Van den Hurk 2006, 274–275.
55. Andrews 1956, 65; Van den Hurk 2006, 274–275.
56. See Dallal, Janowitz, and Stone 2011:48–49.
57. Knight 1901, 621.
58. Dallal, Janowitz, and Stone 2011, 48.
59. Gerhauser 2010, 91.
60. Rothschild, Wall, and Boesch 1987.
61. NYC LPC 1965.
62. NYC LPC 1966.
63. Maika 2005, 103.
64. Jacobs 2009, 81.
65. Jacobs 2009, 86. Burgomasters were the equivalent of mayors; schepens and schouts had varied duties in courts, handling civil and criminal affairs. The British kept these offices, renaming them mayors, aldermen, and sheriffs.
66. Maika 2005, 107.
67. Minutes of Common Council, September 30, 1655, 93.
68. Klooster 2005, 67.
69. Rothschild 2008, 147.
70. Fabend 2017, 113.
71. Taylor 2002, 256.
72. Fabend 2017, 66.
73. Seed 1995.
74. Cronon 2003.
75. Maika 2005, 104.
76. Shorto 2018, 16.
77. Jacobs 2009, 252.
78. Jacobs 2009, 254.
79. Jacobs 2009, 254.
80. Fabend 2017, 18.

3. The British Colonial City and the Nascent Republic, 1664–1800

1. Burrows and Wallace 1999, 77.
2. Rothschild 2008, 87.
3. Rothschild 2008, 14.
4. Rothschild 2008.
5. Rosenwaike 1972, 10. The Lyne-Bradford Plan of 1728 (figure 3.21) illustrates that the city had nearly doubled in area in the sixty-eight years subsequent to the drafting of the Castello Plan in 1660.

6.   Balmer 1989; Voorhees 1994.

7.   Richmond 1871, 48; Stokes 1915, 184.

8.   Burrows and Wallace 1999, 85.

9.   Minutes of the Common Council, November 13, 1697 in New York City 1905, Vol. 2, 18 [278];
     Rothschild, Wall, and Boesch, 1987.

10. Rockman and Rothschild 1984.

11. Veit and Huey 2014.

12. AKRF and URS 2011, 6–18.

13. Richmond 1871, 48; Stokes 1915, 184.

14. Stokes 1915, 184.

15. Blakey and Rankin-Hill 2004, 270–271.

16. Blakey and Rankin-Hill 2004, 153, 269; Cantwell and Wall 2001, 168; 2015, 32.

17. Lepore 2005, 60.

18. Harris 2003, 12; Lepore 2005, 60; 2006, xii.

19. Lepore 2006, 78.

20. Lepore 2006, 79.

21. Burrows and Wallace 1999, 163.

22. Lepore 2005; 2006.

23. Lepore 2006.

24. See Lepore 2006 for a full accounting of the 1741 "conspiracy" and the undercurrent of
     white resentment and economic competition that contributed to the white response to the
     uprising.

25. Howson, Mahoney, and Woodruff 2009.

26. NYC LPC 1993, 25.

27. Blakey and Rankin-Hill 2004, 269–273.

28. Perry, Howson, and Bianco 2009, 370.

29. Bankoff and Loorya 2008, 342.

30. Beaudry 2006, 185

31. Rothschild 2008, 140; Rothschild 2010, 51.

32. Rothschild 2013.

33. Glasse 1760, 96.

34. Rothschild 2008, 146.

35. Rothschild 2008, 148; Pipes 2018.

36. AKRF and URS 2011, 51.

37. Kalm 1771, 225.

38. Rothschild 2008.

39. Kurlansky 2007.

40. Gunn, Baudouin, and Olsen 2011.

41. Evanson 2016, 63.

42. Wild 2004.

43. Burrows and Wallace 1999, 108, 124; Ukers 1922, 116.

44. AKRF and URS 2011, 43.

45. Burrows and Wallace 1999, 120; Nash 1979, 66.

46. Steinberg 2014, 23.

47. Steinberg 2014, 24.

48. Steinberg 2014, 24; Seymann 1939, 252.

49. Steinberg 2014, 26.

50. Steinberg 2014, 27.

51. Steinberg 2014, 345–346.

52. Rothschild and Pickman 1990.

53. Reid 2018.

54. Rothschild and Pickman 1990.

55. Martinón-Torres, Rehren, and Freestone 2006.

56. Maghrak 2013; Rothschild and Pickman 1990.

57. Maghrak 2013.

58. Brooklyn Historical Society 2018.

59. Janowitz 2008; Janowitz and Wall 2017, 166–167.

60. Janowitz 2008.

61. Janowitz 2008; Chrysalis and URS 2013; Bankoff and Loorya 2008.

62. Shaffer et al, 2011.

63. Cohen and Augustyn 1997, 54.

64. Lyne-Bradford Plan, 1730, in Cohen and Augustyn 1997, 54–56.

65. Anbinder 2016, 159–160.

66. Burrows and Wallace 1999, 130.

67. Nash 1979, 35.

68. Lyon 1984.

69. Burrows and Wallace 1999, 116–117.

70. Nash 1979, 45, 35.

71. Blackmar 1989, 5.

72. Wall 1994.

73. Burrows and Wallace 1999, 188.

74. Burrows and Wallace 1999, 138–140.

75. Baugher 2001.

76. Nash 1979, 254.

77. Minutes of the Common Council, January 17, 1734/35, in New York City 1905, Vol. 4, 240–241 [342–343]; Minutes of the Common Council, March 31, 1736, in New York City 1905, Vol. 4, 307–311 [392–395].

78. New York City 1905, Vol. 4, 309 [393].

79. White 2005, 57–63.

80. NYC LPC 1990, 55–60.

81. Hughes and Lester 1981, 177.

82. Albert and Kent 1949, 25.

83.   See White 2005, table 3.3, 53–55.

84.   Nash 1979, 66.

85.   Mintz 1986.

86.   Simmons 1798: 27–29, 31.

87.   Burrows and Wallace 1999, 120–122; Mintz 1986, 39–42; Smith 2005, 25.

88.   Pares 1956.

89.   AKRF and URS 2012; Smith 2005, 25.

90.   Magid 2005, 2.

91.   Magid 2005, 2.

92.   AKRF and URS 2011, 43.

93.   Warner 2011, 7.

94.   Burrows and Wallace 1999, 661.

95.   NYC LPC 2007.

96.   Wondrich 2010, 167–168.

97.   Burrows and Wallace 1999, 119.

98.   Burrows and Wallace 1999, 119, 195–196.

99.   Burrows and Wallace 1999, 196; Miller 1943.

100.   Nash 1979, 252.

101.   AKRF and URS 2011, 5–19, AKRF and URS 2012.

102.   Conolly and Lane 2006; Van Wyngaarden and Waters, 2007.

103.   Louis Berger 2003.

104.   AKRF, Inc., URS Corporation, and Linda Stone 2012.

105.   Nash 2005, 466; 1979, 262; 2005, 93.

106.   Burrows and Wallace 1999, 199, 207, 213.

107.   Burrows and Wallace 1999, 227.

108.   Nash 2005, 241.

109.   Gilje 1992.

110.   Burrows and Wallace 1999, 248.

111.   Hodges 1992, 21–23.

112.   Gilje 1992.

113.   Foote 2004, 211.

114.   Margino 2014.

115.   Wood 2009.

116.   Nash 2005, 449.

117.   Wood 2009, 25–9

118.   Burrows and Wallace 1999, 268–269.

119.   Burrows and Wallace 1999, 306.

120.   Burrows and Wallace 1999, 288.

121.   Burrows and Wallace 1999, 304.

122.   George and Kurchin 2019, 265.

123.   Wall 1994.

124.   Wall 1994, 2; Burrows and Wallace 1999, 307.

125.   Wall 1994, 56.

4. Growing Pains, 1800–1840

1. New York City, 428.

2. Rosenwaike 1972, 18, table 2.

3. Van der Donck (1653) 2008. Van der Donck commented on the purity of the water, as well as the abundance of fruit and game, in his description of the Dutch colony.

4. Rothschild and Pickman 1990.

5. Koeppel 2000, 86.

6. Geismar 2005.

7. Chrysalis Archaeological Consultants 2007.

8. Hunter (1989) 2017, 6.

9. Galusha 1999, 29–30; Koeppel 2000, 215–217.

10. Wegmann (1896) 2006.

11. Burrows and Wallace 1999, 596.

12. Cornog 1998.

13. Levy 2003; Bernstein 2005; Barone 2013; McNeur 2014, 45–46.

14. Barone 2013.

15. Barone 2013.

16. Miller 2008.

17. Rosenwaike 1972, 22.

18. Barone 2013.

19. See the following City Hall Reports for details of excavations from 1988 to 2013: Grossman and Associates 1988, 1991; Hunter Research 1994, 1995; Redding et al. 1995; LPC 1990; Kise Straw and Kolodner, Inc., and The Public Archaeology Laboratory 2000; Hartgen Archaeological Associates 2003; Bankoff and Loorya 2008; Chrysalis Archaeological Consultants and URS Corporation 2013.

20. Rothschild, Wall, and Boesch 1987.

21. Dallal 1994.

22. Janowitz 2013.

23. Of the two primary forms of coal, anthracite has a higher carbon content and fewer impurities; it is found only in Pennsylvania. It ignites with difficulty but burns hotter and longer than bituminous coal, with a short, blue, smokeless flame. Sub-bituminous and lignite are the other two forms of coal used for fuel. Pappalardo 2012, 19–20.

24. Pappalardo 2012, 20.

25. Janowitz 2013, 101.

26. Janowitz 2013, 103.

27. Gerhard 1910, 35.

28. Janowitz 2013, 100–101.

29. Nelson 2002, 13.

30. AKRF 2013.

31. Chappelle 1935; see also "Sailing Ship Rigs," Maritime Museum of the Atlantic, Nova Scotia Culture and Heritage, accessed March 25, 2021, https://maritimemuseum.novascotia.ca /research/sailing-ship-rigs.

32. Rothschild and Pickman 1990.

33. Maryland Archaeological Conservation Laboratory 2008.

34. Wedgwood 1980 [1787], 66–68.

35. Edwards 1994, 87; Lewis 1999, 99; Parramore 2008, 17–43.

36. Nöel Hume 2011.

37. Janowitz 2008.

38. Nöel Hume 2011.

39. Nöel Hume 2011.

40. Chrysalis Archaeological Consultants 2018, 5.64–5.67; 7.13–7.49.

41. NYC LPC 2020.

42. White 2004.

43. Burrows and Wallace 1999, 479.

44. Askins 1980, 1989; Geismar 2009a, 2009b; Wall, Rothschild, Linn, and Copeland 2018.

45. Wellman 2017; Askins 1989.

46. Schuyler 1974, 1980.

47. Florance 1984; Askins 1980, 1989; AKRF 2012. Note that the associated archaeological collection is with the Sandy Ground Historical Society.

48. NYC LPC 2011.

49. Cotz and Lenik 1982, 13.

50. Franz 1982, 185–186.

51. Kurlansky 2007.

52. Franz 1982, 186.

53. Billion Oyster Project n.d.

54. Kaestle 2013.

55. Andrews 1830.

56. Bourne 1870.

57. Bankoff and Winter 1987.

58. Historical Perspectives, Inc., 2001.

59. Meade 2020; Keisler 2011.

60. Geismar 2012, 22.

61. Historical Perspectives, Inc. 2006.

5. Development of the Modern City, 1840–1898

1. Gregory n.d.

2. Burrows and Wallace 1999, 736.

3. Burrows and Wallace 1999, 476.

4. Burrows and Wallace 1999, 1223.

5. Burrows and Wallace 1999, 736.

6. Orser 2007, 88.

7. HPI 2017, 3.42.

8.   HPI 2017, 1–2.

9.   HPI 2017, 10.1–10.7.

10. Burrows and Wallace 1999, 738.

11. GCI 1994.

12. NPS 2021.

13. NYC LPC 1965.

14. AKRF, Inc., and URS Corp., 2011; 2012.

15. Rules of NYC n.d.

16. Orser 2007, 110.

17. Kelly 2000.

18. See Yamin 2000.

19. Linn 2010, 74.

20. Linn 2010.

21. Rothschild, Wall, and Boesch 1997.

22. Schultz et al. 1980, 116–117.

23. Rothschild, Wall, and Boesch 1987; Wall et al. 2018. See also Geismar 1995 for discussion of the D. L. Ormsby bottling works in the Bronx.

24. URS 2008; AKRF 2007.

25. URS 2008.

26. Burrows and Wallace 1999, 556.

27. Crist, Novak, Crist 2008, D-55.

28. Hosek, Warner-Smith, and Watson 2020.

29. Dunlap 2014.

30. Howson 1993, 154.

31. Mattick 1993, 166.

32. McGowan 2000.

33. Sharrow 2001, 231–239.

34. Howson 1993, 147.

35. Fike 2006, 199. See also Bureau of Land Management/Society for Historic Archaeology, n.d, section on Medicinal/Chemical/Druggists bottles.

36. Czerkowicz 2016; Rothschild, Wall and Boesch 1997; 40, 45, 176.

37. Geismar 2016, 21.

38. "Old Druggist Dead" 1907.

39. BLM/SHA n.d.

40. Howson 2013.

41. AKRF 2014.

42. AKRF 2014.

43. Crawford and Gabriel 2019.

44. AKRF 2014.

45. AKRF 2014.

46. Flegl 2008.

47. NYC LPC 1987.

48. Milne and Crabtree 2000.

49. Liebman 2018.

50. Burrows and Wallace 1999, 860.

51. Burrows and Wallace 1999, 860.

52. Quigley 2005.

53. The name Seneca Village, as far as we know, is unrelated to the Seneca Nation of Indians. Some have thought that it may derive from the antislavery sentiments expressed by the first-century philosopher Lucius Annaeus Seneca.

54. Wall et al. 2018

55. Rosenzweig and Blackmar 1998.

56. Wall, et al. 2018, 231–239.

57. Wall, et al. 2018.

58. Landon and Dujnic 2007; Warner 1998; Fennell, Martin, and Shackel 2010; Praetzellis and Praetzellis 2004; Geismar 2009a.

59. Wall et al. 2018, 76.

60. Burrows and Wallace 1999, 867.

61. Soodalter 2011.

62. Burrows and Wallace 1999, 884.

63. Burrows and Wallace 1999, 886.

64. Burrows and Wallace 1999, 897; NYC LPC 2009.

65. NYC LPC 2009, 14.

66. Burrows and Wallace 1999, 921.

67. NYC Department of City Planning n.d.; World Population Review n.d.

68. Burrows and Wallace 1999, 921.

69. Yamin 2000, 99–104.

70. Popson 2002.

71. Geoarchaeology Research Associates 2016.

72. Burrows and Wallace 1999, 920; McNeur 2014, 234–235.

73. NYC LPC 1993.

74. Hartgen Archaeological Associates 2003, 68.

75. Hartgen Archaeological Associates 2003, 119.

76. Burrows and Wallace 1999, 931.

77. NYC LPC 1977, 4.

78. NYC LPC 1977.

79. Solecki 1980. The associated collection is curated by the New York State Museum.

80. NYC LPC 2015.

81. NYC LPC 2015.

82. AKRF and URS Corporation 2010.

83. Szcygiel and Hewitt 2000.

84. About Green-Wood n.d.

85. Jacobson 1980; NYC LPC 2021.

86. Hammack 2010, 306.

87. Salvo and Lobo 2010, 1019; Burrows and Wallace 1999, 1228.

Conclusion

1. Blakey and Rankin-Hill 2009.
2. George 2019.
3. Novak 2019.

WORKS CITED

Introduction

Burrows, Edwin G. and Mike Wallace. 1999. *Gotham: A History of New York City to 1889*. Oxford: Oxford University Press.

Cantwell, Anne-Marie and Diana diZerega Wall. 2001. *Unearthing Gotham: The Archaeology of New York City*. New Haven, CT: Yale University Press.

NYC LPC. 2018. "Guidelines for Archaeological Work in New York City." hhttps://www1.nyc.gov /assets/lpc/downloads/pdf/2018_Guidelines%20for%20Archaeology_Final_high%20res.pdf.

Sanderson, Eric W. 2009. *Mannahatta: A Natural History of New York City*. New York: Abrams.

Salwen, Bert. 1973. "Archaeology in Megalopolis." In *Research and Theory in Current Archaeology*, ed. C.L. Redman, 151 New York: John Wiley & Sons.

——1978. "Archaeology in Megalopolis: Updated Assessment." *Journal of Field Archaeology*, 5:453

Thomas Jefferson Monticello. nd. "People Enslaved at Monticello." Accessed May 20, 2020. https://www.monticello.org/slavery/people-enslaved-at-monticello/.

1. Indigenous Peoples Before the City

Boesch, Eugene. 2016. "An Overview of Life Before New Amsterdam." New York City Archaeological Repository. http://archaeology.cityofnewyork.us/collection/digital-exhibitions/life-before -new-amsterdam/page/1/view_as/grid.

Bolton, Reginald P. 1920. *New York City in Indian Possession (Indian Notes and Monographs)*. Vol. II, no. 7. New York: Museum of the American Indian, Heye Foundation.

——. 1922. *Indian Paths in the Great Metropolis (Indian Notes and Monographs)*. Misc. Series #23. New York: Museum of the American Indian, Heye Foundation.

Boudreau, Jeff. 2008. *A New England Typology of Native American Projectile Points*. Ashland, MA: Freedom Digital.

Bridges, P. S. 1994. "Prehistoric Diet and Health in a Coastal New York Skeletal Sample." *Northeast Anthropology* 48:13–23.

Cantwell, Anne-Marie. 1980. "Middle Woodland Dog Ceremonialism in Illinois." *Wisconsin Archaeologist* 61(4): 480–497.

——. 2013. "Penhawitz and Wapage and the Seventeenth-Century World They Dominated." In *Tales of Gotham: Historical Archaeology, Ethnohistory, and Microhistory of New York City*, ed. Meta F. Janowitz and Diane Dallal, 7–30. New York: Springer.

Cantwell, Anne-Marie, and Diana diZerega Wall. 2001. *Unearthing Gotham: The Archaeology of New York City*. New Haven, CT: Yale University Press.

——. 2015. "Looking for Africans in Seventeenth-Century New Amsterdam." In *The Archaeology of Race in the Northeast*, ed. Christopher N. Matthews and Allison M. McGovern, 29–55. Gainesville: University Press of Florida.

Ceci, Lynn. 1977. "The Effect of European Contact and Trade on the Settlement Patterns of Indians in Coastal New York, 1524–1655." PhD diss., City University of New York.

——. 1989. "Tracing Wampum's Origins: Shell Bead Evidence from Archaeological Sites in Western and Coastal New York." In *Proceedings of the 1986 Shell Bead Conference: Selected Papers*, ed. C. Hayes III and Lynn Ceci. Rochester, NY: Rochester Museum and Science Center.

Cronon, William. 2003. *Changes in the Land: Indians, Colonists, and the Ecology of New England*. New York: Hill and Wang.

Dixon, Boyd. 1987. "Surface Analysis of the Ochee Spring Steatite Quarry in Johnston, Rhode Island." *Man in the Northeast* 34:85–98.

Geoarchaeological Research Associates (GRA). 2014. "Geomorphology/Archaeological Boring and GIS Model of the Submerged Paleoenvironment in the New York/New Jersey Harbor and Bight in Connection with New York and New Jersey Harbor Navigation Project, Port of New York and New Jersey." Report on file at LPC. http://s-media.nyc.gov/agencies/lpc/arch_reports/1795.pdf.

——. 2016. "Phase I and II Geoarchaeological Investigation of the Riverside Project Area, Parcel 2, Volume I, Background, Research Design, Results, and Conclusions." Report on file at LPC. http://s-media.nyc.gov/agencies/lpc/arch_reports/1682.pdf.

Goddard, Ives. 1978. "Delaware in Northeast." *Handbook of North American Indians, Vol. 15*, ed. Bruce Trigger. Washington, DC: Smithsonian Institution Press.

Grossman, Joel W. 2011. "Archaeological Indices of Environmental Change and Colonial Ethnobotany in Seventeenth-Century Dutch New Amsterdam." In *Environmental History of the Hudson River: Human Uses That Changed the Ecology, Ecology That Changed Human Uses*, ed. Robert E. Henshaw, 77–122. Albany: State University of New York Press.

Grumet, Robert S. 1981. *Native American Place Names in New York City*. New York: Museum of the City of New York.

——. 2009. *The Munsee Indians: A History*. Norman: University of Oklahoma Press.

Hamell, George R. 1983. "Trading in Metaphors: The Magic of Beads." In *Proceedings of the 1982 Glass Trade Bead Conference*," sponsored by the Arthur C. Parker Fund for Iroquois Research, ed. Charles F. Hayes III, 5–28. Research record No. 16. Rochester, NY: Rochester Museum and Science Center.

Hart, John P., Eleanora A. Reber, Robert G. Thompson, and Robert Lusteck. 2008. "Taking Variation Seriously: Testing the Steatite Mast-Processing Hypothesis with Microbotanical Data from Hunter's Home Site, New York." *American Antiquity* 73(4): 729–741.

Jacobson, Jerome. 1980. *Burial Ridge: Tottenville, Staten Island, New York: Archaeology at New York City's Largest Prehistoric Cemetery*. Staten Island, NY: Staten Island Institute of Arts and Sciences.

Justice, Noel D. 1987. *Stone Age Spear and Arrow Points of the Midcontinental and Eastern United States*. Bloomington: University of Indiana Press.

Kerber, Jordan E. 1997. "Native American Treatment of Dogs in Northeastern North America: Archaeological and Ethnohistorical Perspectives." *Archaeology of Eastern North America* 25:81–95.

Lopez, Julian, Julius, and Stanley Wisniewski. 1958. "Discovery of a Possible Ceremonial Dog Burial in the City of Greater New York." *Bulletin of the Archaeological Society of Connecticut* 29:14–19.

Loren, Diana DiPaolo. 2008. *In Contact: Bodies and Spaces in the Sixteenth- and Seventeenth-Century Eastern Woodlands*. Lanham, MD: AltiMira.

New York Times. 1925. "Manhattan Yields Mastodon's Bones." March 26, 1925. https://timesmachine.nytimes.com/timesmachine/1925/03/26/104168916.html?auth=login-email&pageNumber=15.

NYC LPC. 1967. "Conference House Park." Report on file at LPC. https://www1.nyc.gov/site/lpc/designations/designation-reports.page.

——. 2021. "Aakawaxung Munahanung (Island Protected from the Wind) Archaeological Site." Report on file at LPC. http://s-media.nyc.gov/agencies/lpc/lp/2648.pdf.

Office of the Federal Register. 2018. *Federal Register* 83, no. 155, Friday, August 10. National Archives Administration. Washington, D.C., Notices 39581–39870. https://thefederalregister.org/83-FR/Issue-155/FR-2018-08-10.pdf.

Otto, Paul. 2006. *The Dutch-Munsee Encounter in America: The Struggle for Sovereignty in the Hudson Valley*. New York: Berghahn.

Public Archaeology Laboratory (PAL). 2016. "New Discoveries at Old Place: The Story of the Old Place Neck Site, Staten Island, New York." http://www.palinc.com/sites/default/files/publications/Old_Place_Neck_Site.pdf.

Rice, Prudence M. 1987. *Pottery Analysis: A Source Book*. Chicago: University of Chicago Press.

Ritchie, William A. 1971. *A Typology and Nomenclature for New York Projectile Points*. New York State Museum Bulletin Number 384 (1961, revised 1971).

——. 1980. *The Archaeology of New York State*. Harrison, NY: Harbor Hill.

Ritchie, William A. and Robert E. Funk. 1971. "Evidence for Early Archaic Occupations on Staten Island." *Pennsylvania Archaeologist* 41(3):45–59.

Rothschild, Nan A. 2003. *Colonial Encounters in a Native American Landscape: The Spanish and Dutch in North America*. Washington, DC: Smithsonian.

Rothschild, Nan A., and Diana diZerega Wall. 2014. *The Archaeology of American Cities*. Gainesville: University Press of Florida.

Sanderson, Eric W. 2009. *Mannahatta: A Natural History of New York City*. Wildlife Conservation Society. New York: Abrams.

Sassman, Kenneth E. 1993. *Early Pottery in the South East: Tradition and Innovation in Cooking Technology*. Tuscaloosa: University of Alabama Press.

Snow, Dean R. 1996. *The Iroquois*. Cambridge: Blackwell.

Tweedie, Mark S. 2014. "Exploratory Steatite Source Characterization in the Long Island Sound Watershed." Master's thesis, Stony Brook University.

U.S. Department of the Interior Indian Affairs. N.d. "Frequently Asked Questions." Accessed March 26, 2021. https://www.bia.gov/frequently-asked-questions.

Ward, H. Henry, and Jay F. Custer. 1988. "Steatite Quarries of Northeastern Maryland and Southeastern Pennsylvania: An Analysis of Quarry Technology." *Pennsylvania Archaeologist* 58(2): 33–49.

Weed, Carol S., and Stephen Warfel. 1990. "Geometrics in Late Woodland/Early Contact Period Ceramics, Quillwork, and Beadwork." Paper presented at the annual meeting of the Society for Pennsylvania Archaeology, Wilkes-Barre, PA.

Weissner, Polly. 1983. "Style and Social Information in Kalahari Stone Projectile Points." *American Antiquity* 48(2): 253–271.

2. Dutch Beginnings, 1624–1664

AKRF. 2016. "Phase IB Archaeological Investigation of the 126th Street Bus Depot, Block 1803 Lot 1, New York." Report on file at LPC. http://s-media.nyc.gov/agencies/lpc/arch_reports/1686.pdf.

AKRF, Inc., and URS Corporation. 2011. "Battery Walls, Sherds, and Clay Pipes: Getting to Know Colonial-Era New Yorkers Through Archaeology at the South Ferry Terminal Site." Metropolitan Transportation Authority. Report on file at LPC. http://s-media.nyc.gov/agencies/lpc/arch_reports/1668.pdf.

AKRF, Inc., URS Corporation, and Linda Stone. 2012. "South Ferry Terminal Project Final Report." Metropolitan Transportation Authority. Report on file at LPC. http://s-media.nyc.gov/agencies/lpc/arch_reports/1439.pdf.

Andrews, Wayne. 1956. "A Glance at New York in 1697: The Travel Diary of Dr. Benjamin Bullivant." *New-York Historical Society Quarterly* 40 (January): 55–73.

Cantwell, Anne-Marie. 2013. "Penhawitz and Wapage and the Seventeenth-Century World They Dominated." In *Tales of Gotham: Historical Archaeology, Ethnohistory, and Microhistory of New York City*, ed. Meta F. Janowitz and Diane Dallal, 7–30. New York: Springer.

Cantwell, Anne-Marie, and Diana DiZerega Wall. 2001. *Unearthing Gotham: The Archaeology of New York City*. New Haven, CT: Yale University Press.

——. 2015. "Looking for Africans in Seventeenth-Century New Amsterdam." In *The Archaeology of Race in the Northeast*, ed. Christopher N. Matthews and Allison Manfra McGovern. Gainesville: University Press of Florida.

Cohen, Paul E., and Robert T. Augustyn. 1997. *Manhattan in Maps: 1527–1995*. New York: Rizzoli International.

Cronon, William. 2003. *Changes in the Land: Indians, Colonists and the Ecology of New England*. New York: Hill and Wang.

Dallal, Diane. 1995. "The People May Be Illiterate but They Are Not Blind: A Study of the Iconography of 17th-Century Dutch Clay Tobacco Pipes Recovered from New York City's Archaeological Sites." Master's thesis, New York University.

Dallal, Diane (AKRF), Meta Janowitz (URS), and Linda Stone. 2011. "Battery Walls, Sherds, and Clay Pipes: Getting to Know Colonial-Era New Yorkers Through Archaeology at the South Ferry Terminal Site." Prepared for Metropolitan Transportation Authority (MTA). http://s-media.nyc.gov/agencies/lpc/arch_reports/1668.pdf.

DeCorse, Christopher. 2001. *An Archaeology of Elmina: Africans and Europeans on the Gold Coast, 1400–1900*. Washington, DC: Smithsonian Institution Press.

Fabend, Firth H. 2017. *New Netherland in a Nutshell: A Concise History of the Dutch Colony in North America*. Albany, NY: New Netherland Institute.

Foote, Thelma W. 1993. "Report on Site Specific History of Block 154, The African Burial Ground." Report on file at LPC. http://s-media.nyc.gov/agencies/lpc/arch_reports/861.pdf.

——. 2004 *Black and White in Manhattan*. New York: Oxford University Press.

Gerhauser, Leslie E. 2010. "Hart Tyles and Histories: Dutch Bible Tiles in Eighteenth-Century New York." In *Soldiers, Cities, and Landscapes: Paper in Honor of Charles L. Fisher*, ed. Penelope Ballard Drooker and John P. Hart, 87–105. Albany: University of the State of New York.

Greer, Allan. 2018. *Property and Dispossession: Natives Empires and Land in Early Modern North America*. Cambridge: Cambridge University Press.

Hammell, George R. 1983. "Trading in Metaphors: The Magic of Beads." In *Proceedings of the 1982 Glass Trade Bead Conference, Sponsored by the Arthur C. Parker Fund for Iroquois Research*, ed. Charles F. Hayes III, 5–28. Research Record No. 16. Rochester, N.Y.: Research Division Rochester Museum and Science Center.

Historical Perspectives, Inc. (HPI). 2013. "Phase IA Archaeological Assessment of the 126th Street Bus Depot, Block 1803, New York, New York." Report on file at LPC. http://s-media.nyc.gov/agencies/lpc/arch_reports/1374.pdf.

Howson, Jean, Barbara A. Bianco, and Steven Barto. 2006. "The Documentary Evidence of the Origins and Use of the African Burial Ground." In "*New York African Burial Ground Archaeology Final Report Volume I*," ed. Warren R. Perry, Jean Howson, and Barbara A. Bianco http://www.npshistory.com/publications/afbg/archaeology-v1.pdf.

Huey, Paul. 1985. "Archaeological Excavations in the Site of Fort Orange, a Dutch West India Trading Fort Built in 1624." In *New Netherland Studies: An Inventory of Current Research and Approaches*, ed. Boudewijn Bakker, 68–79. Utrecht: Bohn, Scheltema & Holkema.

Jacobs, Jaap. 2005. *New Netherland: A Dutch Colony in Seventeenth-Century America*. Boston: Brill.

——. 2009. *The Colony of New Netherland: A Dutch Settlement in Seventeenth-Century America*. Ithaca, NY: Cornell University Press.

Jameson, J. F., ed. 1967. *Narratives of New Netherland 1609–1664*. Reprint ed. New York: Barnes & Noble Imports.

Janowitz, Meta, and Richard Schaefer. 2021. "By Any Othehr Name: Kookpotten or Grapen? Little Pots, Big Stories." In *The Archaeology of New Netherland: A World Built on Trade*, eds. Craig Lukezic and John P. McCarthy, 201–222. Gainesville: University Press of Florida.

Klooster, Willliam. 2005. "The Place of New Netherland in the West India Company's Grand Scheme." In *Revisiting New Netherland: Perspectives on Early Dutch America*, ed. Joyce Goodfriend, 57–70. Leiden: Brill.

Knight, Sarah Kemble. 1901. *The Private Journal of Sarah Kemble Knight; Being the Record of a Journey from Boston to New York in the Year 1704*. Norwich, CT: Academy Press.

Lucas, Robin. 1998. "Dutch Pantiles in the County of Norfolk: Architecture and International Trade in the Seventeenth and Eighteenth Centuries." *Post-Medieval Archaeology* 32(1): 75–94.

Maika, Dennis J. 2005. "Securing the Burgher Right in New Amsterdam: The Struggle for Municipal Citizenship in the Seventeenth Century Atlantic World." In *Revisiting New Netherland: Perspectives on Early Dutch America*, ed. Joyce Goodfriend, 93–128. Leiden: Brill.

Moore, Christopher. 2005. "A World of Possibilities: Slavery and Freedom in Dutch New Amsterdam." In *Slavery in New York*, ed. Ira Berlin and Leslie Harris, 31–56. New York: New Press.

NYC LPC. 1965. "Pieter Claesen Wyckoff House." Report on file at LPC. http://s-media.nyc.gov/agencies/lpc/arch_reports/841.pdf.

——. 1966. "Saint Mark's-in-the-Bowery." Report on file at LPC. http://s-media.nyc.gov/agencies/lpc/lp/0229.pdf.

——. 1983. "Street Plan of New Amsterdam and Colonial New York." Report on file at LPC. http://s-media.nyc.gov/agencies/lpc/lp/1235.pdf.

Rink, Oliver A. 2009. "Seafarers and Businessmen: The Growth of Dutch Commerce in the Lower Hudson River Valley." In *Dutch New York: The Roots of Hudson Valley Culture*, ed. Roger Panetta, 7–34. New York: Fordham University Press.

Rothschild, Nan A. 2003. *Colonial Encounters in Native North America: The Spanish and Dutch in North America*. Washington, DC: Smithsonian Press.

——. 2008. *New York City Neighborhoods: The Eighteenth Century*. 2nd ed. Clinton Corners, NY: Percheron Press.

Rothschild, Nan A., Diana diZerega Wall, and Eugene Boesch. 1987. "The Archaeological Investigation of the Stadt Huys Block: A Final Report." Report on file at LPC. http://s-media.nyc.gov/agencies/lpc/arch_reports/514.pdf.

Rothschild, Nan A., and Arnold Pickman. 1990. "The Archaeological Excavations on the 7 Hanover Square Block." Report on file at LPC. http://s-media.nyc.gov/agencies/lpc/arch_reports/511.pdf.

Schama, Simon. 1987. *The Embarrassment of Riches: An Interpretation of Dutch Culture in the Golden Age*. London: Fontana.

Seed, Patricia. 1995. *Ceremonies of Possession in Europe's Conquest of the New World, 1492–1640*. Cambridge: Cambridge University Press.

Shorto, Russell. 2005. *The Island at the Center of the World: The Epic Story of Dutch Manhattan and the Forgotten Colony that Shaped America*. New York: Doubleday.

——. 2018. "Laying the Groundwork, 1640–1800." In *New York Rising: An Illustrated History from the Durst Collection*, ed. Kate Ascher and Thomas Mellins, 15–42. New York: Monacelli Press.

Stiles, Henry R. 1884. *A History of the City of Brooklyn, Volume 1*. Brooklyn, NY: published by subscription.

Taylor, Alan. 2002. *American Colonies: The Settling of North America*. New York: Penguin.

Thomas, Hugh. 1997. *The Slave Trade: The Story of the Atlantic Slave Trade, 1440–1870*. New York: Simon & Schuster.

Trelease, Allen W. 1960. *Indian Affairs in Colonial New York: The Seventeenth Century*. Ithaca, NY: Cornell University Press.

University of Massachusetts Amherst. 2003. Archaeological Overview and Assessment of Governors Island National Monument. National Parks Service.

Van den Hurk, Jeroan. 2005. "The Architecture of New Netherland Revisited." In *Building Environments: Perspectives in Vernacular Architecture*, ed. Kenneth A Breisch and Alison K Hoagland, 135–152. Knoxville: University of Tennessee Press.

——. 2006. "Imagining New Netherland: Origins and Survival of Netherlandic Architecture in Old New York." PhD diss., University of Delaware.

Van der Donck, A. 2008. *A Description of New Netherland* [1656]. Ed. C. T. Gehring and W. Starna. Trans. D. W. Goedhuys. Lincoln: University of Nebraska Press.

Van Laer, Arnold J. F., ed. 1924. *Documents Relating to New Netherland 1624–1626 in the Henry E. Huntington Library*. San Marino, CA: Henry E Huntington Library and Art Gallery.

Wheeden, William Babcock. 1899. *Economic and Social History of New England, 1628–1779*, vol. 1. Boston: Houghton Mifflin.

3. The British Colonial City and the Nascent Republic, 1664–1800

AKRF, Inc., and URS Corporation. 2011. "Battery Walls, Sherds, and Clay Pipes: Getting to Know Colonial-Era New Yorkers Through Archaeology at the South Ferry Terminal Site." Metropolitan Transportation Authority. Report on file at LPC. http://s-media.nyc.gov/agencies/lpc/arch_reports/1668.pdf.

AKRF, Inc., URS Corporation, and Linda Stone. 2012. "South Ferry Terminal Project Final Report." Metropolitan Transportation Authority. Report on file at LPC. http://s-media.nyc.gov/agencies/lpc/arch_reports/1439.pdf.

Albert, Lillian Smith, and Kathryn Kent [Schwerke]. 1949. *The Complete Button Book*, reprinted 1971. Stratford, CT: J. Edwards.

Anbinder, Tyler. 2016. *City of Dreams: The 400-Year Epic History of Immigrant New York*. Boston: Houghton Mifflin Harcourt.

Balmer, Randall. 1989. "Traitors and Papists: The Religious Dimensions of Leisler's Rebellion." *New York History* 70(4): 341–372.

Bankoff, H. Arthur and Alyssa Loorya. 2008. "The History and Archaeology of City Hall Park, New York, New York." Report on file at LPC. http://s-media.nyc.gov/agencies/lpc/arch_reports/1046_D.pdf.

Baugher, Sherene. 2001. "Visible Charity: The Archaeology, Material Culture, and Landscape Design of New York City's Municipal Almshouse Complex, 1736—1797." *International Journal of Historical Archaeology* 5(2):175–202.

Beaudry, Mary Carolyn. 2006. *Findings: The Material Culture of Needlework and Sewing*. New Haven, CT: Yale University Press.

Blackmar, Elizabeth. 1989. *Manhattan for Rent, 1785–1850*. Ithaca, NY: Cornell University Press.

Blakey, Michael L., and Lesley M. Rankin-Hill, eds. 2004. *The New York African Burial Ground: Skeletal Biology Final Report, Volume I*. http://npshistory.com/publications/afbg/skeletal-biology-v1.pdf.

Brooklyn Historical Society. 2018. "Guide to the Pelletreau Family Papers. ARC.142." Accessed April 4, 2019. http://dlib.nyu.edu/findingaids/html/bhs/arc_142_pelletreau/bioghist.html.

Burrows, Edwin G., and Mike Wallace. 1999. *Gotham: A History of New York City to 1898*. Oxford: Oxford University Press.

Cantwell, Anne-Marie and Diana DiZerega Wall. 2015 "Looking for Africans in Seventeenth-Century New Amsterdam." In *The Archaeology of Race in the Northeast*, ed. Christopher N. Matthews and Allison Manfra McGovern, 29–55. Gainesville: University Press of Florida.

Chrysalis Archaeological Consultants, Inc., and URS Corporation. 2013. "City Hall Rehabilitation—Archaeology Project 2010–2011." Report on file at LPC. http://s-media.nyc.gov/agencies/lpc/arch_reports/1555.pdf.

Cohen, Paul E., and Robert T. Augustyn. 1997. *Manhattan in Maps 1527–1995*. New York: Rizzoli.

Conolly, James, and Mark Lane. 2006. *Geographic Information Systems in Archaeology*. Cambridge: Cambridge University Press.

Evanson, Sara C. 2016. "Consuming Trade in Mid-Eighteenth Century Albany." Master's thesis, Virginia Polytechnic Institute, Blacksburg.

Foote, Thelma Wills. 2004. *Black and White Manhattan: The History of Racial Formation in Colonial New York City*. New York: Oxford Press.

George, Diane F., and Bernice Kurchin, eds. 2019. *Archaeology of Identity and Dissonance: Contexts for a Brave New World*. Gainesville: University Press of Florida.

Gilje, Paul A. 1992. "Introduction: New York in the Age of the Constitution, 1775–1800." In *New York in the Age of the Constitution, 1775–1800*, ed. Paul A. Gilje and William Pencak, 13–19. New York: New York Historical Society.

Glasse, Hannah. 1760. *The Art of Cookery Made Plain and Easy*. 7th ed. London: Printed for A. Millar, J. and R. Tonson, W. Strahan, P. Davey, and B. Law.

Gunn, Bee F., Luc Baudouin, and Kenneth M. Olsen. 2011. "Independent Origins of Cultivated Coconut (*Cocos nucifera L.*) in the Old World Tropics." *PLoS ONE* 6(6).

Harris, Leslie M. 2003. *In the Shadow of Slavery: African Americans in New York City, 1626–1863*. Chicago: University of Chicago Press.

Hodges, Graham Russell. 1992. "Black Revolt in New York City and the Neutral Zone: 1775–1783." In *New York in the Age of the Constitution, 1775–1800*, ed. Paul A. Gilje and William Pencak, 20–41. London: Associated University Presses.

Howson, Jean, Shannon Mahoney, and Janet L Woodruff. 2009. "Pins and Shrouding." In *The New York African Burial Ground: Unearthing the African Presence in Colonial New York: The Archaeology of the African Burial Ground Project, Volume 2*, ed. Warren R. Perry, Jean Howson, and Barbara A. Bianco, 247–263. Washington, DC: Howard University Press. media.nyc.gov/agencies/lpc/arch_reports/1300.pdf.

Hughes, Elizabeth, and Marion Lester. 1981. *The Big Book of Buttons*. Boyertown PA: Boyertown Publishing

Janowitz, Meta F. 2008. "New York City Stonewares from the African Burial Ground." *Ceramics in America*, ed. Robert Hunter, pp. 41–66. Milwaukee, WI: Chipstone Foundation. pp. 41–66.

Janowitz, Meta F. and Diana diZerega Wall. 2017. "New York, New York." *Ceramics in America*, ed. Robert Hunter and Angelika R. Kuettner, 158–179. Milwaukee, WI: Chipstone Foundation.

Kalm, Peter. 1771. *Travels Into North America: Containing Its Natural History*. Vol. 2. Trans. Johann Reinhold Forster. London: William Eyes, Printer.

Kurlansky, Mark. 2007. *The Big Oyster: History on the Half Shell*. New York: Random House.

Lepore, Jill. 2005. "The Tightening Vice: Slavery and Freedom in British New York," in *Slavery in New York*, ed. Ira Berlin and Leslie M. Harris, 57–89. New York: New-York Historical Society.

——. 2006. *New York Burning: Liberty, Slavery, and Conspiracy in Eighteenth-Century Manhattan*. New York: Vintage.

Louis Berger and Associates, Inc. 2003. "Proposed New South Ferry Terminal, Lower Manhattan, NY NY, Phase 1A Archaeological Assessment." Report on file at LPC. http://s-media .nyc.gov/agencies/lpc/arch_reports/490.pdf.

Lyon, Isaac S. 1984. *Recollections of an Old Cartman*. New York: New York Bound.

Maghrak, Theodor M. 2013. "The Huguenot Home: Consumption Practices and Identity in Early Eighteenth-Century New York City." MA Thesis, University of Massachusetts Boston.

Magid, Barbara H. 2005. "Sugar refining Pottery from Alexandria and Baltimore," *Ceramics in America*, ed. Robert Hunter, 223–229. Milwaukee, WI: Chipstone Foundation.

Margino, Megan. 2014, "Evacuation Day: New York's Former November Holiday," New York Public Library on-line exhibitions. https://www.nypl.org/blog/2014/11/24/evacuation-day-new -york-holiday.

Miller, John C. 1943. *Origins of the American Revolution*. Boston: Little Brown.

Mintz, Sidney W. 1986. *Sweetness and Power: The Place of Sugar in Modern History*. New York: Penguin.

Martinón-Torres, Macos, Thilo Rehren, and Ian C. Freestone. 2006 "Mullite and the Mystery of Hessian Wares." *Nature* Vol. 444(23):437–438.

Nash, Gary B. 1979. *The Urban Crucible: Social Change, Political Consciousness and the Origins of the American Revolution*. Cambridge: Harvard University Press.

——. 2005. *The Unknown American Revolution: The Unruly Birth of Democracy and the Struggle to Create America*. London: Viking.

New York City. 1905. *Minutes of the Common Council of the City of New York, 1675–1776*. Volume 2. New York: Dodd, Mead.

New York City. 1905. *Minutes of the Common Council of the City of New York, 1675–1776*. Volume 4. New York: Dodd, Mead.

NYC LPC. 1990. "The Archaeological Investigation of the City Hall Park Site, Manhattan." Report on file at LPC. http://s-media.nyc.gov/agencies/lpc/arch_reports/495.pdf.

——. 1993. African Burial Ground and the Commons Historic District Designation Report. Report on file at LPC. http://s-media.nyc.gov/agencies/lpc/lp/1901.pdf.

——. 2007. Havemeyers & Elder Filter, Pan, & Finishing House Landmark Designation Report. http://s-media.nyc.gov/agencies/lpc/lp/2268.pdf.

New-York Gazette, September 14, 1730. Accessed December 5, 2017. https://nyshistoricnewspapers .org/.

Pares, Richard. 1956. *Yankees and Creoles: The Trade between North America and the West Indies before the American Revolution*. Cambridge: Harvard University Press.

Perry, Warren R., Jean Howson, and Barbara A. Bianco. 2009. "Summary and Conclusions." Chapter 15 in *The New York African Burial Ground: Unearthing the African Presence in Colonial New York: The Archaeology of the African Burial Ground Project, Volume 2*, ed. Warren R. Perry, Jean Howson, and Barbara A. Bianco, 367–374. Washington, DC: Howard University Press. http://s-media .nyc.gov/agencies/lpc/arch_reports/1300.pdf.

Pipes, Marie-Lorraine. 2018. "A Class Apart: Shifting Attitudes about the Consumption of Fish." Paper presented at the 51st Annual Conference of the Society of Historical Archaeology. January 3–6. New Orleans, LA.

Reid, John, Jr. 2018. "History Now: Indenture Agreement, 1742, Spotlight on a Primary Source." Gilder Lehrman Institute of American History Collection. https://www.gilderlehrman.org /sites/default/files/inline-pdfs/T-3107.02668.pdf.

Richmond, Reverend J. F. 1871. *New York and Its Institutions 1609–1871*. New York: E. B. Treat.

Rockman, Diana diZ., and Nan A. Rothschild. 1984. "City Tavern, Country Tavern: An Analysis of Four Colonial Sites." *Historical Archaeology* 18(2): 112–121.

Rosenwaike, Ira.1972. *Population History of New York City*. Syracuse, NY: Syracuse University Press.

Rothschild, Nan A. 2008. *New York City Neighborhoods: The Eighteenth Century*. 2nd ed. Clinton Corners, NY: Percheron.

——. 2010. "Digging for Food in Early New York City." In *Gastropolis: Food and New York City*, ed. Annie Hauck-Lawson and Jonathan Deutsch, 50–67. New York: Columbia University Press.

——. 2013. "Maria and Alida: Two Dutch Women in the English Hudson Valley." In *Tales of Gotham: Historical Archaeology, Ethnohistory and Microhistory of New York City*, ed. Meta F. Janowitz and Diane Dallal, 89–105. Heidelberg: Springer.

Rothschild, Nan A., Diana diZerega Wall, and Eugene Boesch. 1987. "The Archaeological Investigation of the Stadt Huys Block: A Final Report." Report on file at LPC. http://s-media.nyc.gov /agencies/lpc/arch_reports/514.pdf

Rothschild, Nan A., and Arnold Pickman. 1990. "The Archaeological Excavations on the 7 Hanover Square Block." Report on file at LPC. http://s-media.nyc.gov/agencies/lpc/arch _reports/511.pdf.

Seymann, Jerrold. 1939. *Colonial Charters, Patents and Grants to the Communities Comprising the City of New York*. New York: The Board of Statutory Consolidation.

Shaffer, Rafe, Zhongqi (Joshua) Cheng, Arthur Bankoff, and Meta Janowitz. 2011. "Fingerprinting Pottery with X-Ray Fluorescence Chemistry." Poster presented at the 45/46 Annual Meeting of the Geological Society of America.

Simmons, Amelia. 1798. *American Cookery*. Hartford, CT: Printed for Simeon Butler, Northampton.

Smith, Andrew F. 2015. *Sugar: A Global History*. London: Reaktion.

Steinberg, Ted. 2014. *Gotham Unbound: The Ecological History of Greater New York*. New York: Simon and Schuster.

Stokes, I. M. 1915. *The Iconography of Manhattan Island*. New York: Robert H. Dodd.

Ukers, William H. 1922. *All About Coffee*. New York: The Tea and Coffee Trade Journal Company.

Van Wyngaarden, Robert, and Nigel Waters. 2007. "An Unfinished Revolution: Gaining Perspectives on the Future of GIS." https://www.researchgate.net/profile/Nigel_Waters/publication/265678191_An_Unfinished_Revolution_Gaining_Perspective_on_the_Future_of_GIS/links/54c944ed0cf2f0b56c2214aa.pdf.

Veit, Richard, and Paul R. Huey. 2014. " 'New Bottles Made with My Crest': Colonial Bottle Seals from Eastern North America, a Gazetteer and Interpretation." *Northeast Historical Archaeology* 43(4): 54–82.

Voorhees, David William. 1994. "The 'fervent Zeale' of Jacob Leisler." *William and Mary Quarterly* 51(3): 447–472.

Wall, Diana diZerega. 1994. *The Archaeology of Gender: Separating the Spheres in Urban America.* New York: Plenum.

Warner, Deborah Jean. 2011. *Sweet Stuff: An American History of Sweeteners from Sugar to Sucralose.* Washington, DC: Smithsonian Institution Scholarly Press.

White, Carolyn L. 2005. *American Artifacts of Personal Adornment, 1680–1820.* Lanham, MD: AltaMira.

Wild, Antony. 2004. *Coffee: A Dark History.* New York: Norton.

Wondrich, David. 2010. *Punch: The Delights (and Dangers) of the Flowing Bowl.* A Perigee Book, 167–168.

Wood, Gordon S. 2009. *Empire of Liberty: A History of the Early Republic, 1789–1815.* New York: Oxford University Press.

4. Growing Pains, 1800–1840

AKRF, Inc. 2012. Phase 3 Data Recovery New York City School Construction Authority: Crabtree Avenue Site Block 7092, Lots 39 and 75 Staten Island, Richmond County, New York SHPO Project Review Number 09PR05955. NYS Office of Parks Recreation and Historic Preservation.

——. 2013. "Final Technical Report: World Trade Center Memorial and Development Plan: Data Recovery and Analysis of the WTC Ship." Report on file at LPC. http://s-media.nyc.gov/agencies/lpc/arch_reports/1612.pdf.

Andrews, Charles. 1830. *The History of the New-York African Free-Schools from Their Establishment in 1787 to the Present Time.* New York: Mahlon Day.

Askins, William. 1980. "The Sandy Ground Survey: Archaeological and Historical Research in Support of a National Register Nomination." New York State Office of Parks and Recreation and Historic Preservation. Report on file at LPC. http://s-media.nyc.gov/agencies/lpc/arch_reports/129.pdf.

——. 1989. "Historical Archaeology of Class and Ethnicity in a Nineteenth-Century Community on Staten Island." PhD diss., City University of New York.

Bankoff, H. Arthur, Alyssa Loorya (The Brooklyn College Archaeological Research Center). 2008. "The History and Archaeology of City Hall Park." (Online report in seven parts, A–G.) Report on file at LPC. http://s-media.nyc.gov/agencies/lpc/arch_reports/1046_A.pdf.

Bankoff, H. Arthur and Frederick A. Winter. 1987. "Erasmus Hall High School: Report of the Trial Excavations Conducted by the Brooklyn College Summer Archaeological Field School." http://s-media.nyc.gov/agencies/lpc/arch_reports/129.pdf

Barone, Michael. 2013. *Shaping Our Nation: How Surges of Migration Transformed America and Its Politics*. New York: Crown.

Bernstein, Peter L. 2005. *Wedding of the Waters: The Erie Canal and the Making of a Great Nation*. New York: Norton.

Billion Oyster Project. n.d. Accessed March 25, 2021. https://www.billionoysterproject.org/.

Bourne, William Oland. 1870. *History of the Public School Society of the City of New York*. New York: Wm. Wood.

Burrows, Edwin G., and Mike Wallace. 1999. *Gotham: A History of New York City to 1898*. Oxford: Oxford University Press.

Chappelle, Howard I. 1935. *The History of American Sailing Ships*. New York: Norton.

Chrysalis Archaeological Consultants. 2007. "Wall Street Water Mains Project, New York, New York, Monitoring and Limited Phase 1A Documentary Report." Volume 1 of 3. Report on file at LPC. http://s-media.nyc.gov/agencies/lpc/arch_reports/979.pdf.

——. 2018. "Fulton Street Phase II Reconstruction Project and Peck Slip Redevelopment Project: Phase II Archaeological Investigations." Report on file at LPC. http://s-media.nyc.gov/agencies/lpc/arch_reports/1788.pdf.

Chrysalis Archaeological Consultants and URS Corporation. 2013. "City Hall Rehabilitation Archaeology Project 2010–2011. Volumes 1–4." Report on file at LPC. http://s-media.nyc.gov/agencies/lpc/arch_reports/1555.pdf.

Cornog, Evan. 1998. *The Birth of Empire: DeWitt Clinton and the American Experience, 1769–1828*. Oxford: Oxford University Press.

Cotz, Jo Ann, and Edward Lenik. 1982. "Cultural Resource Sensitivity Study: Sharrott Estates Archeological Project: Sandy Ground National Register District." Report on file at LPC. http://s-media.nyc.gov/agencies/lpc/arch_reports/663.pdf.

Dallal, Diane. 1994. "A Possible Turkish Pipe in New York City." *Society of Clay Pipe Research Newsletter* 42: 38–40.

Edwards, Diana. 1994. *Black Basalt: Wedgwood and Contemporary Manufacturers*. Suffolk, UK: Antique Collectors' Club.

Florance, Charles. 1984. National Register of Historic Places Nomination Form for Sandy Ground Historic Archeological District (A085-01-2258-D03).

Franz, David. 1982. "An Historical Perspective on Molluscs in Lower New York Harbor, with Emphasis on Oysters." In *Ecological Stress and the New York Bight: Science and Management*, ed. Gary F. Mayer. Columbia, SC: Estuarine Research Federation.

Galusha, Diana. 1999. *Liquid Assets: A History of New York City's Water System*. Fleischmanns, NY: Purple Mountain Press.

Geismar, Joan. 2012. "Washington Square Park, Phase 2 Construction Work, New York, New York." Report on file at LPC. http://s-media.nyc.gov/agencies/lpc/arch_reports/1479.pdf.

——. 2005. "Construction of Coenties Slip: Report on the Log Water Main Discovery and Monitoring. Report on file at LPC." http://s-media.nyc.gov/agencies/lpc/arch_reports/864.pdf.

Geismar, Joan. 2009a. "Archaeology at the Hunterfly Road Houses (Weeksville), 1878–1982 and 2000–2003, Brooklyn, New York. NYS Site No. (USN) A04701.015991." Report on file at LPC. http://s-media.nyc.gov/agencies/lpc/arch_reports/1160_A.pdf.

——. 2009b. "Archaeology at the Hunterfly Road Houses (Weeksville), 1878–1982 and 2000–2003, Brooklyn, New York. NYS Site No. (USN) A04701.015991." Volume 2. Catalogs. Report on file at LPC. http://s-media.nyc.gov/agencies/lpc/arch_reports/1160_B.pdf.

——. 2012. "Washington Square Park, Greenwich Village, New York: Phase 2 Construction Field Testing Report." Report on file at LPC. http://s-media.nyc.gov/agencies/lpc/arch_reports/1479.pdf.

"Green-Wood History: A Treasure Since 1838," n.d. Accessed January 7, 2022. https://www.green-wood.com/history/

Gerhard, William Paul. 1910. "Kitchens and Laundries." *Domestic Engineering and the Journal of Mechanical Contracting* 53(2): 35–39.

Grossman and Associates, Inc. 1988. "Archaeological Sensitivity Evaluation and Testing Recommendations for the Proposed Subterranean Utilities Corridor between City Hall and Tweed Court House, City Hall Park, New York City." Report on file at LPC. http://s-media.nyc.gov/agencies/lpc/arch_reports/348.pdf.

——. 1991. "The Buried History of City Hall Park: The Initial Archaeological Identification, Definition and Documentation of Well-Preserved Eighteenth-Century Century Deposits and the Possible Structural Remains of N.Y.C.'s First Almshouse." Report on file at LPC. http://s-media.nyc.gov/agencies/lpc/arch_reports/349.pdf.

Hartgen Archaeological Associates. 2003. "Tweed Courthouse Archaeological Survey and Data Retrieval Investigations. Two volumes." Report on file at LPC. http://s-media.nyc.gov/agencies/lpc/arch_reports/365_A.pdf.

Historical Perspectives, Inc. 2001 "Stage 1B Archaeological Investigation P.S. 325-K, Church and Bedford Avenues, Brooklyn, New York." Report on file at LPC. http://s-media.nyc.gov/agencies/lpc/arch_reports/858.pdf.

——. 2006. "Memorandum: 235 Bowery Street, Block 426/ Lot 12, Manhattan, Archaeological Field Investigation." Report on file at LPC. http://s-media.nyc.gov/agencies/lpc/arch_reports/909.pdf.

Hunter, Gregory. (1989) 2017. *The Manhattan Company: Managing a Multi-Unit Corporation in New York, 1799–1842.* London: Routledge.

Hunter Research Associates. 1994. "Analysis of Cultural Materials Including Human Skeletal Remains Retrieved from Soils Originating from Chambers Street North of Tweed Courthouse at City Hall, New York, New York." Report on file at LPC. http://s-media.nyc.gov/agencies/lpc/arch_reports/446.pdf.

——. 1995. "Archaeological Investigations in City Hall Park Electrical Conduit Trench Tweed Courthouse to Broadway Borough of Manhattan City of New York, New York State." Report on file at LPC. http://s-media.nyc.gov/agencies/lpc/arch_reports/447.pdf.

Janowitz, Meta F. 2008. "New York City Stonewares from the African Burial Ground." *Ceramics in America*, ed. Robert Hunter, 41–66. Milwaukee, WI: Chipstone Foundation.

——. 2013. "Decline in the Use and Production of Red-Earthenware Cooking Vessels in the Northeast, 1780–1880." *Northeast Historical Archaeology* 42: 92–110.

Kaestle, Carl F. (1973) 2013. *The Evolution of an Urban School System: New York City 1750–1850*. Cambridge: Harvard University Press.

Keisler, Douglas. 2011. *Stories in Stone New York: A Field Guide to New York City Area Cemeteries*. Newburyport, MA: Gibbs Smith.

Kise Straw and Kolodner, Inc., and The Public Archaeology Laboratory. 2000. "Bioarchaeological Monitoring of Water Main Repairs and Identification of Associated Human Skeletal Remains, Chambers Street Between Broadway and Centre Street, Lower Manhattan, New York City." Report on file at LPC. http://s-media.nyc.gov/agencies/lpc/arch_reports/475.pdf.

Koeppel, Edward. 2000. *Water for Gotham*. Princeton, NJ: Princeton University Press.

Kurlansky, Mark. 2007. *The Big Oyster: History on the Half Shell*. New York: Random House.

Landmarks Preservation Commission and Brooklyn College Archaeological Research Center. 1990. "The Archaeological Investigation of City Hall Park." Report on file at LPC. http://s-media.nyc.gov/agencies/lpc/arch_reports/495.pdf.

Levy, Janey. 2003. *The Erie Canal: A Primary Source History of the Canal That Changed America*. New York: Rosen Central.

Lewis, Griselda. 1999. *A Collector's History of English Pottery*. Suffolk, UK: Antique Collectors' Club.

Maryland Archaeological Conservation Laboratory. 2008. "Post-Colonial Ceramics: Painted Wares." Accessed October 8, 2019. https://apps.jefpat.maryland.gov/diagnostic/Post-Colonial%20 Ceramics/PaintedWares/index-paintedwares.htm.

McNeur, Catherine. 2014. *Taming Manhattan: Environmental Battles in the Antebellum City*. Cambridge: Harvard University Press.

Meade, Elizabeth. 2020. "'Prepare for Death and Follow Me': An Archaeological Survey of the Historic Period Cemeteries of New York." PhD diss., City University of New York.

Miller, Kerby. 2008. *Ireland and Irish America: Culture, Class and Transatlantic Migration*. Dublin: Field Day.

National Museum of American History Behring Center. John Remmey III, Stoneware Jar, identification number CE.300894.007. Accessed October 6, 2019. https://americanhistory.si.edu /collections/search/object/nmah_1404173.

Nelson, Bruce. 2002. *Divided We Stand: American Workers and the Struggle for Black Equality*. Princeton, NJ: Princeton University Press.

New York City. 1905. *Minutes of the Common Council of the City of New York, 1675–1776*. Volume 1 (1675–1696). New York: Dodd, Mead.

Noël Hume, Ivor. 2011. "Cap-Hole Oyster Jars: A Racial Message in the Mud, or, Shipping, *Ostreidae Crassostrea Virginia*." *Ceramics in America*, ed. Robert Hunter. Milwaukee, WI: Chipstone Foundation.

NYC LPC. 1990. "The Archaeological Investigation of the City Hall Park Site, Manhattan." Report on file at LPC. http://s-media.nyc.gov/agencies/lpc/arch_reports/495.pdf.

——. "Rossville A.M.E. Church Designation Report." Report on file at LPC. http://s-media .nyc.gov/agencies/lpc/lp/2416.pdf.

——. 2020. "New York City and the Path to Freedom." https://storymaps.arcgis.com/stories /69963f59071f4ecca36e19a4a64f875c.

Pappalardo, Michael. 2012. "Phase II: Tappan Zee Hudson River Crossing: Investigation and Evaluation of Submerged Archaeological Resources, Rockland and Westchester Counties, New York." Survey Number: 12SR61441.

Parramore, Lynn. 2008. *Reading the Sphinx: Ancient Egypt in Nineteenth-Century Literary Culture*. New York: Palgrave Macmillan.

Redding, Mark, Mauricio Ferreira, Kate Morgan, and Anthousa Ridge. 1995. "City Hall Park/2 Archaeological Site Report: The J. C. Decaux Public Lavatory Pilot Installation Project in NYC's City Hall Park." Report on file at LPC. http://s-media.nyc.gov/agencies/lpc/arch_reports/510.pdf.

Rosenwaike, Ira. 1972. *Population History of New York City*. Syracuse, NY: Syracuse University Press.

Rothschild, Nan A. and Arnold Pickman. 1990. "The Archaeological Evaluation of the Seven Hanover Square Block: A Final Report." Report on file at LPC. http://s-media.nyc.gov/agencies/lpc/arch_reports/511.pdf.

Rothschild, Nan A., Diana diZerega Wall, and Eugene Boesch. 1987. "The Archaeological Investigation of the Stadt Huys Block: A Final Report." Report on file at LPC. http://s-media.nyc.gov/agencies/lpc/arch_reports/514.pdf.

Schuyler, Robert L. 1974. "Sandy Ground: Archaeological Sampling in a Black Community in Metropolitan New York." *Conference on Historic Site Archaeology Papers* 7(1972): 13–51. Columbia, SC: Institute of Archaeology and Anthropology, University of South Carolina.

——. 1980. "Sandy Ground: Archaeology of a Nineteenth-Century Oystering Village." In *Archaeological Perspectives on Ethnicity in America*, ed. Robert L. Schuyler, 48–59. Farmingdale, NY: Baywood.

Van der Donck, Adrien. (1653) 2008. *A Description of New Netherland*. Lincoln: University of Nebraska Press.

Wegmann, E. (1896) 2006. *The Water-Supply of the City of New York, 1658–1895*. New York: Wiley.

Wall, Diana diZerega, Nan A. Rothschild, Meredith B. Linn, and Cynthia R. Copeland. Institute for the Exploration of Seneca Village History, Inc. 2018. "Seneca Village, A Forgotten Community: Report on the 2011 Excavations." Report on file at LPC. http://s-media.nyc.gov/agencies/lpc/arch_reports/1828.pdf.

Wedgwood, Josiah. 1980. [1787]. *Catalogue of Cameos, Intaglios, Medals, Bas-Reliefs, Busts and Small Statues with a General Account of Tablets, Vases, Escritoires, and other Ornamental and Useful Articles. Reprint*. New York: The Wedgwood Society of New York.

Wellman, Judith. 2017. *Brooklyn's Promised Land: The Free Black Community of Weeksville, New York*. New York: New York University Press.

White, Shane. 2004. *Somewhat More Independent: The End of Slavery in New York City, 1770–1810*. Athens: University of Georgia Press.

5. Development of the Modern City, 1840–1898

AKRF, Inc. 2007. "Topic Intensive Documentary Study, Spring Street Presbyterian Church [Cemetery], 244-246 Spring Street, New York, NY." Report on file at LPC. http://s-media.nyc.gov/agencies/lpc/arch_reports/1139.pdf.

——. 2014. "Phase IB/2 Archaeological Investigation, Evaluation, and Data Recovery for New York City College of Technology Academic Building, 285 Jay Street, Brooklyn, NY." Report on file at LPC. http://s-media.nyc.gov/agencies/lpc/arch_reports/1626.pdf.

AKRF, Inc., and URS Corporation. 2010. "Unanticipated Discovery of Brick Feature Beneath the Corbin Building, 192 John Street, New York, NY." Report on file at LPC. http://s-media.nyc.gov/agencies/lpc/arch_reports/1237.pdf.

——. 2011. "Battery Walls, Sherds, and Clay Pipes: Getting to Know Colonial-Era New Yorkers Through Archaeology at the South Ferry Terminal Site." Metropolitan Transportation Authority. Report on file at LPC. http://s-media.nyc.gov/agencies/lpc/arch_reports/1668.pdf.

AKRF, Inc., URS Corporation, and Linda Stone. 2012. "South Ferry Terminal Project Final Report." Metropolitan Transportation Authority. Report on file at LPC. http://s-media.nyc.gov/agencies/lpc/arch_reports/1439.pdf.

Bankoff, H. Arthur, Frederick A. Winter, and Christopher Ricciardi. 1992. "Archaeological Excavations at Van Cortlandt Park, The Bronx 1990–1992." Report on file at LPC. http://s-media.nyc.gov/agencies/lpc/arch_reports/27.pdf.

Bureau of Land Management/Society for Historical Archaeology (BLM/SHA). n.d. Historic Glass Bottle Identification & Information Website. Accessed May 20, 2020. https://sha.org/bottle/index.htm.

Burrows, Edwin G., and Mike Wallace. 1999. *Gotham: A History of New York City to 1898*. Oxford: Oxford University Press.

Crawford, Matthew James, and Joseph M. Gabriel, eds. 2019. *Drugs on the Page: Pharmacopeias and Healing Knowledge in the Early Modern Atlantic World*. Pittsburgh, PA: University of Pittsburgh Press.

Crist, Thomas A., Shannon A. Novak, and Molly H. Crist. 2008. "Analysis of Human Remains Spring Street Presbyterian Church Burial Vaults, New York, New York." Report on file at LPC. http://s-media.nyc.gov/agencies/lpc/arch_reports/1140.pdf.

Czerkowicz, Camille. 2016. "Lost Cures: Jacques & Marsh Druggists." MCNY Blog: New York Stories. Accessed June 11, 2020. https://blog.mcny.org/2016/06/07/lost-cures-jacques-marsh-druggists/.

Dunlap, David W. 2014. "Burial Vaults Inspire a Celebration of Church Opposed to Slavery." *New York Times*, October 8, 2014. https://www.nytimes.com/2014/10/09/nyregion/burial-vaults-window-on-sohos-past-inspire-a-celebration-of-an-anti-slavery-church.html.

Fennell, Christopher C., Terrance J. Martin, and Paul A. Shackel, editors. 2010. "New Philadelphia: Racism, Community, and the Illinois Frontier." Historical Archaeology (thematic issue), Vol. 44, No. 1.

Fike, Richard. 1986. *The Bottle Book: A Comprehensive Guide to Historic, Embossed Medicine Bottles* Caldwell, New Jersey: Blackburn.

Flegl, Amanda. 2008. "A Brief History of the Bagel." *Smithsonian Magazine*, December 17, 2008. https://www.smithsonianmag.com/arts-culture/a-brief-history-of-the-bagel-49555497/.

Geismar, Joan H. 1995. "1A Archaeological Assessment of the 33rd Precinct Project Site Block 2112, Lots 10–42, Manhattan." Report on file at LPC. http://s-media.nyc.gov/agencies/lpc/arch_reports/307.pdf

——. 2013. "Washington Square Park, Phase 3 Construction Field Testing Report." Report on file at LPC. http://s-media.nyc.gov/agencies/lpc/arch_reports/1631.pdf.

——. 2016. "Reconstruction of the Gazebo and Construction of the Asphalt Pathways, Rufus King Manor, Jamaica Queens, Archaeological Monitoring Report." Report on file at LPC. http://s-media.nyc.gov/agencies/lpc/arch_reports/1872.pdf.

Geoarchaeology Research Associates. 2016. "Phase I and II Geoarchaeological Investigation of the Riverside Project Area." Report on file at LPC. http://s-media.nyc.gov/agencies/lpc/arch_reports/1682.pdf.

Gonzalez, Sara. 2017. "Hunyadi Janos, Fights Ottomans and Constipation!" Posted February 26, 2017. Accessed May 20, 2020. https://blogs.uw.edu/gonzalsa/2017/02/26/hunyadi-janos-fights-ottomans-and-constipation/.

Greenhouse Consultants, Inc. (GCI). 1994. "Archaeological Investigations of the Chilled Water Line, Manhattan Psychiatric Center, Wards Island, New York." Report on file at LPC. http://s-media.nyc.gov/agencies/lpc/arch_reports/337.pdf.

Gregory, James. n.d. "The Southern Diaspora (Black, White, and Latinx)." America's Great Migrations Project, University of Washington. Accessed May 24, 2021. https://depts.washington.edu/moving1/diaspora.shtml.

Hammack, David. 2010. "Consolidation." In *The Encyclopedia of New York City: Second Edition*, ed. Kenneth T. Jackson. pp. 305–306. New Haven, CT: Yale University Press.

Hartgen Archaeological Associates. 2003. "Tweed Courthouse Archaeological Survey and Data Retrieval Investigations." Report on file at LPC. http://s-media.nyc.gov/agencies/lpc/arch_reports/365_A.pdf.

Historical Perspectives, Inc. (HPI). 2017. "Phase IB, II, and III Field Investigation for the Staten Island Criminal Court and Family Court Complex, Staten Island, New York." Report on file at LPC. http://s-media.nyc.gov/agencies/lpc/arch_reports/1774.pdf.

Hosek, Lauren, Alanna L. Warner-Smith, and Cristina C. Watson. 2020. "The Body Politic and the Citizen's Mouth: Oral Health and Dental Care in Nineteenth-Century Manhattan." *Historical Archaeology* 54: 138–159.

Howson, Jean E. 1993. "The Archaeology of Nineteenth-Century Health and Hygiene at the Sullivan Street Site, New York City." *Northeast Historical Archaeology* 22(1):137–160.

——. 2013. "The Archaeology of First Street: 8 Households in Nineteenth-Century Newark." Paper given at the New York State Archaeological Association Metropolitan Chapter.

Jacobson, Jerome. 1980. "Burial Ridge: Tottenville, Staten Island: Archaeology at New York City's Largest Prehistoric Cemetery." Staten Island, NY: Staten Island Institute of Arts and Sciences.

Kelly, Tamara. 2000. "Father Theobald Mathew." In *Tales of Five Points: Working-Class Life in Nineteenth-Century New York*, ed. Rebecca Yamin. *Vol. 2, An Interpretive Approach to Understanding Working-Class Life*, 265–271. http://s-media.nyc.gov/agencies/lpc/arch_reports/5.pdf.

Landon, David, and Teresa Dujnic. 2007. "Investigating the Heart of a Community: Archaeological Excavations at the African Meeting House, Boston, Massachusetts." Boston: Andrew Fiske Memorial Center for Archaeological Research, University of Massachusetts, Boston.

Liebman, Bennett. 2018. "The Quest for Black Voting Rights in New York State." *Albany Government Law Review* 11(2): 386–421.

Linn, Meredith. 2010. "Elixir of Emigration: Soda Water and the Making of Irish Americans in Nineteenth-Century New York City." *Historical Archaeology* 44(4): 69–109.

Mattick, Barbara E. 1993. "The History of Toothbrushes and Their Nature as Archaeological Artifacts." *Florida Anthropologist* 46(3): 162–184.

McNeur, Catherine. 2014. *Taming Manhattan: Environmental Battles in the Antebellum City*. Cambridge, MA: Harvard University Press.

McGowan, Gary S. 2000. "Cottage Industries at Five Points." In *Tales of Five Points: Working-Class Life in Nineteenth-Century New York*, ed. Rebecca Yamin. *Vol. 2, An Interpretive Approach to Understanding Working-Class Life*, 305–310. Report on file at LPC. http://s-media.nyc.gov/agencies/lpc/arch_reports/5.pdf.

Milne, Claudia, and Pam Crabtree. 2000. "Faunal Remains from Additional Features and Analytical Strata on Block 160." In *Tales of Five Points: Working-Class Life in Nineteenth-Century New York*, ed. Rebecca Yamin. *Vol. 2, An Interpretive Approach to Understanding Working-Class Life*, C-1. Report on file at LPC. http://s-media.nyc.gov/agencies/lpc/arch_reports/5.pdf.

National Parks Service (NPS). 2021. "Castle Clinton: History & Culture." Accessed October 2, 2020. https://www.nps.gov/cacl/learn/historyculture/index.htm#:~:text=The%20Immigration

NYC Department of City Planning. n.d. "New York City Population: Population Facts." Accessed April 19, 2019. https://www1.nyc.gov/site/planning/data-maps/nyc-population/population-facts.page.

NYC LPC. 1965. "Castle Clinton." Designation Report. http://s-media.nyc.gov/agencies/lpc/lp/0029.pdf.

——. 1977. "Fulton Ferry Historic District: Designation Report." Report on file at LPC. http://s-media.nyc.gov/agencies/lpc/lp/0956.pdf.

——. 1987. "The Archaeological Investigation of the Matron's Cottage Snug Harbor Cultural Center, Staten Island, New York." Report on file at LPC. http://s-media.nyc.gov/agencies/lpc/arch_reports/778.pdf.

——. 1993. "African Burial Ground and the Commons Historic District: Designation Report." Report on file at LPC. http://s-media.nyc.gov/agencies/lpc/lp/1901.pdf.

——. 2009. "Lamartine Place Historic District: Designation Report" Report on file at LPC. http://s-media.nyc.gov/agencies/lpc/lp/2324.pdf.

——. 2015. "Corbin Building." Designation. Report on file at LPC. http://s-media.nyc.gov/agencies/lpc/lp/2569.pdf.

——. 2021. "The Aakawaxung Munahanung (Island Protected from the Wind) Archaeological Site," Designation Report. Report on file at LPC. http://s-media.nyc.gov/agencies/lpc/lp/2648.pdf.

"Old Druggist Dead." 1907. *Pharmaceutical Era* 37: 161.

Orser, Charles E., Jr. 2007. "The Irish in New York City." In *The Archaeology of Race and Racialization in Historic America*. Gainesville: University Press of Florida.

Popson, Colleen P. 2002. "Cultural Loss in New York City." *Archaeology*, June 19, 2002. Accessed June 6, 2019. https://archive.archaeology.org/online/features/wtcartifacts/.

Praetzellis, Mary, and Adrian Praetzellis. 2004. "Putting the 'There' There: Historical Archaeologies of West Oakland: I-880 Cypress Freeway Replacement Project." Oakland, CA Anthropological Studies Center, Sonoma State University, DOT, District 4, Cultural Resource Studies Center.

Quigley, David. 2005. "Southern Slavery in a Free City: Economy, Politics, and Culture." In *Slavery in New York*, ed. Ira Berlin and Leslie M. Harris. New York: New Press.

Rosenzweig, Roy, and Elizabeth Blackmar. 1998. *The Park and the People: A History of Central Park*. Ithaca, NY: Cornell University Press.

Rothschild, Nan A., Diana diZ. Wall, and Eugene Boesch. 1997. "The Archaeological Investigation of the Stadt Huys Block: A Final Report." Report on file at LPC. http://s-media.nyc.gov /agencies/lpc/arch_reports/514.pdf

Rules of NYC. n.d. "Title 16: Department of Sanitation." Accessed June 12, 2020. https://rule -sofnyc.readthedocs.io/en/latest/c07/.

Salvo, Joseph, and Arun Peter Lobo. 2010. "Population." In *The Encyclopedia of New York City: Second Edition*, ed. Kenneth T. Jackson, pp. 1018–1020. New Haven, CT: Yale University Press.

Schultz, Peter D., Betty J. Rivers, Mark M. Hales, Charles A. Litzinger, and Elizabeth A. McKee. 1980. "The Bottles of Old Sacramento: A Study of Nineteenth-Century Glass and Ceramic Retail Containers, Part I." California Archaeological Reports, No. 20. Sacramento, CA Cultural Resource Management Unit, Department of Parks and Recreation.

Sharrow, Victoria. 2001. *For Appearance' Sake: Historical Encyclopedia of Good Looks, Beauty and Grooming*. Westport, CT: Oryx Press.

Solecki, Ralph. 1980. "Archaeological Survey: The Archaeology and History of the Empire Stores, 2–14 Main Street, Brooklyn." Report on file at LPC. http://s-media.nyc.gov/agencies/lpc /arch_reports/271.pdf.

Soodalter, Ron. 2011. "The Union's 'Shoddy' Aristocracy." *New York Times*, May 9, 2011.

Szcygiel, Bonj, and Robert Hewitt. 2000. "Nineteenth-Century Medical Landscapes: John H. Rauch, Frederick Law Olmsted, and the Search for Salubrity." *Bulletin of the History of Medicine* 74(4): 708–734.

URS Corporation. 2008. "Archaeological Investigations of the Spring Street Presbyterian Church Cemetery, New York, New York." Report on file at LPC. http://s-media.nyc .gov/agencies/lpc/arch_reports/1138.pdf.

Wall, Diana diZerega, Nan A. Rothschild, Meredith B. Linn, and Cynthia R. Copeland. Institute for the Exploration of Seneca Village History, Inc. 2018. "Seneca Village, A Forgotten Community: Report on the 2011 Excavations." Report on file at LPC. http://s-media.nyc.gov /agencies/lpc/arch_reports/1828.pdf.

Warner, Mark S. 1998. "Food and the Negotiation of African American Identities in Annapolis, MD and the Chesapeake." PhD diss., University of Virginia, Charlottesville.

"World Population Review: Population Density by City," n.d. Accessed January 7, 2022: https:// worldpopulationreview.com/world-city-rankings/population-density-by-city

Yamin, Rebecca, ed. 2000. *Tales of Five Points: Working-Class Life in Nineteenth-Century New York: Vol. 1, A Narrative History and Archeology of Block 160*. Report on file at LPC. http://s-media .nyc.gov/agencies/lpc/arch_reports/462.pdf.

Conclusion

Blakey, Michael L., and Lesley M. Rankin-Hill, eds. 2009. *Skeletal Biology of the New York African Burial Ground, Part I*. Washington, DC: Howard University Press.

George, Diane F. 2019. " 'Sacred to the Memory of Washington': National Identity Formation in Post-Revolutionary New York City." In *Archaeology of Identity and Dissonance*, ed. Diane F. George and Bernice Kurchin, 251–276. Gainesville: University Press of Florida.

Novak, Shannon. 2019. "Barn Burning: Where Species Meet on Spring Street." Paper presented at the Theoretical Archaeology Group (TAG) Conference, Syracuse, NY.

INDEX

Page numbers in *italics* indicate figures, maps, tables, or boxed text.

Aakawaxung Munahanung (Island Protected from the Wind), Staten Island, *xii*, *16*, *24–26*, *39–40*, *207*, *218–219*, *221*, *232*, 250n25; European colonist artifacts at, 52

abolitionists, 160–161, 196, *196*

advertisements, *124*, *125*, 139–140, *155*, *155*, *175*, 184

Africa, 15, 87, 101, 193

African Burial Ground, lower Manhattan, 98–102, *100*, *102–103*, 113, 221, 232

African burial grounds, *14*, *102–103*, 163, 178 Elmhurst African Burial Ground, *xii*, 86, 102, *218–219*, 234; Flatbush African Burial Ground, *xii*, 86, 102, *218–219*, 235; Harlem African Burial Ground, *xii*, 50, 60–61, 86, *102–103*, *218–219*, 236; Hunts Point African Burial Ground, *xii*, *14*, 89, 102, *218–219*, 237; Inwood African Burial Ground, *xii*, 86, 102, *218–219*, 237; Sankofa Park, *xii*, 86, 102, *218–219*, 242.

Africans, enslaved, *14*, 15, 62–63, *63*, 64, *17*, *99*, 101; in British New York, 96, 98; children of, 96, 101, 160; by Dutch colonists, 47, 53, 55, 57, 63–66; in New York City, 160–161, 189; Revolutionary War and, 130–132; sugar produced by, 122; trade involving, 62–63, *63*. *See also* free Black people; labor, enslaved African

Africans, half-emancipation, 64–65, *65*

African Union Methodist Church, 191

agriculture, 47, 54, 65, 81–82, *83*; Woodland period, 32–33, 35

Albany, New York, 51, 52, 58, 60

Algonquian language, 45, 48, 252n79; peoples 54

Allum, William, *6*, 134

Almshouse, 146, 161, 180, 201–202, *202*; bone buttons produced at, 118, *119*, 120, 233

American Colonization Society, 157

American Cookery (Simmons), 122

American Museum of Natural History, 8, *39*, 207, 221

American Revolution, 1–2, *39–40*, 129–131, *130*, 135, 163

A.M.E. Zion Church Cemetery, 160, 189, 227

Anglican Christians, 95–96, 117

Anglo-French wars, 128

Anglo-Spanish wars, 128

Angola, 57

anthracite coal, 125, *147–149*, 257n23

apprenticeships, *109–110*, 117–118

archaeobotanical analysis, 46, 47, 184–185, *185*

archaeological context, 5, 8, 13–14, 30–31, 35, 157, 159, 174, 180, 280; depositional context, 5, 30; lack of, 5, 30–31, 35. *See also individual entries.*

Archaeological feature(s), 1, 5, 9, 91, 109, 146, 185, 197, 201, 204; cellar midden 159; ceramic dump, 150–153, 152, 153; cesspool, 197, 199; cooking hearth, 24; Lovelace barrel feature, 91–92, 92, 93; middens, 110; privies, 89, 179, 183–185, 197–200, 198–199; privies, artifacts from, 150, 179, 183–185, 184, 185; root cellar, 209; shaft feature, 204; shell middens, 25–27, 38, 234, 243; well, stone-lined, 146. *See also* cemeteries, burial grounds, landfill

archaeological process in NYC: curation plan, 12; documentary study 11; excavation (mitigation) 13; testing 11–13

archaeological record, 2, 8, 19, 43, 120, 149, 249n2; ceramics in, 72–75, 72–75; Indigenous peoples in, 21–22, 23, 31; rituals evidenced by, 33; trade evidenced in, 122

archaeologists, 8, 11, 89–91, 249n4; avocational, 20, 20–21, 22, 28, 32; field schools for, 207–211

archaeology, definition of, 1; history of in NYC, 8; review, 11–13; analysis, 14–15. *See also* *specific topics*

Archaic period, 17, 18, 38; Early, 22–25, 25, 39; Late, 22–23, 26–28, 27, 28; Middle, 22–23, 25–26, 26; Transitional, 22–23, 28–32, 30, 31, 35, 35, 36

architectural styles, 69, 204, 204–205; class-based, 118; wooden, 64, 67–68, 118, 139

architectural styles, Dutch, 64, 66, 66–70, 68, 70; surviving, 78, 78–80, 79

arrowheads (chipped stone), 26, 28, 40, 41; *see also* projectile points, specific types

artifacts, 1, 5–8, 24, 52, 172, 212; as time markers 72–74; urban planning as, 58

artifacts, Indigenous, 19–21, 24–27, 26; Transitional Archaic, 29, 35, 35

artisans, 64, 117–118, 128, 132, 167

Art of Cookery Made Plain and Simple, The (Glasse), 103

Astor, John Jacob, 143

Australia, 87, 169

avocational archaeologists, 20, 20–21, 22, 28, 32

axes, stone, 23, 23, 27

Ayer's Cherry Pectoral cough medicine, 181, 181

Baltimore, Maryland, 143

Bankoff, H. Arthur, *vii*, 207–208, 216

Bank of New York, 132, 134, 141

baptisms, 63, 191

barracks, 120, 130, 201, 233

barrels, wine, 92–93, 94

Battery Park, Manhattan, 13, 14, 95, 128, 171

Battle of Brooklyn, 129

Bayard, Nicholas, 124–125, 125

Bayard family, 112

Bay Terrace, Queens, *xii*, 16, 29–31, 30, 218–219, 233

beads, 38, 45-46,52, 54, 81, 101, 232

beaver trade, 46, 49, 51, 55, 81, 83; Dutch colonists spurring, 53–54

Beekman Street Reconstruction, Manhattan, 135, 141, 233

beer, 75, 77, 94, 155, 173, 177, 191–192

Bellevue Hospital, 180

Bentley, Thomas, 155, 155

Billiou-Stillwell-Perine House, Staten Island, 222, 254n48

Bill of Rights, U.S., 132

Bird, Edward, 73

bituminous coal, 147–149

blackberries, 184–185, 185

Black communities: Sandy Ground as, 160, 241; Seneca village as, 160, 189, 190, 191–193; Weeksville as, 160, 166, 192, 244

Blakey, Michael, 100

Board of Commissioners of Emigration, 170–171

Boesch, Eugene, 89–90

Bogardus, Dominie Evarardus, 63

Bolton, Reginald P., 20, 23

bones, animal 7, 21, 25, 92, 104, 179, 180, 185–188, 216; buttons made of, 118, 119, 120, 122–123, syringe made of, 212

van de Border, Wellen Abramsen, 76, 77

boroughs, New York City, 2, 48, 168, 168–169, 210, 211; Indigenous pathways across, 33–34

Boston, Massachusetts, 69, 108, 116, 129, 143

bottles, *181–183*; from Stadt Huys, 91–92, *93*, *176–177, 176–177*; wine, 75, 93, *93, 95, 95*

Boudinot, Elias, 110

Bowne House, Queens, *222*, 254n48

Bradford, William, 115

brandy, 127

Brazil, 51, 83 106, 195

bricks, 66, 67–69, *68*, 118

Bridewell Prison, 146

Bridges, Charles, 88

Britain, U.K., 253n1

British colonies, 51, 70, 107; Dutch colonies compared to, 53, 83, 87

British military, 128–130

British soldiers, 131, 202–203

Bronx, 26, 32, 37, 142, 168, 210; Indigenous peoples in, *33–34, 48. See also specific sites*

Brooklyn, *33–34*, 59–60, 203, *203*, 210. *See also specific sites*

Brooklyn Bridge, 203, *203*, 222

Brooklyn Institute of Arts and Sciences (Brooklyn Museum), 207, *222*

Brooks Brothers, 194, *195*

brown jasper tools, 35, *35*

brownstone, 96

building code, 197–198

Bullivant, Benjamin, 69–70

burgomasters (governance), 81, 255n65

burial grounds, 29, 32, 33, 38, 60, 80, 102, 205; excavations of: African Burial Ground, 98–102, *100*, 197, Almshouse and Bridewell (City Hall Park) 146, 201–202;Elmhurst African Burial Ground, 234; Emigrant Refuge and Hospital, 170; Flatbush African Burial Ground, 235; Harlem African Burial Ground, 60–61, *61*; Indigenous Peoples, 19, 21; Quarantine Grounds 169–170; second African Burial Ground, 163, Spring Street Presbyterian Church (Trump SoHo), 178, Washington Square Park (potter's field) 163.

Burr, Aaron, 140–141

Burr, David, *168*

Bush, George, 109

buttons, 118, *119*, 120, *122–123*, 131

Calver, William I., 20

Canada, 48, 49, 130–131

canals, 21, *149*; Erie, 136, 143, 145, *145*, 150, 215

Canarsee peoples, 43, *44*, 48

canoes, 27, *54*, *59*

Caribbean, sugar plantations in, 107, 122, 124–125, 150

Castello Plan, *60*, 78, 88, 89, 103, 255n5

Castelo de São Jorge da Mina in Elmina (fortress/prison), 63, *63*

cast-iron stoves, *149*

Castle Clinton (Castle Garden), Manhattan, 171, *172*, *222*, 242

Catholicism, 53, 54, 66, 88, 110, 117, 172; on temperance movement, 173

cemeteries, 83, 146, 162, *164*, 169–170; A.M.E. Zion Church, 160, 189, 227; Cypress Hills, 163; Gravesend (Old Gravesend Cemetery), *xii*, 79–80, 86, 218–219, 227, 236; Green-Wood, 163, 205, *206*, 224; St Mark's-in-the-Bowery Church, 80; Trinity Church, 96, 98; Woodlawn Cemetery, *61*, 163, 205

censuses, 145, 157, *158*, 160, 161, 183, 191–192

Central Park, Manhattan, *9*, 143, 222

ceramics, 150–151, 173, *174*; Abbot Zoned Incised, 37; Bowman's Brook Stamped 37; Chinese porcelain, *7*, 73–74, *75*, 84, 151, 154, 191, 192; creamware, 151–153, *152*, Eastern Incised, *41*; Gothic-style, 183, *184, 193*, 198, *198*, *212*; ironstone or white granite, *180, 183, 184, 212*; material culture of, 72–75, *72–75, 84*; pearlware, 135, 151, *152–153*, 154, *212*; redware, 69, *72–73*, 75, *149–150*, 154, *212*; Soumaine workshop, 110, *111–112*; salt-glazed stoneware, 157, 173, *176*; tin-glazed earthenware, 71, 72, 74–75, 83–84, *94*, 127; Whickham Punctate, *37*; Van Cortlandt Stamped, *41*; Woodland period, 33, *36–37*, *36–38, 40–42, 41. See also* decorative type, ceramic; earthenware ceramics; potteries; stoneware ceramics

cesspools, 197, *199*

chamber pots, 197, *198*

Chambers Street, 98, *99*, 118, 120, 125, 141, 161

Charles II (King), 87–88

charters, 82, 107–109, 118

Chicago, Illinois, 143, 210

children, 63, 64, 65, *121*, 195; deaths of, 101, 110; education for, 140, 161, 191–192, *192*; of enslaved Africans, 96, 101, 160

China, 7, *7*, 51

chipped stone, 23, 24, 27, 35, 40; tools, 23, 40; axes 23, *23*; adze 23; biface 21, 27, 35; drill 21; graver 21; knives 21, 24, 27, 35; scraper 21, 24, 35

cholera, 142, 169, 181

Christianity, 101, 172

churches, 64, 88, 95–96, 116–117, 178; in Black communities, 192. *See also specific churches*

Citizens' Association, New York Council of Hygiene and Public Health, 198–199

City Hall, Manhattan, 146, *146*, 222

City Hall Park, Manhattan, *xii*, 156, 218–219, *219*; African Burial Ground and, *100*, 101, 146; as excavation site, 15, *102*, 104–105, *119*, 146, 233–234, 259n19

Civil War, 167, 189, *194*–196, *194*–197

Claessen, Pieter, 78, *78*–79

class, 143, 161, 163, 215; conflicts, 117–118, 143, 167; diet and, 103–104, 185, *186*–188; hygiene standards and, 179–180; middle, 103, 118, 136, 191–192, 195; working, 98, 122, 178–179, *186. See also* merchant class

clay smoking pipes, 14, 72, *73*, 75, 91, *90*, *92*, 194

Clinton, DeWitt, 143, *145*, 161

Clinton, George, 131, 143

Clovis points, 21–22, *22*

coal, 150, 179; anthracite, 125, *147*–149, 259n23

coconuts, 106, *106*

Coenties Slip, Manhattan, *xii*, *138*, 139, 141, *141*, 218–219, 234

coffee, *106*, 106–107

cold-creams, 180, *180*

Collect Pond, Collect Pond, 65, 113, 124, 139, 141

College Point, Queens, *xii*, 16, 218–219, 234; excavations at, 25–26, *26*, 28, *28*, 220

colonialism, 43, 51, 53–54, 56, 59, 66, 87

colonists, European, 17, 34, 42, 51–52

colonization. *See* Contact Period (European Contact); *specific colonizing countries*

Colored Orphan Asylum, 195

Colored School No. 3, 191

Commeraw, Thomas, 157, *157*–158, 159

commerce, 14, 53, 150–151, *152*–153, 167

Commissioners' Plan (1811), 143, *144*, 145, 163, 202

Common Council (governance), 91, 118, 139–143

Confederate States of America (the South), 194–197

Conference House (Billop House), Staten Island, 24, *39*–40, 223

conflicts, 132; class, 117–118, 143, 167; Dutch colonists and Munsee peoples, 47, 62, 64–66, 81, 83–84; for enslaved Africans, 96, 98, *99*; French-British, 88, 95, 117, 128–129

Congress of the Confederation, 132–133

Connecticut, 32, *48*, 58

conservation, artifact, *207*

consolidation, 2, 167, 210

Constitution, U.S., 132, 134, 189

Contact period (European Contact), 1–2, 17, 42–43, *44*, 45, 47, 249n4; Dutch colonists in, 51–53; wampum as currency in, *45*–46

Continental Congress, 129

contract archaeology, 8, 11

cookbooks, 103, 122, *186*

cooking, *76*, 149, *186*–188; by Indigenous Peoples, 24–25, *25*, 31–32

cookware, 14, *149*

Corbin Building, Manhattan, *xii*, *166*, 204, *204*, 218–219, 222, 234

Corlear's Hook, Manhattan, 157, 158

corn (maize), 32–33, 35, 37, *37*, 64, 96, 107

corruption, 167, 200–201

cotton, 150, 194

cows, *187*

Cox, Samuel, 178

creamware ceramics, 151–153, *152*

Crolius, Willem, 113–115, *114*–115, 157

Cronon, William, 19

Croton River, 142–143, 163, 210

crucibles, 110, *111*–112

Cubberly-Britton Cottage, Staten Island, *223*

cultural bias, 5, 43

currency, 6, *6*, 132, 134, *134*; wampum as, 45, *45–46*, 53, 81

Cypress Hills Cemetery, 163, 177

Dalton points, 22, 250n19

Dalzell, James, 96

Dalzell, Mary, 96, *97*

Davis, Epiphany, 189

deaths, 101, 110, 163, 169–170, 184; from Draft Riots, 195–196; of enslaved Africans, 96, 98; of Indigenous peoples, 64–66

debts, war, 132, 134, 194

Declaration of Independence, U.S., 109

decorative type, ceramic, 113, 134, *135*, 136, *152–153*, *193*; cobalt, 70; *157*, *157*, *136*; corn cob dentate, *37*; hand painted porcelain, *7*, 192; incised, *36*, *37*, *41*, 157; polychrome painted, 151, *152–153*, 154, *212*; manganese, 70; punctate, *37*, *41*; stoneware, 113; *157*; swag and tassel (pattern) 157; transfer printed, *135*, *152*, 191, 192, *193*, 198; shell-impressed, *41*; stamped, *36*, *37*, *41*; Woodland period, 40–42, *41*

Delaware Tribe of Indians, *34*, *40*, 47–48, 252n79

Democratic Republic of the Congo, 57

demographics, 82, 96, 160. *See also* censuses

dendrochronology analysis, 13, 150

density, of New York City, 140, 163, 197, 210

dental care, 178–179, *179*

descendants, of Indigenous Peoples, 47–48

designation, Landmarks, ix, 2, 11, 221

desserts, 122

Diderot, Denis, 120, *123*

die, bone, 5, *6*

diets, 101, 183–184, *186–187*; Archaic period, 25–26, 31–32; Contact period, 47, 81–82; of elite families, 103, 106, 185; middle class, 103–104; oysters in, 104–105, 157, 159, *159*, 161; Woodland period, 35

Dinkins, David, 100

diseases, 49, 169, 173–174, 198–199

diversity, ethnic, 2, 15, 82, 116–117, 132

D. L. Ormsby bottles, 176, *177*, 261n23

documents (documentary record), 2, 6–8, 11, 43, *54–55*, 104; censuses as, 145, 157, *158*; Dutch colonist, 67; Indigenous Peoples lacking, 17; limits of, 146–147; recording enslaved Africans, 57. *See also* maps

Dogan Point (shell midden), 25, *234*

dog burials, 33, 38, 251n73

domesticated animals, 38, 47, 104

Dongan, Thomas, 107

Dongan Charter (1686), 107–108

Draft Riots, 195–197, *196*

drills, *46*, *123*

drinking water, 140–143, *142–143*, 167

Dronken tamboer met roemer en toorts (Gole), 77

Dr. O'Toole's Cough Remedy, 181, *181*

druggists, medicines from, 180–183, *181–183*

Durand, John, *121*

Dutch colonies, 51, 53

Dutch colonists, *46*, 51, *60–61*; Africans enslaved by, 47, 53, 55, 57, 63; Indigenous peoples and, 53–54, *54*; Munsee people and, 43, 45, 47, 49

Dutch East India Company (Vereenigde Oost-Indische Compagnie, VOC), *52*, 53

Dutch Golden Age, 53

Dutch-Indigenous wars, 81

Dutch-Munsee war, 64–66

Dutch West India Company, 59

Dyckman House, Manhattan, 223, 254n48

Early Archaic period, 23–25, *25*, 39

Early Woodland period, 35–36, *35–36*

earthenware ceramics, 72–73, *74–75*, 83–85, *92*, *149*, 152; at Lovelace Tavern, *94*; molds, 125; punchbowl as, *127*; tiles as, *71*

East River, 2, 67, 108, *116*, 203

economy, 49, 84, 129, 145, 189, 194; artifacts relating to, 5, *6*; of Indigenous people, 55

education, 63, 140, 161–162, *162*, 167; for Seneca Village children, 191–192, *192*

Egypt, 154–155

84 Tillary Street, Brooklyn, 183–185, *185*, 243

elites, 88, 117, 124, 163, 180, 195; buttons as status symbol for, 120, *121*; diets of, 103, 106, 185

Ellis Island Historic District, Manhattan, 171, 223

Elmendorf Reformed Church, 61, 103

Elmhurst African Burial Ground, Queens, xii, 86, 102, 218–219, 234

Elmina, Ghana, 62–63, 63

Elting, John, 151

Emancipation from enslavement, New York, 157, 160–161, 189

Emancipation Proclamation, U.S., 195

Emigrant Refuge and Hospital, 169–171, 170–171

eminent domain, 9, 177, 191, 242

Empire State Building, Manhattan, 2, 223

Empire Stores, Brooklyn, xii, 166, 203, 203, 218–219, 235

Encyclopedie (Diderot), 120, 123

England, U.K., 79, 95, 110, 117, 154, 167, 173, 193

Enlightenment principles, 131–132

enslavement, 63, 194, 209; in British New York, 96, 98; emancipation from, 157, 160–161, 189. See also Africans, enslaved

environmental changes, 8, 18–19, 22–23, 81–82, 188; British New York causing, 104–105; European colonists causing, 47, 49, 83

epidemics, 110, 117, 142

eras, archaeological, 17, 18. See also specific periods

Erasmus Hall High School, Brooklyn, xii, 138, 209, 218–219, 223, 235; as excavation site, 162, 162

Erie Canal, 136, 143, 145, 145, 150, 215

Esopus War, 81

Ethiopia, 106

Evacuation Day, 131

excavation, archaeological, 13, 19–21, 27, 162, 162; City Hall Park, 15, 102, 104–105, 119, 233–234; College Point, 25–26, 26, 28, 28, 220; Conference House, 24, 25, 38–40; Lovelace Tavern, 11, 12, 75, 75–77, 77; Riverdale Archaeological Research Project, 25, 27–28, 27–28, 35, 198, 200; Sailors' Snug Harbor, Staten Island, 40, 41, 148, 185, 186; Sandy Ground, 160; Seneca Village, 23, 160, 138, 166, 177; Seven Hanover Square, 50, 66–67, 74, 78, 86, 104, 109–110, 112, 127, 138, 140, 150, 152, 213; South Ferry Terminal, 45, 71, 105–106, 107, 108, 129; Stadt Huys, 10, 75, 75–78, 77, 154, 174, 179, 180, 182, 182; Tweed Courthouse, 6, 119, 174, 201–202; Van Cortlandt House, 71, 156, 180, 180–181, 181, 209; World Trade Center Ship, 138, 151, 219

Exchange Coffee House, 107

Exhibits, archaeological: x, 13, 207; Five Points surviving, 197; related to Seneca Village, 193; at Stadt Huys, 91; Walls Within Walls (South Ferry Terminal, Battery Park), 171

exports, 5, 7, 57, 92, 108, 129; to Great Britain, 87, 107, 129

extinctions, 21, 22, 188

families, 62, 109, 112, 136; Black, 160–161; Havemeyer, 125, 225; McEwen, 183–185; potteries run by, 113–115; W. Wilson, 191–193, 192–193

famine, 117, 145, 169, 172

farming, 33, 35, 47, 54, 60, 83, 103, 124

faunal analysis, 104, 186, 186–188, 191–192

federal government, U.S., 48, 132

Federal Hall National Memorial, 132, 133

Female Association, 161

field schools, archaeological, 207–210

Fifteenth Amendment, U.S. Constitution, 189

fire cracked rock, 24, 25

fires, 31–32, 56, 67, 129, 139–140; in British New York, 98; Draft Riot, 195–197, 196; stone tools and, 24–25, 25. See also hearths

First Dutch War, 87

fishing, 33, 35, 40, 104, 187, 215

Five Nations, 252n96

Five Points, Manhattan, xii, 166, 174, 194, 218–219, 235; cesspool at, 197, 199; faunal analysis at, 186–187

565 and 569 Bloomingdale Road Cottages, Staten Island, 221

Flatbush, Brooklyn, 40

Flatbush African Burial Ground, Brooklyn, xii, 86, 102, 218–219, 235

Flatbush District No. 1 School, Brooklyn, 162, 223

Flatbush Dutch Reformed Church, Brooklyn, *224*

Flatlands, Brooklyn, *78, 78–79*

Fletcher, Benjamin, 88, 92–95, *95*

Flushing, Queens, 82, *102*

Foley Square, Manhattan, *139, 156*

food, 167, 185

food resources, 103–107, *105–106*

forests, 22, 23, 26, 28, 214–215

Fort Greene Historic District, Brooklyn, 2, *209, 224*

fortifications, defensive, 128–129, *130*, 171, 215

Fort Orange, New Netherland, 51–52, 59–60

Fox Creek spear point, 38

France, 88, 95, 110, 117, 143

Franklin, Benjamin, *39–40*

Fraunces Tavern, 131

Fredericksz, Crijn, 58–59

free Black men, 150, 157, *157–158, 159*, 189, 191

free Black people, 157, 160, 189, *190*, 191–193

Free School Society, 161

French and Indian War, 128–129

French-British conflicts, 88, 95, 117, 128–129

French colonists, 49, 54, 66

fresh water, 18, 19, *65*, 167

Friends Meeting House (Quaker house of worship), Queens, 82, *82*, 117, *224*

Fugitive Slave Act of 1850, U.S., 189

Fulton Ferry Historic District, Brooklyn, 203, *203, 224*

Fulton Street and Peck Slip Reconstruction, Manhattan, *xii, 138, 218–219, 219, 235*

Gannett, George A., 139–140

gardens, 47, 103, 118, 139, 215

Gauntlet family, makers' mark, *73–74*

gender, 22, 38, 41–42, *121, 123*

General Services Administration (GSA), U.S., *98, 100*

geographic information system (GIS) programs, 13, *129*

George II (King), 108

George L. Peck Hall of Pharmacy, 182, *183*

Gerdes, Hendrik, *74*

German immigrants, 113–115, 167, 191

Germany, 110, 113, 117, 176

germ theory, 169, 205

Ghana, 62–63, *63*

Gibbons, Abby, *196*

Gibbons, James Sloan, *196*

Gilje, Paul, 131

GIS. *See* geographic information system

glaciers, 18, 21

glass, 52, 54, *149*; bottles, 93, 95; roemers, 75–76, *77*

Glasse, Hannah, 103

Glorious Revolution of 1688, 88

Gole, Jacob, *77*

Gothic-style ceramics, 183, *184*, 193, 198, *198*

Govaert, Aeltje, *73*

governors, British New York, 91, 107, 108; Colonel Nicolls as, 83; Leisler as attempted, 88; Fletcher as, Sir Francis Lovelace as, 91, 88, 92–95 Dongan as, 107, John Montgomerie as, 108

governors, New Amsterdam, 53, 55, 62, 83; Peter Minuit as, 62; Kieft as, 64–66; Stuyvesant, Peter, as, 81–84

governors, New York State, 143, 195; Clinton as, 131, 143; Seymour as, 195

Governor's Island (Noten Eylant, Nut Island), Manhattan, *12, 44, 50, 56–58, 57*, 68, *218–219, 224, 236*

GPR. *See* ground-penetrating radar

Gravesend, Brooklyn, 79–80, *80, 236*

Gravesend Cemetery, Brooklyn (Old Gravesend Cemetery), *xii*, 86, *218–219, 227, 236*

graveyards. *See* cemeteries and burial grounds.

Great Britain, U.K., 88, 122, 124, *130*, 147, 253n1; exports for, 87, 107, 129

Great Fire (1835), 139–140, *140*, 142, 236

Great League of Peace, 46, 252n96

Greenwich Village Historic District, Manhattan, 136, 163, 192–193, *224*

Green-Wood Cemetery, Brooklyn, 163, 205, *206, 224*

Grim, David, *119*

grocers, 124, *124*, 183

ground-penetrating radar (GPR), 13, *14, 237, 238*

ground stone tools, 24, 25, 27, 29–30, *30*; celt (axe) 24; pestle hammerstone mano (multitool), 29, *30*

Grumet, Robert, *40*

GSA. *See* General Services Administration

gunny bags (burlap sacks), 139–140, *140*

Hackensack peoples, 43, *48*

Halve Moon (VOC ship), 51, *52*

Hamilton, Alexander, 132, 134, 141

Harlem African Burial Ground, Manhattan, *xii*, *50*, *60–61*, *86*, *102–103*, *218–219*, *236*

Harlem Canal, 21

Harlem River, *60*, 128

Hartger, J., *54*

hats, 55, *55*, *194*

Haudenosaunee, 46, 49

Havemeyers & Elder Filter, Pan and Finishing House, Brooklyn, *125*, *225*

hearths, 24–25, *25*, 38, 69–70, *71*, *149–150*

Hendrick I. Lott House, Brooklyn, *xii*, *166*, *209*, *218–219*, *225*, *238*

H. F. Hollowell Site, Staten Island, *xii*, *16*, 24, *218–219*, *237*

Hirst family, 192–193

Historical Archaeology, 1–2, 5, 15, 43, 197

hive syrup, *182*

Holland, 53, 56, 73, 79, 81–82, 110

Horsmanden, Daniel, *99*

houses, 64, *66*, *149*, *167*, 197–198, 200; Dutch style, 66–70, *68*, *70*, *78*, *78–79*; workplaces as separate from, 117–118

Howe (Lord), *39–40*

Hudson, Henry, 51, *52*, 249n4

Hudson River, 2, 18, 118, *149*

Hudson Valley, 62, 117

Huguenot families, 110, 116–117

Hunterfly Road Houses (Weeksville), Brooklyn, *225*

hunter-gatherers, 21, 25, 40

hunting, 18, 32, *54*, 81–82; in Archaic period, 23, 26–28, *27–28*, 29

Hunts Point Burial Ground, Bronx, *xii*, *14*, *86*, *102*, *218–219*, *237*

Hunyadi Janos mineral-water, *175*

Hurricane Sandy, 108–109

hygiene, 178–180, *179–180*

Illinois, 143

immigrants, European, 15, 62, 64, 118, 132, 172, 214; Dutch, 53, 66; German, 69, 72–73, 75, *149–150*, 154; Huguenot, 110, 116–117; Palatine German, 132; Irish, 117, 145, 167, 169, 172–174; population growth due to, 140, 145, 167–169; quarantining for, 169–171, *170–171*, Walloon 56, *60–61*, 67

imports, 107, 124, 142, *147*; coconuts, 106; coffee, 106–107, *106*, 122, 128, 203; ceramics, 66, 107, 122, 134, 150–154, *152*, *153*; glassware, 66, 75, 107, 150, 154, *155*; glass beads, 52, 53–54; mineral water, 174, *175–177*, *176–177*; textiles and cloth, 45, 54, 57, 122, 128; smoking pipes, 122; sugar, 107, 122, 124–127, *124*, *126*, 128, 203; wine 75, 92–93, *93*, *94*, 128

imports, New Amsterdam, 66–67, 81–82, 84; tile and brick, 67–71, *68*

indentured servants, 47, 109, *109–110*, 110, 117

Indigenous Peoples, 1–2, 15, 17–19, *18*, 132, *214*, 237; Algonquian peoples as, *45*, 48, *54*; Canarsee peoples as, 43, *44*, *48*; descendants of, *47–48*; Dutch colonists interacting with, 53–54, *54*; Hackensack peoples as, 43, *48*; Lenape people as, 34, 40, 47–48; pathways of, *33–34*; Raritan peoples as, 64–66; wars against, 64–66, 81. *See also* Munsee peoples

Indigenous Peoples Archaeology, 1, 8, 14, 20–21, *39–41*, 207, 215

Indonesia, 51, 53

industrialization, *46*, 117–118

inflation, economic, 194

inkwells, stoneware, 154–155, *155*, *173*

in situ artifacts, 24, *154*

international commerce, 150–151, *152–153*

Inwood, Manhattan, 21, 26–27

Inwood African Burial Ground, Manhattan, *xii*, *86*, *102*, *218–219*, *237*

Inwood Hill Park, Manhattan, *xii*, *16*, *218–219*, *237*

Ireland, 117, 145, *164* , 167, 169, 173

Irish immigrants, 117, 145, 167, 169, 172–174

Ironstone or white granite, 180, 183, *184*, 212

Iroquois Confederacy, 252n96

Iroquois people. *See* Haudenosaunee

Isotope analysis, 35, 251n63

Jackson, James, 163, *164*

Jacob J. Teufel & Bros. thermometer, 201–202, *202*

Jacques and Marsh Druggists, *179*, 180, 182, *182*

Jamaica, 107

Jamaica, Queens, 33–34, 43, *175*, 182

James II (King), 87

Jamestown, Virginia, 51, 87

Janowitz, Meta, 89–90

Jay, John, 134

Jefferson, Thomas, 5, 134, 207

Jewish people, 172, 185, *187*

Johnson, Daniel, 157, 159

Jonah pipe, *72*

JP Morgan Chase. *See* Manhattan Water Company

Kanien'kehaka, 34

Kaeser, Edward, 20–21, 38

Kalm, Peter, 104

Kemble, Sarah, 69–70

Kempson, Peter, *134*

Keshaechquereren Village, 40

Kieft, Willem, 64–66

kilns, 69, 113, 156

King's Arms coffeehouse, 107

Kings County, Brooklyn, 79

Kingsland Homestead, Queens, *227*, 254n48

Kingston, New York, *149*

Know Nothing Party, 172–173

labor, 145, 169, 170

labor, enslaved African, 57–58, *58*, 64, 195, 215; in British New York, 96, 98; in sugar production, 122, 124

Lamartine Place Historic District, Manhattan, *196*, 225

Lamoka projectile points, 28, *28*, 29

landfilling, 2, *4*, 13–14, 25, 47, 79, 89, 171–172, 104, 107–109, *108*, *126*, 171–172, 198, 200, 203; artifact from, *173*; in British New York, 89, 104, 107–109; ship buried in, 150, *151*

land grants, *65*

Landmarks Law, 11

landmarks, 2, 221–230. *See also specific landmarks*

Landmarks Preservation Commission (LPC), New York City, 2, 11, 39–40, 91, 101, 178, 185

Late Archaic period, 22–23, 26–28, *27*, *28*

Late Woodland period, 40–42, *41–42*, 239, 252n79.

Laurentide Ice Sheet, 18

Lee, James, *6*, *134*

legislation, 47, 48, 83, 160; Common Council, 140, 142

Leisler, Jacob, 88, 124

Leisler Rebellion, 88, 95

Lenape people, *34*, 40, *40*, 47–48

Lenapehoking, 252n79

Lent Homestead, Queens, 225, 254n48

Levanna points, 40, *41*

limestone, 96

Lincoln, Abraham, 195

Livingston, Robert, *109*, *109–110*

loaf sugar, refined, *124*, 124–125, *127*

London, England, 95, 110, 117, 167

longhouses, Indigenous, 43, *44*

Long Island, 33–34, 48, 210

Longshoremen, 150

Lopez, Julius, 20–21, 251n73

Lott House (Brooklyn), *xii*, *166*, 209, 218–219, 225, *238*

Louisiana Purchase, U.S., 143

Lovelace, Francis, 91

Lovelace Tavern, *90–92*, 91–92, *94*, 242; excavation of, 11, *12*, *75*, 75–77, *77*

LPC. *See* Landmarks Preservation Commission

Lyne, James, 115, *116*

Lyne-Bradford Plan of 1730, *4*, 115–117, *116*, 255n5

MacLean, Jessica Striebel, *vii*, 216

macrobotanical analysis, see archaeobotanical analysis

Madagascar, 96

Madison, James, 134

Maerschalck Plan (1755), 98, *100*, 113

makers' marks, 72, *73–74*, 157, *157*

Male Ozorovice (Kiss-Azar), 147, *147*

mammals, hunting of, 21–22

Manatus map, 43, *44*, 56–58, *57*

Manhattan, 2, 26, 33–34, 57. *See also specific
      sites*

Manhattan Company, 140–142

Manhattan Life Insurance Company Building,
      204

Manhattan Water Company (JP Morgan
      Chase), 142, *234*

Manley, John, 151

Manumission Society, 160–161

Map of the City of New York (Burr, D.), *168*

maps, *x–xi*, *xii*, 16, *50*, 86, *138*, 166, 211, *218–
      219*; Burr's Map, 168; Castello plan as, *60*,
      78, 88, *89*; Commissioner's Plan of 1811,
      144; Grim Plan (1742), *119*; Hooker's Plan
      (1838), *172*; Lyne-Bradford Plan of 1730,
      4, 115–116, *116*; Manatus map, 43, *44*, 56,
      57; of New Netherland, *59*; Ratzer Map,
      130; Risse Map, *211*, Lyne-Bradford Plan
      of 1730, 4, 115–116, *116*; Manatus map, 43,
      44, 56, *57*; Maerschalck Plan (1755), *100*,
      Ratzer Map, *130*; Risse Map, *211*; Viele
      (1855) survey, *190*

Marine Park, Brooklyn, 40, *209*

markets, 81, 87, 88, 96, 103, 106–107, 113, 134

Mark-Viverito, Melissa, 103

marshland, 18, 23, 26, 33, 34, 42, *79*, *213*

Maryland, 143, 160

Massachusetts, 32, 79, 87; Boston, 69, 108, 116,
      129, 143

mast forests, 26, 250n34

mastodon, 21, 22

material culture, 2, 17, 64, 66, 214; ceramics as,
      72–75, *72–75*, 84; of Dutch, 66–70, 83–84

Mathew (Father), 173, *174*

mayors, New York City, 100, 143, 161, 194

McEwen, Janette, 183–184

McEwen, Robert, 183

Meal Market, 96, 107

meats, 103–104, 183–184, 185, *186–188*; nut
      meat, 26, 29

medicines, 180–184, *181–183*

merchant class, 88, 107, 117–118, 121, 128, *149*;
      fire impacting, 139–140

Merchants' Coffee House, 107

merchant token, 5, *6*

metal cookware, *149*

Metropolitan Board of Health, 198, 200

Metropolitan Museum of Art, Manhattan, 110,
      112, 193, 207, *226*

middens, 25–27, 38, 110, 234, 237, 243

Middle Archaic period, 22–23, 25–26, *26*

middle-class, 103, 118, 136, 191–192, 195

Middle Woodland period, 36–38, *37*, *39–40*, 45

migration, Indigenous, 26, 29

militaries, 128–129

milk, 127, *127*

mineral water, 174, *175–177*, *176–177*

minimum number of individuals (MNI),
      faunal analysis, *186*

Minuit, Peter, 62

MNI. *See* minimum number of individuals

Mohican people, *34*, *40*, 48

molasses, 124, 125, 128

Molasses Act of 1733, 128

monopolies, 55, 65, 128, 141

Montgomerie, John, 108

Montgomerie charter, 108–109, 118

Monticello (plantation), 5

Moody, Deborah, 79–80, *80*

Morris-Schurtz Site. *See* Throgs Neck, Bronx

Morse, Samuel F. B., 195

municipal institutions, 9, 118, *119*, 120, 146

Munsee dialect, 48, 252n79, 253n111

Munsee peoples, 33, 34, 40, *40*, 54, 252n79;
      descendants of, *47–48*; Dutch colonists
      and, 43, 45, 47, 49; Kieft waging war with,
      64–66; on property ownership, 62

Murray Hill Reservoir, 142

nailbrushes, *179*

Nan A. Rothschild Research Center
      (NYC Archaeological Repository), *x*, 2, 3,
      213, *216*

Napoleonic wars, 154

National Historic Preservation Act, U.S., 11, 98

National Museum of the American Indian, 8, 254n21

Native Americans. *See* Indigenous Peoples

nativist ideology, 172–174

Netherlands (United Provinces), 56, 67, 68, 69, 75, 81–82, 214; immigrants from, 53, 66; pipes from, *73–74, 122*

New Amsterdam, as town, 81–84, *90*

New Amsterdam, Dutch colony, 15, 51–52, *66*, 89, 214; architecture of, 66–70, *68, 70*, 254n48; British taking control of, 1–2, 49, 83–84; ceramics in, 72–75, *72–75*; enslaved Africans in, 53, 55, 58, 64–66, 253n106. *See also* governors, New Amsterdam

New England, 33, 118, 120–121, 129, 145, 150

New Jersey, 21, 40, 129–130

New Netherland, 51, *59*, 67, 69, 139

New Orange, 83, 84

New Utrecht Reformed Dutch Church Cemetery, Brooklyn, 226

New World, European colonists and, 53

New York (State), *48, 158*; building code by, 197–198; emancipation in, 157, 160–161

New York, British colony, 1–2, 49, 83–84, 87–89; food for, 103–107, *105–106*; Revolutionary War in, 129–131, *130*; sugar in, 122, 124–125, *124–126, 127–128*

New York City, 1, 8, *9*, 200–201, 210; cemeteries in, 162–163, *164*, 178; during Civil War, *194–196, 194–197*; drinking water for, 140–143, *142–143*, 167; education in, 161–162, *162*; emancipation in, 160–161, 189; following Revolutionary War, 131–132, 134, 136; free Black people in, 157; hygiene in, 178–180, *179–180*; mineral water popular in, 174, *175–177, 176–177*; pollution impacting, 139, 142, *149*, 167; as port, 143, 155, 167; quarantining implemented in, 169–171, *170–171*; sanitation in, 167, 197–198, *198–200*, 200; sewage system for, 143, 167, 197, 200, 202; skyscrapers in, 204, *204–205*; stoneware pottery in, 154–157, *154–159, 159*; urban density for, 140, 163, 197, 210. *See also*

New Amsterdam, as Dutch colony; *specific boroughs*

NYC Archaeological Repository. *See* Nan A. Rothschild Research Center

New York City Landmarks Preservation Commission, see Landmarks Preservation Commission

New York Commercial Advertiser, 155, *155*

New York Council of Hygiene and Public Health, 198, 200

New York Courthouse. *See* Tweed Courthouse, Manhattan

New-York Gazette, 124

New York Harbor, 33, 35, 52, 128, 150

New-York Historical Society, Manhattan, 8, 143, *226*

New York Journal of Commerce, 139

New York Public Library, Manhattan, 142, *142*, *226*

New York Stock Exchange, 59, *60, 226*

Nicolls (Colonel), 83

Nieuw Haarlem, *60–61*

Nine Men (governance), 81

NISP. *See* number of identifiable specimens

Noten Eylant (Nut Island). *See* Governors Island

Novi Belgii Novaeque Angliae (map), *59, 66*

number of identifiable specimens (NISP), faunal analysis, *186*

Officer and a Laughing Girl (Vermeer), 55, 75–76

Ohio, *48*

Old Place Neck, Staten Island, *xii*, 21–22, *22, 24*, *16*, 218–219, 238

Old Towne (of) Flushing Burial Ground, Queens, *xii*, 86, 102, 218–219, 238

Onderdonck Site (Adrian and Ann Wyckoff Onderdonk House), Queens, *xii*, 50, 79, 218–219, 230, 239, 254n48

Oneroad, Amos, 26

onion bottles, 92–93, *93*

oral history, 17, 42–43, 209, 252n79

orchards, 103, 118

Ormsby, D. L., 176–177, *177*

oysters, 8, 33, 104–105, *106*, 157, 159–161
oyster jars, 14, 157, 159, *159*

Palatine German Immigrants, 132
Paleo-Indian period, 17, *18*, 21–22, *22*
Parker, Arthur C., 20–21
Parliament, U.K., 128
passenger pigeons, 92, *188*
Patent Office, U.S., *149*
Patroonship Plan, WIC, 63
Peach War, 81
pearlware ceramics, *135*, 151, *152–153*, 154, 212
Peck, George L., 182
Pelham Bay Park, Bronx, *xii*, 19–20, *16*, 218–219, *219*, *239*
Pelletreau, Elias, 110
pencils, 76–77, *77*, 162, 191, *192*
Pennsylvania, 32, 48, 117, 130, 143; coal from, *147–149*, 150, 259n23
Pennsylvania Station, *vii*, 11; demolition of, *xi*
Pepper, George Hubbard, 207
Perris Map (1857), *204*
personal care, 180–183, *181–183*
Peter Curtenius & Co. New York Air Furnace, 122
Petrie, William Flinders, 207
Philadelphia, Pennsylvania, 108, 116, 143, *150*
Philip II (King), 53
pickled oysters, 104–105, 159, *159*
Pickman, Arnold, 89–90
pigeons, passenger, 92, *188*
pigs, 47, 65, *186–187*, 216
pins, shroud, 101, *102*
pipes, smoking, 14, 33, 35, *72–74*, 90, 92, 122, 147, 162, 174; *194*
pipes, water, 141, *141*, 142–143
plantations, sugar, 107, 122, 124–125, 150
points, projectile (chipped stone), 21–26, *26*, 27, 28, 29, 40, *212*, 243; arrowheads 26, *28*, 40, *41*; spear points, 21, *22*, 24, 26, *27*, 212
pollution, 139, 142, *149*, 167
poor people and poverty, 88, 98, 118, *119*, 120, 129, 142, 167, 180, 216
population growth, 15, 87, 143, 161, 210; for British New York, 88, 117–118; coal contributing to, *147–148*; for Dutch

colonists, 57–58; immigrants causing, 140, 145, 167–169; for Indigenous Peoples, 22, 26
porcelain, Chinese, *7*, 73–74, *75*, 84, 151, 154, 191, *192*
pork, *186–187*, 216
Port Mobil, Staten Island, *xii*, 22, *22*, 16, *218–219*, *239*
Port of New York, 155, 169
Portuguese colonists, 62–63
postwar (Civil War), 200–203
potatoes, 169
Potato Famine of 1845 to 1849, 145
Pot Baker Hill, Manhattan, 113, 156–157, 159
potteries, 113–115, *114–115*, 154–156
pottery. *See* ceramics
poultry, *187*, 215; chicken, 92; chicken, goose, and turkey, 104; turkey, 22, 26, 28, 29, 38, 92, 103–104
prehistoric archaeology, *see* Indigenous Peoples Archaeology
preservation law, 9, 11, 98; Landmarks Law, 11
Presbyterianism, 117, 178
privatization, 107
privies, 89, 179, 183–185, 197–200, *198–199*
profiteering, wartime, 194, *195*
property ownership, 47, 62, 132; by free Black men, 189, 191–193; Indigenous Peoples on, 17; women and, 79–80, *80*
Prospect Park Scenic Landmark, Brooklyn, 205, *227*
protein, in diets, 104
Protestantism, 53, 54, 88, 110, 145, 172
prunts, roemer, *77*
public health, 140, 142, 163, 198, 205; quarantining and, 169–171, *170–171*
Public School Society, 161
public transportation, 169, 202
punch (alcoholic beverage), 127, *127*
Pure Food and Drug Act of 1906, 181

Quakers, 82, *82*, 117, 160
Quarantine Grounds, Staten Island, *xii*, *166*, 169–170, *170*, 218–219, 240
Queens, 26, *33–34*

racism, 143, 178, 191, 195–197

radiocarbon dating, 24, 25, 35, 234

railroads, 149, 167

Raleigh, Walter, 72

Randel, John, Jr., 143, 144

Rapalje Children, The (Durand), 121

Raritan peoples, 64–66

Ratzer Map, 130

raw sugar, 122, 124–125

recipes, 106, 127, 159

redware ceramics, 69, 72–73, 75, 149–150,
    154, 212

refined sugar, 124, 124–125, 127, 127–128

Reformed Church, Staten Island, 96, 227

Reformed Low Dutch Church of Harlem,
    60–61

regulations, archaeological, 8, 11, 11–13

Reid, John, 109–110

religions, 5, 6, 63, 70, 71, 82, 178; of European
    colonists, 53, 54; temperance movement
    and, 172–173, 174

religious freedom, 54, 56, 72, 80

religious persecution, 79, 116–117, 178

Rementer, Jim, 40

Remmey, Johannes, 113–115, 114–115, 157

Remmey, John, III, 156

Repository. *See* Nan A. Rothschild Research
    Center.

republic, American, 131–132, 134

reservoirs, 141, 142, 142

Reverend Isaac Coleman and Rebecca Gray
    Coleman House, Staten Island, 160, 222

Revolutionary War, 1–2, 39–40, 129–131, 130,
    135, 163

Rhode Island, 32

Richards, Smith, 124

Richmond Hill, Staten Island, *xii*, 24, 16,
    218–219, 240

rights, 83, 132, 160, 189

rituals, 29, 33, 38, 101, 209

Riverdale Archaeological Research Project,
    Bronx, *xii*, 16, 218–219, 240; excavations at,
    25, 27–28, 27–28, 35, 198, 200

Robson family, 192–193

roemers (drinking glass), 75–76, 77

Ronalds, Thomas A., 155, 155

roof tiles, 67–68, 68

root-beer, 177, 177

Rossville A.M.E. Zion Church, Staten Island,
    160, 227

Rothschild, Nan A., *vii*, 89–91

Rufus King Manor, Queens, 175, 182, 183, 227, 238

rum, 124, 125, 127–128

Rutledge, Edward, 39–40

Rynder, Elizabeth, 124

Sailors' Snug Harbor, Staten Island, 228–229,
    240; excavations at, 40, 41, 148, 185, 186

Saint Catherine Labouré Miraculous Medal, 6

Saint Mark's-in-the-Bowery Church,
    Manhattan, 80, 228

Saint Paul's Chapel and Graveyard,
    Manhattan, 228

Saint Philip's Protestant Episcopal Church,
    Manhattan, 228

salt, 74

Salwen, Bert, 8, 239

Sandy Ground, Staten Island, *xii*, 138, 160–161,
    218–219, 222, 227, 241

sanitation, 167, 197–198, 198–200, 200

Sankofa Park, Brooklyn, *xii*, 86, 102, 218–219, 242

Savage, Gus, 100

sawmill, WIC, 56, 57, 68, 236

schepens (governance), 81, 255n65

schout (governance), 81, 255n65

Schuyler, Alida, 109

sea levels, 2, 18, 21, 33; during Archaic period,
    25, 26, 28

segregation, 60–61

segregation, cemetery, 98

segregation, in grave-sites, 60–61

Seneca Village, Manhattan, *xii*, 14, 138, 166,
    218–219, 242, 262n53; as Black community,
    160, 189, 190, 191–193; excavations at, 8,
    176–177, 177, 192, 193

7 Hanover Square, Manhattan, *xii*, 4, 4, 218–
    219, 236; ceramic sherds found at, 152–153;
    excavations at, 10, 74, 76, 109–110, 110–111,
    127; faunal analysis at, 104; fire evidence
    at, 140

1765 the Stamp Act, 129

Seventh Ward, Manhattan, 157, 158, 160–161

Seven Years War, 129

sewage systems, 143, 167, 197, 200, 202

Seymour, Horatio, 195

Shanscomacocke Village, 40

Shearith Israel Graveyard, Manhattan, 117, 229

Sheepshead Bay, Brooklyn, 104

shellfish, 23, 25–26, 33, 104, 105, 160. See also oysters

shell middens, 25–27, 38, 234, 243

shells, wampum made from, 45, 45–46

sherds (fragments), ceramics, 150–151, 152–153

Shinnecock peoples, 48

ship, buried in landfill, 150, 151

shorelines, 2, 4, 18, 25, 107–109

shroud pins, 101–102, 102

Sierra Leone, 157

silversmiths, 110, 111–112

du Simitière, Pierre Eugene, 69, 70

Simmons, Amelia, 122

Singletary, Patricia A., 103

Sinoway peoples, 48

sites, archaeological, 232–241; see also individual discussions

Skinner, Alanson, 26

skyscrapers, 204, 204–205

slate pencils, 76–77, 77, 191, 192

Slave "Conspiracy" of 1741; 96, 98, 99, 110, 265n24

Slavery. See enslavement

Slovakia, 147, 147

smallpox, 110, 169, 198

soda water, 174, 176, 177, 177, 212

Solecki, Ralph S., 20

Soumaine, Simeon, 110, 111–112, 114, 116–118

South Ferry Terminal, Battery Park, Manhattan, xii, 16, 86, 166, 218–219, 242; excavations at, 45, 50, 71, 105–106, 107, 108, 129; GIS used at, 129

Spain, 53

Spanish colonists, 51, 54, 66

spear point (chipped stone), 21, 22, 24, 26, 27, 212

Spring Street Presbyterian Church (Trump Soho), xii, 166, 178, 218–219, 243

Stadt Huys, Manhattan, xii, 16, 50, 86, 138, 166, 242; bottles found at, 91–92, 93, 176–177, 176–177; ethnic diversity evidenced at, 146–147, 147; excavations at, 10, 75, 75–78, 77, 154, 174, 179, 180, 182, 182; faunal analysis at, 104; in Lyne-Bradford Plan, 4; Rothschild on, 89–91. See also Lovelace Tavern

standards, archaeological, 8, 11, 11, 13, 21

Stanly Stemmed points, 25, 26

state legislature, New York, 140, 160, 170

Staten Island, 33–34, 160; Indigenous Peoples in, 22, 22, 24, 26, 40, 48; quarantining on, 169–171, 170–171. See also specific sites

States General (Dutch government), 53

Statue of Liberty, Manhattan, 171, 229

steatite vessels, 31, 31–32, 36

stone, as building material, 64, 67, 69, 70

Stone Street, Manhattan, xii, 77, 50, 218–219, 242

stone tools, 26; Archaic, 23, 23, 25, 28–30, 30; chipped, 21, 23, 23, 24, 27, 35, 40; ground, 24, 25, 27, 29–30, 30; Paleo-Indian, 21–23, 22; Woodland period, 35, 35

see ground stone and chipped stone.

stoneware ceramics, 111, 113–115, 114–115, 134, 154–156, 154–156, 159, 212; by Commeraw, 157, 157, 159

St. Paul's Chapel and Graveyard, 114

St. Philip's Church, 163

Strachey, Henry, 39–40

Stratigraphy, archaeological, 9, 200

Street Plan of New Amsterdam and Colonial New York, Manhattan, 59, 60, 89, 229

Stuyvesant, Peter, 80–84, 87–88, 124

Stuyvesant, Petrus, 66

sugar, 107, 112, 178; in British New York, 122, 124–125, 124–126, 127–128; trade, 51, 83, 122, 124, 128, 150

Sugar Act of 1764, 128

sugar molds, 14, 125, 126

surviving Dutch architecture, 78, 78–80, 79

Sutphin, Amanda, vii

Talbot, Allum, & Lee one-cent token, 6, 134, *134*

Talbot, William, 6, *134*

taverns, 11, *90–91*, 92, 107, 116, 131, 139. *See also* Lovelace Tavern

taxes, 64, 81, 124, 128, 207

teaware, *112*, *134*, 183, *184*, *193*

technologies, archaeological, 13–15, *14*, 24, 110, *129*, *150*; European, 72, *149*, 203; Indigenous, 17, 23, 25, 27, 28–29, 33, *41*

temperance movement, 172–173, 174, *174*

Tenement House Law, 197

terminus post quem (TPQ), for artifacts, 172

T'Fort Nieuw Amsterdam op de Manhatans (illustration), *54*

thermometer, 201–202, *202*

Thomas, John, and Joseph Mayer pottery, *193*

Throgs Neck (Morris-Schurtz Site), Bronx, *xii*, 38, *16*, *218–219*, *219*, 243, 251n70

tiles, Dutch, 66–70, *68*, *69*, *71*, 84, 212

Times Square, *42*

tin-glazed ceramics, 71, 72, *74–75*, 83–84, *94*, 127

tobacco, 73, *150*

Tom (enslaved African; Soumaine), 110

Tomlinson, Roger, *129*

tools, *46*, 118, 120, *123*; woodworking, 23, *23*, 24, 27. *See also* ground stone tools, chipped stone tools

toothbrushes, *179*, 191

Topographic Survey of Central Park (Viele), *190*

Tories (British allies), 132

Total Station (Theodolites), 13, 208

Tottenville, Staten Island, 35, 38, *39–40*, 207, 232

TPQ. *See* terminus post quem

trade networks, 29, 38, 55; British New York in, 88, *106*, 106–108; enslaved Africans in, 62–63, *63*, 160; sugar, 51, 83, 122, 124, 128, 150. *See also* beaver trade

transatlantic trade, *106*, 106, 150

Transitional Archaic period, 28–32, *30*, *31*, 31–32, 35, 36

Travels Into North America (Kalm), 104

treaties, 49

Treaty of Paris in 1783, 131

Tribal Nations, 21, 40, *48*

Trinity Church and Graveyard, 83, 95–96, *97*, 98, 110, 117–118, 229

Trump SoHo. *See* Spring Street Presbyterian Church

Tubby Hook, Manhattan, *xii*, *218–219*, 26, *16*, 243

tuberculosis, 181

tuition, 161

Tumblety, Francis, 184

Turkish smoking pipe, *147*, 147

Tweed, William M., 200

Tweed Courthouse (New York Courthouse), Manhattan, *xii*, 7, 113, 226, *218–219*, 243; corruption and, 200–201, *201*; excavations of, 6, *119*, *174*, 201–202

typhoid, 117, 142

Underground Railroad, 209

Union states (the North), 194–197

United Kingdom (U.K.), 169, 253n1

United Provinces. *See* Netherlands

United States (U.S.), 98, 143, *149*, 249n5; Revolutionary War, 129–132, *130*, *131*

Unkechaug peoples, *48*

upper class, 118, 136

Urban Archaeology, 5, 8 11, 13, 15, 90, 178, 217, 249n5

urban planning, 142, 215, 229; for British New York, 89, *89*; Commissioners' Plan (1811), 143, *144*, 145, 163, 202; by Dutch colonists, 53, 58–59, *59*; post civil war, 202–203

U.S. *See* United States (U.S.)

U.S. Customs House (Federal Hall National Memorial), Manhattan, 8, *59*, 223, 229, 254n21

Van Cortlandt House, Bronx, *xii*, *50*, 138, *166*, *218–219*, 229, 244; excavations at, 7, *71*, 156, 180, *180*–181, *181*, 209

van der Donck, Adriaen, 139, 259n3

Van Rensselaer family, 62, 103

Vereenigde Oost-Indische Compagnie. *See* Dutch East India Company (VOC)

Vermeer, Johannes, 55, 75–76

da Verrazzano, Giovanni, 249n5

Viele, Egbert, *190*

Virginia, 5, 51, 87, 207
Vissher, Nicolaes, *59, 66, 67*
VOC. *See* Dutch East India Company
Vosburg-type projectile point, *27, 27*, 29
voting rights, 132, 160, 189, 191
de Vries, David Peietersz, 64

Wading River–type point, 28
Wall, Diana, *89–90*
Walloon settlers, 56, *60–61*, 67
Wall Street, Manhattan, 58, 87, 96, 124, 215
wampum, 45, *45–46*, 53, 81, 252n79
Ward's Island, Emigrant Refuge, Manhattan, *xii, 166*, 170, *171*, 218–219, 244
Ward's Point, 253n4. *See also* Aakawaxung Munahanung (Island Protected from the Wind), Staten Island
War of 1812, *147*, 171
wars, 47, 53, 64–66, 81, 107. *See also specific wars*
Washington, DC, 134
Washington, George, 129, 132, *133*, 134, *135*, 143
Washington Square Park, 163, *244*
water, 101, 136, 139, 173; drinking, *140–143, 142–143*, 167; fresh, 18, 19, *65*, 167; mineral, 174, *175–177, 176–177*
waterfronts, *4, 168*
water lots, 107–108
water mains, wooden, *141, 142–143*, 234
Water Street, *10*
Webster, George, *124*
Webster, Noah, 88
Wecquaesgeek peoples, 48, 64
Wedgewood, Josiah, *154–155, 155*
Weeksville, Brooklyn, *xii, 138, 218–219*; as Black community, 160, *166*, 192, *244*
wells, 89, 139, 141, *146*, 234
West Africa, 96
West India Company (WIC), 53, 55, 58, *58–59*, 63, 81, 83–84; enslaved Africans and, 62–64, *63*; monopoly over beaver pelts for, 54, 64. *See also* New Amsterdam, Dutch colony
White granite or ironstone, *180*, 183, *184, 212*
white people, 98, 160, 189, 192–193
Whritenour, Ray, *40*
WIC. *See* West India Company (WIC)
Wilkins, Sharon, 103
Williams, Andrew, 189
Wilson, William Godfrey, 191
Wilson family, *9*
windmills, *44, 57*
wine, 75, *91–95, 93, 94, 95, 95*
Wisniewski, Stanley H., *20–21, 21*, 251n73
women, 65, 83, 123, 132, 136, *193*; as archaeologists, *90*; enslaved African, 64; Indigenous, 38, 66; property ownership for, 79–80, *80*
wood, as fuel, 120, *147*, 149; architecture, 64, 67–68, 118, 139; pipes for water, *141, 141, 142–143*
Wood, Fernando, 194
Woodland period, 17, *18*, 33–34; Early, 28, *32–33, 35–36, 35–36*; Late, *32–33*, 36, 40–42, *41–42*; Middle, *32–33*, 36, *36*–38, *37, 39–40, 45*
Woodlawn Cemetery, *61*, 163, 205
Woodward, Anthony, *23*
woodworking tools, *23, 23*, 24, 27
working-class, 98, 122, 178–179, *186*
workplaces, home as separate from, 117–118, 136
World Trade Center ship, *xii*, 150–151, *151*, 197, *218–219, 244*
Wyckoff House, Brooklyn, *78, 78–79, 230*, 254n48

X-ray fluorescence (XRF) spectrometers, 14–15, 110, 113–114

yellow fever, 136, 142, 163, *164*, 169
Yemen, 106